VISIONS OF
SCOTLAND'S PAST

Frontispiece: John R Hume, OBE

Visions of Scotland's Past

Looking to the Future

Essays in Honour of John R Hume

<small>EDITED BY</small>

Deborah C Mays

Michael S Moss

Miles K Oglethorpe

<small>FOREWORD BY</small>

Donald Dewar

TUCKWELL PRESS

First published in Great Britain by
Tuckwell Press
The Mill House
Phantassie
East Linton
East Lothian EH40 3DG
Scotland

Copyright © The editors and contributors severally, 2000

ISBN 1 86232 072 1

The publishers and editors gratefully acknowledge
the support of the following in the production of this volume:

The Russell Trust

Sir William Lithgow

The Ballast Trust

Charles Craig

The New Lanark Conservation Trust

British Library Cataloguing-in-Publication Data
A catalogue record for this book is available
on request from the British Library

Typeset by Carnegie Publishing Ltd, Lancaster
Printed by The Cromwell Press, Trowbridge, Wiltshire

Contents

Illustrations

J.R.H.

MORTLACH DISTILLERY
DUFFTOWN   1974

Abbreviations

AHSS	The Architectural Heritage Society of Scotland
AIIMHS	Association of Independent Industrial Museums and Heritage Sites
CANMORE	Computer Application for National Monuments Record of Scotland
CBA	Council for British Archaeology
CSA	Council for Scottish Archaeology
DOCOMOMO	Documentation and Conservation of the Modern Movement
FOMOCO	Ford Motor Company
GD	Gift Deposit
HAA	Honorary Archaeological Adviser
IA	Institute of Architects
LMS	London Midland and Scottish Railway
LNER	London and North Eastern Railway
NER	North Eastern Railway
NGR	National Grid Reference
NGS	National Galleries of Scotland
NLCT	New Lanark Conservation Trust
NMRS	National Monuments Record of Scotland
NMS	National Museums of Scotland
NTS	National Trust for Scotland
RIAS	Royal Incorporation of Architects in Scotland
RICS	Royal Institute of Chartered Surveyors
RCAHMS	Royal Commission on the Ancient and Historical Monuments of Scotland
RIBA	Royal Institute of British Architecture
RMS	Royal Museum of Scotland
RSA	Royal Scottish Academician
SCRAN	Scottish Cultural Resources Access Network
SCWS	Scottish Co-operative Wholesale Society
SDD	Scottish Development Department
SIAS	Scottish Industrial Archaeology Survey
SIHS	Scottish Industrial Heritage Society
SIWA	Scottish Inland Waterways Association
SNBR	Scottish National Buildings Record
SRO	Scottish Record Office
SSPHM	Scottish Society for the Preservation of Historic Machinery
SusTrans	Sustainable Transport
SVBWG	Scottish Vernacular Buildings Working Group

Acknowledgements

An exercise of collation such as this is not possible without a great deal of good will and assistance. The editors wish to thank all those who have contributed their time, knowledge and funds to the realisation of this volume. The sponsors gave generously to provide the financial backing which was a *sine qua non*: United Distillers and Vintners kick-started the process and were followed by the Russell Trust, the Royal Commission on the Ancient and Historical Monuments of Scotland, Sir William Lithgow, Bill Lind and the Ballast Trust, and Charles Craig. We are most grateful to them all.

Similarly, thanks are due to the various authors whose work is the substance of the Festschrift. Illustrations have been provided by a wide number of organisations, public bodies and individuals, all of whom are acknowledged individually with each figure, but we take this opportunity to thank them *en masse*. A number of individuals have contributed to the realisation of the book, notably, Nick Haynes, Pauline Laing, Frank Lawrie, Miriam McDonald, Roger Mercer, Seán O'Reilly, Derek Smart, Geoffrey Stell and Ruth Wimberley, to name but a few. The publishers, John and Valerie Tuckwell, stayed with the volume through the stops and starts of its genesis, and their patience and quality of production are much appreciated.

The companion conference has materialised thanks to the endeavours of Jim Arnold, Lorna Davidson, and Stephen Owen at New Lanark, and the invaluable services of the Architectural Heritage Society of Scotland. The Scottish Industrial Heritage Society, Historic Scotland, and the Association for Industrial Archaeology also kindly helped to circulate information about the event, ensuring that as many as possible could participate.

It is not possible to name all those who have played a part in this tribute to John Hume, but we here offer our full acknowledgement of their contribution and considerable support. Not least among the wider majority are the staff of the Photography Department at RCAHMS. In addition, medals should be struck for the staff of the Metropole Café, Edinburgh, compatriots in an intrigue where much was hatched and advanced, and for Matthew Hume, who withheld the secret throughout.

Editors' Note

THE extraordinary variety of the papers within this Festschrift accurately portrays the huge range of activities with which John Hume has been associated during the last four decades. Although the balance of the volume inevitably reflects a pervasive interest in Scotland's immensely significant entrepreneurial and industrial heritage, it also represents wide-ranging interests in other subjects equally central to the understanding and appreciation of Scottish history and its built heritage. Indeed, in the first of the papers, Michael Moss stresses the close links that bind together business and industry with a broad range of historical themes, including aristocracy and religion.

In addition to David Walker's paper on the Royal College, several other contributions have links to the University of Strathclyde, and in particular to the Department of History, where John Hume embarked upon his career in the early 1960s. These papers tackle topics such as the development of ports in Britain, and 'Remembering Work', the latter tying in well with Matthew Hume's piece on industrial museums. Also emanating from Strathclyde University are the themes of recording industrial heritage, and especially the power of photography as a recording medium. These combine well with papers considering the importance of archival records, and in particular, film archives.

A significant number of these papers were delivered at a conference held in John Hume's honour at New Lanark on 27 February 1999. It is appropriate, therefore, that one of the papers provides a detailed account of the survival and development of New Lanark mills and village, and of the evolution of the New Lanark Conservation Trust. Subsequent contributions pay particular attention to Scotland's roads, canals, railways and associated bridges. In a diversion away from the overtly industrial theme, there are also papers on the inventory of Scottish Churches, and on the extraordinary library at Newhailes. Finally, very much with the future in mind, consideration is given to imaginative ways in which industrial and other categories of buildings can be successfully re-used and re-vitalised.

The extensive nature of John Hume's professional and charitable activities has meant that he has worked with a broad cross section of individuals and institutions within Scotland and beyond. This volume attempts to provide a balanced selection of contributions reflecting these interests. Inevitably, it has not been possible to embrace elements from all the many strands of his career. This Festschrift can only represent a sample of a much bigger whole, but is nevertheless intended to stand as a tribute on behalf of everyone who has worked with John over the years.

Meanwhile, retirement rarely means a quieter life, and with a fresh career beckoning in several institutions, we fully expect to find ourselves working even more closely with him in the coming years.

Mill Number One after conversion to The New Lanark Mill Hotel in 1997.

Foreword

I AM delighted to have the opportunity to write a foreword for this volume dedicated to John Hume.

Throughout his career John has worked to ensure a future to the great treasury which is Scotland's cultural heritage, and especially its ecclesiastical and industrial heritage. A man of vision with a pioneer's energy, he has remained undaunted by the volume of the tasks he has taken on board. In documenting and evaluating the built heritage of church and industry, he has laid an essential foundation for succeeding generations. Through his many publications and in his official capacity within The Scottish Office, John has given wise and positive counsel on how conservation and sustainability can be balanced with necessary development and economic growth.

His powers of communication and his ability to motivate have been invaluable, in his work with students as a lecturer at the University of Strathclyde and through his key role in private and government-led initiatives. It is so often the case that John has been in 'right at the start', from the saving and regeneration of New Lanark, to nationwide programmes such as the Scottish Industrial Archaeology Survey and the Inventory of Churches. As someone who enjoys and marvels at the scale and significance of New Lanark, I am personally grateful and have very directly benefited from his efforts. He is rightly respected and liked. A crucial factor in John's success in promoting his ideas is his ability to explain things clearly to expert professional and amateur alike.

Since 1984, John has been based at Historic Scotland, latterly as Chief Inspector of Historic Buildings, where he has succeeded in ensuring that what we have inherited from past generations is recognised and valued by today's generation. This book reflects his wide range of interests and his achievements and as such provides the reader with inspiration and cause for thought. It is also 'a good read', which in many ways is the most relevant way of recognising John's contribution to our cultural heritage.

Donald B. Dewar.

The Rt Hon Donald Dewar, MA, LLB, MP, MSP
First Minister of The Scottish Parliament

Notes on Contributors

JAMES EDWARD ARNOLD was born in Glasgow in 1945. After primary education in a mining village in Dumfriesshire, his family moved to Coventry in 1956. He took a BA in History at the University of York, awarded 1967, followed by a Certificate in Education at the University of London, 1967, an Honours MA from the University of Strathclyde in 1990, and an Honours MUniv from the Open University, 1998. He gained an MBE in 1989 and became a Fellow of the Royal Scottish Academy in 1992. His employment prior to his current role at New Lanark included teaching and FOMOCO. He became Village Manager at New Lanark in 1974, and has collected various awards on behalf of the village. He has been or is currently chairman, director or committee member of several industrial and developmental bodies.

W HAMISH FRASER is Professor of Modern History at the University of Strathclyde. He shared a room with John Hume in the early days of the Department of History. He is the author of many books and articles on aspects of labour and social history including: *Trade Unions and Society 1850–1880, The Struggle for Acceptance; The Coming of the Mass Market; Conflict and Class, Scottish Workers 1700–1838; Alexander Campbell and the Struggle for Socialism.* Most recently he edited with Irene Maver, *Glasgow, Vol II, 1830–1912.*

JANE GEDDES read History at Cambridge University and completed an MA and PhD at the Courtauld Institute, with a thesis on 'Medieval Decorative Ironwork'. She worked as an Inspector of Ancient Monuments with English Heritage before moving to Aberdeen. She has produced the computer database 'The Inventory of Scottish Church Heritage' for the Council for Scottish Archaeology. She is currently lecturer in architecture and medieval art at Aberdeen University, in the History of Art Department.

IAN GOW was born in Edinburgh and educated at George Heriot's School, where his interest in architecture was first stimulated, and Trinity College, Cambridge, where he read the History of Art. After three years in the Inspectorate of Ancient Monuments (London), where his responsibilities included Audley End, he transferred to The National Monuments Record of Scotland where he served seventeen years, latterly as Curator of Collections. In 1998 he was appointed Curator of The National Trust for Scotland. He has written extensively on the decorative arts and architecture of Scotland, including many guidebooks, and his publications include *The Scottish Interior* (1992). He has been a frequent contributor to *Country Life* and published *Scottish House and Gardens from the Archives of Country Life* (1997).

MATTHEW J HUME was born in Glasgow in 1969 and educated at Hyndland Secondary School. He then attended the University of Glasgow where he took an Honours degree in the Humanities, awarded 1990. In 1995, he supplemented this with a Postgraduate Diploma in Museum and Gallery Studies from the University of St Andrews. Archival work experience with Glasgow University as a volunteer in vacations 1987–89, and a contract to list the records of John Hastie Ltd, Greenock in 1990, were followed by voluntary work at Summerlee Heritage Trust. In 1991 he became Assistant Curator (Industrial History) at Summerlee, and on Local Government reorganisation, Curator of Industrial History, North Lanarkshire Council.

GUTHRIE HUTTON was born in Scotland and raised in Australia, arriving back in Glasgow in 1962 at a time when the debate about the future of the Forth and Clyde Canal was in full swing. He took early retirement in 1994 on the grounds of redundancy after a thirty-two year career at BBC Scotland as a television set designer, and latterly as a programme planner. He began a second stint as chairman of the Forth and Clyde Canal Society in 1995, and played a leading role in the voluntary sector's contribution in the campaign to win funding for the Millennium Link.

GORDON JACKSON is Reader in Economic History at the Department of History in the University of Strathclyde. His research focuses on maritime history, and in addition to papers in many books and journals, he has authored several books, including *The History and Archaeology of Ports*, *Hull in the Eighteenth Century*, and *The Whaling Trade*. He is also a member of the International Commission for Maritime History, and is Chairman of the British Commission.

FRANK LAWRIE is Director of Heritage Policy in Historic Scotland. He joined the Agency's predecessor body in 1988 as Deputy Director and Head of Historic Buildings Division, having moved across from looking after co-ordination of EC agricultural policies within the Scottish Office. A career civil servant, he has had a lifelong interest in industrial archaeology, including particularly the archaeology and history of railway development in the United Kingdom. He is an Assessor to the Railway Heritage Trust, and is a member of the United Kingdom judging panel for the Ian Allan Railway Heritage Awards. A keen cricketer and qualified cricket coach, he is also heavily involved in the promotion of sport for the young.

JANET MCBAIN graduated in Scottish History at Edinburgh University, and then trained as an archivist at Glasgow University Archives. In the mid-1970s she was employed as survey officer on the Western Survey of the National Register of Archives, and then on a temporary contract with the Scottish Film Council to examine a collection of nitrate films in a garden shed! One of the more successful of the early Job Creation schemes, this led to the establishment of the Scottish Film and Television Archive. As Curator of the Archive, she has contributed to several television programmes and film retrospectives on aspects of Scotland on the screen, and has published a number of articles on Scottish film history. She is also the author of *Pictures Past: Recollections of Scottish Cinemas* (1986) and the filmography 'Scotland in Feature Film' in *From Limelight to Satellite* (1990).

MICHAEL MOSS was educated at the University of Oxford and trained as an archivist at the Bodleian Library. He was appointed Registrar of the Western Survey of the National Register of Archives Scotland in 1970 to locate and list records in private hands in what was to become the Strathclyde Region. Over the next four years he collaborated closely with John Hume in rescuing the records of the Clyde's shipbuilding and heavy engineering industries. He became archivist of the University of Glasgow in 1974 and was awarded a personal chair in archival studies in 1997. He has written widely on a variety of topics including (with John Hume) shipbuilding and engineering, the history of Scottish universities, the dynamics of wealthholding, and issues in historical methodology. He is currently writing a history of Standard Life, the Edinburgh life assurance office, to celebrate the company's 175th anniversary in the year 2000.

MILES K OGLETHORPE completed BA Honours and PhD degrees at Durham and Glasgow Universities respectively before joining the Scottish Industrial Archaeology Survey (SIAS) at the Department of History in the University of Strathclyde in 1982, assisting its Survey Officer, Graham Douglas, and working under the directorship of

John Hume. SIAS was transferred in 1985 to the Royal Commission on the Ancient and Historical Monuments of Scotland in Edinburgh, where he now works in the Buildings Division's Industrial Survey. Recent publications have included *Explosives in the Service of Man: Ardeer and the Nobel Heritage* (1996), jointly authored with John E Dolan, formerly of ICI Explosives.

EDWINA PROUDFOOT, educated at Edinburgh University, lectured at universities in Durham, Edmonton and Calgary (Canada), and St Andrews (Adult Education). She has excavated Bronze Age burial mounds in England, and recently at Dun, Angus, for The National Trust for Scotland. Other excavations include the Hallow Hill, Fife, an early Christian cemetery. She directed the Fife Archaeological Index of archaeological research in Fife. She has served on numerous committees including the National Trust for Scotland's Executive, and currently as Past President, the Council for Scottish Archaeology. Her current research interests include the Island of Bute, a survey of graveyards, and the Inventory of Scottish Church Heritage.

TED RUDDOCK MBE is an Honorary Fellow of the Department of Architecture in the University of Edinburgh, and former Senior Lecturer and Head of Department. A Civil Engineer by profession, he has for over twenty-five years combined practice in the conservation of historic buildings and bridges – prime examples being Alloa Tower and Nasmyth Bridge – with lecturing and writing both about their history and their conservation. He has received national awards for both areas of his work.

DAVID WALKER OBE was born in 1933 at Dundee, which formed the subject of his first architectural researches. He studied at the College of Art there. After a period of study in Glasgow he joined the Scottish Office's Historic Buildings division in Edinburgh in 1961, where he became Chief Inspector of Historic Buildings until 1993. He is currently Associate Professor at the School of Art History, University of St Andrews, and Assessor to the Heritage Lottery Fund.

MARK WATSON is a Principal Inspector of Historic Buildings within Historic Scotland, engaged on listed building and conservation area consent casework. He has previously worked at the Ironbridge Gorge and Scottish Mining Museums. A Dundonian, he is author of *Jute and Flax Mills in Dundee* (1990) and a contributor to the *Blackwell Encyclopedia of Industrial Archaeology* (1992).

MICHAEL MOSS

John Hume and a Vision of Scotland's Heritage

I fiRST MET John Hume in 1970 (see Figure 1), not long after I had taken up my appointment as Registrar of the Western Survey of the National Register of Archives (Scotland) with the task of surveying records of historical interest, broadly defined, in what was to become the short-lived Strathclyde Region. I can vividly recall going to see him for the first time – even then he bore a remarkable resemblance to Mr Pickwick, and his office was a cross between the Old Curiosity Shop and an engineer's store. John was recommended to me as an industrial archaeologist – at the time an expanding field with which I had some familiarity. My Headmaster, H M Porter, a distinguished Anglo-Saxon historian of the West of England, had taken an interest in the preservation of the fine mill buildings of the Somerset woollen industry [1] and I had walked to school along the banks of the then disused Kennet and Avon Canal. Consequently, I was aware that this new branch of our discipline had a rigorous scholarly dimension rooted in the best traditions of English antiquarianism – where archival research is the key to interpreting and understanding the physical remains, and where the physical remains contextualise and illuminate the archives. This was and is John Hume's *credo*, and for that very reason our interests meshed precisely. John wanted to record the plant and I wanted to survey and more often than not save the archives. However there is more to John Hume's perspective on the past than just industrial archaeology, if by that we mean the recording and, perhaps, the preserving of remains of our manufacturing and mercantile heritage. Despite or perhaps because of his training in chemistry, he is an historian with a genuine appreciation of

geschichte as a science with its own methodologies and pre-occupations, particularly the dynamics of change. He understands better than most that technical advances are often sudden, at least in their impact, and bring in their wake massive and sometimes unforeseen changes. He also understands the powerful effect of economic forces on national economies which can have bewildering ramifications on enterprises and people caught up in vortexes beyond their control. In a sense, for John Hume the physical object is a metaphor for much that lies beyond and not a thing to be interpreted simply for itself.

Looking back, it is very hard to describe what the west of Scotland was like in 1970. It was profoundly depressing, leading Sydney Checkland to publish his fatalistic and at the time much acclaimed *Upas Tree* in 1976.[2] If you came as I did from the south west of England, it was unimaginable. I was not wholly unprepared. My Scottish grandmother lived on the Tyne, and during my summer holidays I had seen a little of a great shipbuilding river in decline; but nothing on the scale of the Clyde. As we gradually came to appreciate, John Hume and I set to work at the very moment the whole industrial fabric of the west of Scotland finally collapsed. Between 1970 and 1974 when we collaborated most intensively, the roll-call of closures of companies which had once been almost household names, was frightening and, of course, included the most important shipyards on the upper Clyde. In approaching the formidable task of recording and rescuing what we could of what had once been 'the Workshop of the British Empire', we were able to draw on the experience of Peter Payne, the first Colquhoun Lecturer in Business History at the University of

Glasgow, and later professor of economic history at the University of Aberdeen, who had started rescuing records in the early 1960s. He edited the book *Studies in Scottish Business History*, which includes summary lists of his surveys, and was not only a most helpful guide, but also set a high standard for others to follow.[3] John Hume himself had been photographing industrial plant and premises and much else besides since he was in shorts; but by joining forces he was able to adopt a more systematic approach, usually (but not always) with the full co-operation of the management. (I well recall John Hume photographing premises, to which he had been refused access, through locked gates and over high fences, and on occasions being pursued by fearsome dogs.) We described the approach we adopted in 'The Techniques of the Western Survey of the National Register of Archives (Scotland)', in

Chapter 8 of our book, *Workshop of the British Empire – Engineering and Shipbuilding in the West of Scotland*.[4] Although written twenty years ago, it still stands the test of time, and there is little I would wish to add. It spells out clearly our commitment (novel at the time) to the creation of an integrated record of an enterprise, where technical records (including surveys of the physical plant) are given as much weight as those of management, and are not stored separately. This view of the history of manufacturing has been central to all our subsequent writing, and has been widely adopted.

Reflecting back across twenty years, which have seen the most profound structural change in the west of Scotland economy probably since the early nineteenth century, what is lacking from our account is some sense of the reality of the fieldwork. At that time, Glasgow and much of the surrounding

Figure 1. John Hume in 1969, shortly before his first encounter with Michael Moss, and five years after joining the Department of History at the University of Strathclyde.

region was in the grip of 'comprehensive development', a euphemism for comprehensive destruction. Through the ruins of handsome tenements and terraces, pre-cast monstrosities were beginning to pierce the skyline, appalling even to our eyes. The vision of city planners was of a concrete Stalinist city where industry was pushed out to the periphery. We did not, though, begin systematic surveying in Glasgow, but in the ironfounding industry of predominantly central Scotland which, as we discovered, had changed little for almost a century.[5] Foundries, which had adopted mechanical handling, injection moulding and new types of alloy were an exception, and even then it had often been done only half-heartedly. However, surprised as we were, we were not there to criticise, only observe and learn. I recollect calling on one primitive foundry which the owner proudly told us could produce the highest quality spheroidal graphite iron. 'Oh', said John Hume, 'how do you make that?', knowing full well that the ingredients had to be measured very precisely. 'Easy', came the reply, 'we just take a shovel full of that and that' – indicating various sacks of ingredients. Everywhere we went, armies of specious consultants had already been, purveying often misleading advice about how to resolve present difficulties. The evidence of their handiwork could often be seen in expensive investments (rotary furnaces being a good example), which had simply failed to work and contributed directly to the company's collapse. Subsequently we were to encounter many similar tragic stories. It was not difficult to see why consultants had recommended investment because much of the plant was out-dated and seemingly hopelessly undercapitalised. The most remarkable foundry and finishing workshop we visited was in Bridgeton, where many of the machine tools (all belt driven) were a century old, and brass screws were still cut by hand using tools and techniques now entirely forgotten. What consultants, caught up in the white heat of technology, did not understand was that such plant could be operated profitably just because it was undercapitalised – new investment within the existing financial and ownership structure spelled disaster. Of course only

recently has it emerged that much of Japan's industry is organised in this way.

As it turned out, ironfounding could not have been a better place to start – most of the firms were small, and the records on the whole were not extensive, but the preservation of even a fraction of the physical plant was almost impossible. Stores were often crammed with wooden patterns, dating back well into the last century, of long disused items such as huge letters for signs, bench ends of bewildering variety, and complex bits of gearing. There was no obvious home for such material, and at that time architectural ironwork was distinctly unfashionable. Although the remarkable primitive lathes from the brass founder in Bridgeton were not large, preservation was only made possible by the efforts of enthusiasts, who formed the Scottish Society for the Preservation of Historical Machinery (SSPHM). In such circumstances, photography was our only resort if an adequate record of the plant was to be made.

Engineering and shipbuilding was an altogether different scale. Many of the shops were vast and the machine tools enormous. At William Beardmore & Co.'s legendary Parkhead Forge, the enormous trepanning machines installed at the turn of the century to bore 16 inch naval guns survived, and were breathtaking to see. John Hume recorded them, but their weight alone put any thought of preservation out of the question. When one of them had been moved to a shadow factory at Linwood on the outbreak of the Second World War, during the night it had plunged through the concrete floor to disappear into the underlying bog. The same was true of all the large works we visited. In many, the number of 'historic' tools was awesome, with serried rows of steam hammers, forging presses and planing machines. We were privileged to have the opportunity to record these extraordinary monuments to the achievement of the Clyde, and to speak to the men (they were all men), who could, without the help of automated controls, machine a gigantic piece of steel to the tolerance of a thou. Like us, they knew that such skills were of little worth in industries dominated by competitors whose yards and shops were equipped with modern numerically controlled machines. There was nothing they could do – they knew, perhaps better than the management, that re-equipping and re-skilling on such a scale was impossible. All they could do was tell us, often with pride, what it had been like to live through the 1930s depression and the Second World War.

As striking as the antiquated plant in the shipbuilding and engineering industries were, so were the records, which often stretched back to the very origins of a business. I remember vividly crawling with John Hume underneath what were the offices of the Fairfield Shipbuilding and Engineering Company in Govan Road (see Figure 2) to find the records from the time the company was founded by Randolph & Elder in the 1850s. John Hume's excitement in unrolling what turned out to be the first drawings of their marine compound engines was infectious. There were many similar experiences. The sheer wealth of material we encountered was overwhelming, and it is hard to believe we collected and recorded so much in such a short space of time. We had to – time was not on our side. As far as possible

we tried to be systematic, but the pace of events was usually against us. We often only had a week before the demolition contractors moved in. We were also working in the dark, not just literally (often the case) but metaphorically. Since the pioneering work of Peter Payne and Tony Slaven, there had been little research, and as a result we had no context into which we could place what we discovered. Peter Payne's own magisterial history of the west of Scotland steel industry was in preparation, but was not to appear until the end of the decade, and Tony Slaven's *The Development of the West of Scotland 1750–1960* was not published until 1975.[6] In any case, it owed much to the survey work we were engaged in, because Tony Slaven himself was an active participant. John Hume's own path-breaking *The Industrial Archaeology of Glasgow* did not come out until 1974.[7] We had therefore to make some intelligent guesses about the future direction of research at a time, it is worth remembering, when research funding in the social sciences seemed assured. In our quest for balance we, undoubtedly, took too many records from the whole of the engineering sector.

Figure 2. Engraving of the Fairfield Engine Works and Shipbuilding Yard, Glasgow, dated 1890. The offices are top left.

Experience has shown that there is little interest in branches of engineering other than shipbuilding and locomotive manufacture, due almost certainly to cuts in funding for research, and an enormous growth in enthusiast interest in ships and railways. It has become difficult for archivists, museum curators and other heritage professionals to justify expenditure in a world driven by the market on areas where there is little demand. Such expense cannot easily be hidden in the archives, and physical objects and plant of heavy engineering trades are very bulky and costly both to record and store. Many archivists and museum curators who care for business records and related artefacts are concerned about how best to address this issue.[8]

Although I coined the phrase 'when in doubt throw it out',[9] I do not subscribe to the view that unused collections should be scrapped in their entirety, but as I have argued elsewhere, some de-accessioning is inevitable. Since it is unlikely the heritage sector will receive much additional funding or new buildings in the near future, we have bluntly to de-accession some material so we can adequately create and preserve a record of more recent industrial and commercial developments.[10] John Hume was amongst the first to advocate recording the contemporary as well as the old in the certain knowledge that modern industrial structures are not built to last. This is not my concern here, however, because what I want to do is to consider how the records of Scottish industry that have been assembled over the last thirty years can be interpreted to a wider audience. There is no doubt in my mind that this is the challenge which confronts all those engaged with industrial heritage, and it is by no means straightforward. Take for example as a metaphor for our times the *Titanic*, completed by Harland & Wolff for the White Star Line in 1912. The most recent film presents this great liner as a British ship, and there is certainly a flavour of American jingoism in the treatment. Nothing could be further from the truth, because by that time the White Star Line was part of an American-owned combine controlled by that mysterious banker, J Pierpoint Morgan. Indeed, the managing director of Harland & Wolff, Sir William Pirrie, had been

vilified for his lack of patriotism in helping to bring the merger about. However he, himself, had been trapped into the merger by the terms of the will of Gustav Schwabe, the uncle of his partner Gustav Wolff. It is impossible effectively to interpret the history of Harland & Wolff, and the many of the liners constructed at Queen's Island, without reference to such connections, but these were only unravelled by John Hume and myself after careful scrutiny of the private ledgers of the firm, which we discovered by chance.[11]

The key to interpretation is usually to be found in finance, but this often presents the greatest obstacles both to research and simple explanation. It is easier to demonstrate how a compound engine worked than to describe the economics of its introduction. The compound engine developed in the mid-1850s by Randolph & Elder had two cylinders, as the name implied, rather than the single cylinder of most existing engines. They were economic to run but expensive to buy. Shipowners had to judge carefully between the need for efficiency and the high initial cost. They made such calculations by drawing on information to be found in their financial records. To many historians such records remain a closed book, although for most enterprises until recently they were the core records, containing most of the information required to manage the business. They are the records which draw together much of the detail of other series, and therefore can illuminate a range of questions, many of which are unrelated in themselves to finance. For example, they provide the names of a company's agents and customers with special relationships. As John Hume and I have demonstrated in both the history of Harland & Wolff and of P MacCallum & Sons, a Greenock firm of iron and steel stockholders, they can be used, in the absence of other records, to unravel the history of an enterprise.[12] Moreover, they can also be used to shed light on patronage, philanthropy, church membership and so on because, until the owners chose to adopt limited liability status, the private ledger contained all the partners' transactions, and even the purchase of household goods.[13]

From the time I first met him, John Hume has

had a feel for the significance of finance – with those searching questions – 'But how much does it cost?' and 'Where did the money come from?' – on the tip of his tongue. I well remember visiting the works of William Doxford in Sunderland to look for some missing Fairfield drawings, and being shown their prototype medium-speed land diesel – the inappropriately named *Seahorse*. There were many problems with medium speed diesels. John Hume watched it vibrating and pulsating on the test bed, listened to the claims of fuel-efficiency, and then said 'How much lube oil does it consume?'. Hurriedly we were led into a small side office, the door closed and came the reply: 'As much lube oil as fuel oil'. John Hume moved not a muscle. It came as no surprise to learn later that the experiment had been a costly failure. In interpreting the past, particularly to our lay public, we need to keep such questions at the forefront because the answers often help to illuminate much of what follows. This applies not just to industrial plant, but also to great churches, houses and castles. Like the *Seahorse*, great churches or houses ill-conceived and built on borrowed money can contribute to the failure of a congregation, or a monastic or noble house. Scotland is littered with examples which are never referred to in wholesome guidebooks, where noble lords rarely do wrong – never gamble or drink. Yet posing such questions adds a human dimension to interpretation, and often helps contextualise a property in a wider scheme of reference, even if it is only the history of the turf, but more often much more than that. It is well known that since medieval times, the aristocracy loved to gamble when deprived of battle; but at the same time, they could aspire to great passions for the latest architectural ideas, agricultural improvements, new theological insights, or simply collecting things. These passions, like gambling, consumed formidable fortunes, often borrowed on the security of their property. Take for example the Earl of Crawford , who applied successfully to Standard Life, the Edinburgh life assurance company, for a loan of £50,000 in 1888. His lawyer reported:

I know the family Establishment expenses are kept as low as possible, and that especially during the 'pinch' of the last few years [a reference to the agricultural depression], household and other expenditure has been reduced to meet the deficiency in income to a very great extent. His Lordship does not bet or gamble in any way and if any of his tastes may be said to be expensive they are in connection with literature and science and these have been and are regulated according to his means. [14]

This was understatement. The Earl borrowed heavily to fund his passion and was obliged to sell both his Dunecht estate in Aberdeenshire and later in 1901 his magnificent *Bibliotheca Lindesiana* to the new John Rylands Library in Manchester for £155,000. This is just one of many examples of similar borrowings, which many would condemn as improvident; but without such recklessness, a great library such as John Rylands, or a great house such as Taymouth Castle, embellished by successive Marquises of Breadalbane, would not exist. The motivation for such behaviour was not greed or envy; but obsession. In a sense, there was little to choose between fine porcelain, fine buildings, fine women and fine horses; they were all expensive. To return to our industrial past, clearly the economics of a sector is a vital ingredient to understanding; but, as the example of the *Titanic* illustrates, exposition must extend beyond cyclical effects to the individual linkages and markets of each concern. Herein lies a crucial problem – if this is so, how are representative sites and objects to be chosen? This is a question that increasingly the whole world of heritage must grapple with.

At some levels the answer is straightforward. We can admit that the linkages of one whisky distillery or grain mill are different, but individual plant have enough in common for examples to be chosen without major disagreement. This is even true for large industrial-scale operations, such as the massive lowland grain distilleries or giant textile mills. We could even extend such a methodology to the preservation of records – a few sets of records of Speyside distilleries would be enough to represent the industry as a whole. Selection would need to be based on a thorough knowledge of the industry to ensure that

collections included some distilleries, such as Mortlach, which continued to market self whiskies after
the rise of blending. However, at the level of the
major Clyde shipbuilding and engineering industries, the answer is enormously complex and open
to considerable disagreement for the simple reason
that many of these businesses were in their time
world leaders with very precise 'niche' markets.
Examples include William Denny of Dumbarton,
with their links to Paddy Henderson and the
Irrawaddy Steam Navigation Co, and Scotts Shipbuilding and Engineering Co with their links to
Swires and the China Steam Navigation Co. The
same can be said for great houses and their occu-
pants, at least until recent times. One has only got
to think of the different roles played by the Dukes
of Argyll and the Viscounts Melville in the history
of Scotland. It is possible to designate New Lanark
as a world heritage site; there is no such mechanism
for designating the record of Fairfields or John
Browns, or even of the Dukes of Argyll, world
heritage collections. I believe there should be such
provision, if only at a European Commission level,
as it is beyond the scope of individual organisations
or the owners effectively to support such significant
holdings. This, of course, would only be a stepping
stone towards the interpretation of a past, which in
many cases has largely vanished with little trace. A
boat trip down the Clyde poignantly illustrates that
little of the mighty shipbuilding industry, which
once dominated the world, survives. For all industrial heritage, this is a major difficulty because
visitors want (partly for their safety) a view of the
past that is so sanitised as to be almost trivial.

This is often as much the fault of the evidence
itself as the exhibition designers and curators. Factory owners made certain that still photographs, and
latterly, film showed plant and products to best
advantage, with a sparklingly clean shop floor and
happy smiling workers. This is not of course to
dismiss such evidence as useless, but to add a note
of caution to any interpretation.[15] Employment and
wage records rarely survive in sufficient quantity to
make it possible to unravel the individual history
of members of the workforce or even to explain,
except in rudimentary terms, how employment was

structured. It is also difficult to convey an impression of the noise and physical exertion of a large
engineering workshop. Nevertheless we must strive
to achieve at least a flavour of such conditions, as
for example in the Annie Macleod Experience at
New Lanark. On the other hand, we must beware
of the danger of presenting all employers as greedy
exploiters of their workforce. We need to show
something of their concerns and the risks they took
in developing their enterprise and leave the visitor
to determine whether their rewards were commensurate. This is usually easier to research from the
perspective of the firm; but it is notoriously difficult
to discover much about the personal opinions of all
but a few men of business. Unlike politicians, they
rarely kept diaries or private correspondence, and
in Scotland at least, usually eschewed the public
stage. When they did record their thoughts and
aspirations, they were more likely to reflect on their
religious attitudes and concerns than their business
outlook, although the one clearly informed the
other.[16]

In the secular society of the late twentieth century, it is very difficult to explain the powerful
influence of religious commitment on the motivation of people in the past. The churches in Scotland,
the majority of which date from the nineteenth
century, are powerful testament to Victorian religious fervour; but in themselves they do not tell of
the excitement of the Disruption of 1843, or of the
long history of secession from the Church of Scotland. At one level, religious differences are easily
explained as being consequences of conflicts over
patronage or provision for the poor; but such interpretation is always simplistic because such causes are
symptoms of profound theological disagreements,
usually about the relationships of the individual with
god. Theological debate in a generation where even
political debate has been trivialised are immensely
difficult to interpret to an audience only familiar
with the outward differences between Protestant
and Catholics. Yet they remain perhaps the most
important motivation for behaviour in all spheres
of life, particularly in Scotland where the political
process was believed to be far removed. This
was very true of the business community, which

contributed most to the building of Free churches and those of other non-conformist Protestant denominations. John Hume has long been interested in the eclectic church architecture of Scotland; but his meticulous recording of buildings was a recognition of the centrality of faith to many of the industrialists whose careers he sought to document. He dismisses out of hand those who view church membership and philanthropy as self-interest, or advance nostrums about social control. Participation in great projects, such as the creation of the Glasgow Royal Technical College, for him are matters of conviction about the wider needs of the whole community or economy, even if there is the potential for personal gain. He stands in a Whig tradition of historical writing which in Scotland stretches back to the Union of 1707.

The next conundrum is where is the industrial and commercial experience of Scotland to be interpreted to a wider audience – given that most industrial-scale sites have gone, or where they survive are too expensive to preserve, or if they are preserved are altered out of all recognition? There is nothing more depressing than some token reminder amidst a modern shopping complex or development of industrial units that this was once the site of a world-famous business. There is everything to commend the reuse of industrial structures, except that their new purpose usually quite properly eclipses the past, making them inappropriate for serious interpretation unless that was the intention from the start. In some projects the past naturally impinges directly on the present, as is the case with the restoration of the Forth & Clyde canal, or the maintenance of road and rail bridges. This does not necessarily make interpretation any more straightforward. The Forth Bridge (see Figure 3) is a spectacular construction, but the achievement of the designers, Sir John Fowler and Sir Benjamin Baker, and the contractor, Sir William Arrol, can only be appreciated in the context of the Tay Bridge disaster, and the complex and unique method of assembly. Explanation requires the use of the remarkable series of construction photographs, which were discovered and catalogued by John Hume and myself in the British Rail collection at the Scottish Record Office. As with railway

structure, it is difficult if not impossible to provide adequate information for users unless the rail franchise operators are willing to collaborate. For most the objects, whether used or unused, remain features in the landscape which would only be *noticed* if they were demolished, or when abandoned were called back to service. Canals, because by their very nature their structures are more accessible than railway lines, present greater opportunities and also dangers. There is no doubt that yachtsmen will welcome an alternative route to the western ocean when the Forth & Clyde Canal is restored. Although in one sense this is the use for which it was intended, in another it is profoundly not. This is what David Lowenthal was getting at in his telling phrase 'the past is a foreign country.'[17] We can recreate an approximation of the past, ships travelling up and down along a disused waterway with all the associated development, but we delude ourselves if we imagine we have recreated past worlds. What we have done is create an opportunity to interpret the past to the present, by for example drawing attention to the remarkable aqueduct which carries the canal over the river Kelvin (NS 562 679), and setting the canal in the wider context of the commercial success of Glasgow in the late eighteenth century, and of the problems of the navigation of the Clyde above the Tail of the Bank. Such exegesis is expensive, and in an outdoor unsupervised setting, a ready target for vandalism, as can be seen all too clearly from the modest signs already in place. It is the confident expectation of the promoters of the restoration that with greater usage will come more security.

There are a few businesses where the past is used directly to reinforce current marketing, no more so than the Scotch whisky industry, which has been one of John Hume and my major interests.[18] When we wrote *The Making of Scotch Whisky*, the number of visitor centres at distilleries could be more or less counted on one hand. Today they are the rule rather than the exception (see Figure 4), reflecting the growth in interest in single malts, and to a lesser extent, the history of leading blends. Although they differ in style, standards are high, and on the whole the presentations are an accurate reflection of the history of the distillery, and sometimes associated

Figure 3. View of the Forth Bridge from North Queensferry during construction in August 1888. (Crown Copyright: RCAHMS)

blends. The Scotch Whisky Heritage Centre in Edinburgh's Royal Mile tells well the history of the whole industry from a cottage craft in the fifteenth century to modern mass production. Nevertheless, in all these visitor attractions there is a sleight of hand – the unspoken assumption that the product is changeless. As anyone who has tasted pre-war, let alone nineteenth-century whisky, knows, nothing could be further from the truth. Suborning the past to present needs is always a threat, and it does not just happen within a commercial context, as the history of the twentieth century reminds us most painfully. With that caveat in mind, the increasing employment of professional archivists, historians, museum curators and librarians by business in Scotland since the 1980s has been a good thing, improving access and the quality of heritage presentation, extending our knowledge of particular sectors, most obviously banking, brewing, insur-

ance, and whisky making. However, for most of Scotland's major industries in the nineteenth century, there is no opportunity to present them in this way because the firms have closed and families switched to other areas of economic activity, if they remain in the world of business at all.

For a long time I have wondered if the best place to display our industrial and commercial inheritance is not so glaringly obvious that we have overlooked it. If we cast our eyes across the landscape of our built heritage, the most numerous sites open to the public are castles and country houses. Their presentation is usually clinical to a fault, scholarly descriptions of the paintings and artefacts, sometimes mention of an advantageous marriage to an American heiress; but rarely are there any reference to economic determents, and yet we all know that the reason so many are in public hands is because of the imperative of capital taxation. It is important

Figure 4. Glenfiddich Distillery, Dufftown – one of the first and most successful visitor centres to be established at a distillery in Scotland. (Crown Copyright: RCAHMS)

of course to understand the intellectual currents that helped shape a great library such as Newhailes, or a fine collection of artefacts such as the Beckford porcelain and silver at Brodick; but it also helpful to know something of the lives and commitments of those responsible. This is something which the *New Dictionary of National Biography* is attempting to correct by including at the most basic level information about a subject's wealth at death, and encouraging contributors to explore in a way which was not done before the practical aspects of careers. There are many houses in Scotland which only exist in their present form because of commercial and industrial wealth, but this scarcely merits a remark in most guidebooks. A tour of Brodick includes paintings of Fonthill, and yet fails to link that extraordinary Gothic fantasy with William Beckford

(1759–1844) and the enormous mercantile fortune he inherited from his father and then left in part to his second daughter, who married the Duke of Hamilton. We surely need to make these connections, illustrating how a legal practice in Edinburgh in the late eighteenth and early nineteenth century gave access to profits from the burgeoning Scottish capital market, which in turn paid for many new houses; how high farming techniques in the 1840s and 1850s may have contributed to a family's fortunes and shaped the landscape of an estate; or how proximity to a railway line in the 1880s may have encouraged the development of dairying; or how owning coal provided a lucrative source of income to pay for elegant Palladian houses in the eighteenth century, and later massive ungainly Victorian extensions, or how the ownership of urban property provided the cash to support Edwardian refurbishment. What we need to do is to alter our frame of reference and ask how much did it cost, and where did the money come from? Once we do that, we can bring our great houses together with our industrial and commercial past to provide visitors with a more complete interpretation. Such an approach will require more rather than less scholarship because these relationships are not always at first obvious, and need to be unravelled from patient investigation of the family archives. This is not to say that industrial museums should or will not exist; they will, but they will never have the attraction of Chatsworth or Culzean. Even if they did, such connections would still need to be made so that the relationship of the New Town of Edinburgh or the West End of Glasgow with the wider economy is understood. There is little purpose in having a Scottish Maritime Museum if it does not do more than catalogue the history of boat and shipbuilding in the country, worthy as such an objective may be. Its interpretation must go further to explore the careers of the entrepreneurs who contributed to its development, the social lives of those who worked in the industries, and the linkages firms established for themselves with shipping companies and overseas markets.

As in many things, the Americans are better at this than we are, probably because culturally they are not embarrassed by wealth and industry; but also, as importantly, they set great store by professional training. At Wintertour, that extraordinary Dupont shrine to American interiors all paid for by chemicals and explosives, the quality of the presentation and the knowledge of the guides and other staff is impressive, and owes much to joint programmes with the University of Delaware. The visitor comes away with the sense that all the staff have a thorough knowledge of the collections and how their area of responsibility fits with the whole. Likewise, the site of the original explosive works

beside the Brandywine River leaves the visitor with a clear impression of how the industry developed, and of the dangers which confronted the workforce. In presenting the whole of our heritage, we urgently need to follow such examples to enrich our visitor experience. Guides need to be better trained so they can set their particular attraction within a wider scheme of reference. Such reformation will be expensive and take time; but what is needed first is a recognition that we need to rethink the ways we approach our past. This is particularly important at time when Scotland is about to embark on a new political future. We must avoid the danger of creating a bogus national identity in tartan-kitsch rather than in the complex tapestry of our historical landscape where being Scottish was defined by residence rather than accent, creed or name.

This is where John Hume has excelled. He has throughout his career challenged the accepted with bold concepts informed by his original interest in Scotland's industry. He rightly sees that Scotland's economic success from the mid-eighteenth century until the First World War was the underlying bedrock of her achievements in other fields, architecture, the sciences, the arts, the church and so on. Without that economic power-house, little would have changed. There would have been no great new country houses and few portraits to paint. However he is no economic determinist, recognising that everything feeds off and informs the other. He is unhappy with concepts of the past as constructs, believing passionately that history is concerned with truth not approximations. His understanding stems from inquisitiveness and desire to ensure that nothing should escape his camera's lens. His contribution has been enormous, and we must ensure that the legacy of his camera and his researches into the largely uncharted territory of Scotland's industrial history are firmly embedded in our interpretation and presentation of historical sites in the future.

NOTES

1. See for example H M Porter, *The Celtic Church in Somerset* (Morgan Books, Bath, 1971).

2. S G Checkland, *The Upas Tree, Glasgow, 1875–1975, A study in Growth and Contraction* (Glasgow, 1976).

3. P L Payne (ed), *Studies in Scottish Business History* (London, 1967).

4. Michael S Moss and John R Hume, *Workshop of the British Empire: Engineering and Shipbuilding in the West of Scotland* (Heinemann, London, 1977).

5. Michael S Moss and John R Hume, 'The Ironfounding Survey', *Newsletter of the Business Archives Council of Scotland*, 1972.

6. P L Payne, *Colvilles and the Scottish Steel Industry* (Clarendon Press, Oxford, 1979), and Anthony Slaven, *The Development of the West of Scotland 1750–1960* (Routledge, Kegan & Paul, London, 1975).

7. John R Hume, *The Industrial Archaeology of Glasgow* (Blackie, Glasgow, 1974).

8. See for example, *Business Records and Business History: Essays in celebration of the 50th Anniversary of The Danish National Business Archives*, Århus, 1998.

9. Michael S Moss, 'When in Doubt Destroy It!', *Proceedings of the Annual Conference 1981 and 1982 of the Business Archives Council*, 1982.

10. See for example Michael S Moss and Lesley M Richmond 'Business records: The Prospect from the Global Village' in James M O'Toole (ed), *The Records of American Business*, Chicago, 1997.

11. Michael S Moss and John R Hume, *Shipbuilders to the World: 125 years of Harland and Wolff, Belfast 1861–1986* (Blackstaff, Belfast, 1986).

12. *Shipbuilders to the World*, op cit, and John R Hume and Michael S Moss, *A Bed of Nails – The History of P MacCallum & Sons Ltd of Greenock 1781–1981 – a study in survival* (Lang & Fulton, Greenock, 1981).

13. See for example N J Morgan and M S Moss, 'Wealthy and titled persons – the accumulation of riches in Victorian Britain – The case of Peter Denny' in Charles Harvey (ed), *Business History Concepts and Measurement* (London, 1989).

14. Standard Life Archives – Minute Book No. 27, A1/1/27, 10 July 1888, p 45.

15. These issues are discussed in Paul Smith (ed), *The Historian and Film* (Cambridge University Press, 1976).

16. See for example A B Bruce, *The Life of William Denny Shipbuilder* (London, 1889). Although a biography, this book contains much autobiographical material.

17. David Lowenthal, *The Past is a Foreign Country* (Cambridge, 1985).

18. Michael S Moss and John R Hume, *The Making of Scotch Whisky: A History of the Scotch Whisky Industry* (James & James, Edinburgh, 1981).

2

MILES OGLETHORPE

Images from an Industrious Past:
John Hume's Contributions to the Collections
of the National Monuments Record of Scotland

Between 1964 and 1984, as part of his research at Strathclyde University, John R Hume took many thousands of photographs every year, mostly of industrial buildings and associated machinery in Scotland (see Figure 1). He also founded a specialist unit, the Scottish Industrial Archaeology Survey (SIAS), which itself generated a large archive covering many hundreds of industrial buildings and structures in Scotland. Since the mid-1980s, he negotiated the transfer of the SIAS and its archive to the Royal Commission on the Ancient and Historical Monuments of Scotland (RCAHMS), gifted portions of his own collections to the National Monuments Record of Scotland (NMRS), and made available for printing a substantial block of his negative archive. This paper evaluates the importance of John Hume's contribution to the NMRS collections, examines ways in which this vast influx of material has been dealt with so far, and considers the opportunities it presents for the future.

Background

In 1964, the newly established Department of Economic and Industrial History at Strathclyde University (formerly the Royal College of Technology) took the unusual decision of appointing a young research chemist, John R Hume, as a lecturer. In the spirit of the new university, his tasks were innovative and inter-disciplinary, involving, for example, the teaching of history of technology to engineering students. In the ensuing twenty years, as well as teaching, he was encouraged by his head of department to undertake research into previously neglected fields. He chose to devote much of his time and energy to work on the history of industrial processes, especially in relation to buildings and machinery.

The results of this two-decade period of intense activity included a sequence of important publications, at the heart of which were the two seminal *The Industrial Archaeology of Scotland*[1] volumes (Lowlands and Borders published in 1976 and Highlands and Islands in 1977), which had been preceded by *The Industrial Archaeology of Glasgow*[2] in 1974. There were, in addition, several co-authored volumes, notably with Michael S Moss[3] (see Figure 2), and many papers and jointly edited publications involving work with colleagues such as John Butt and Ian Donnachie.[4] The publications, however, are merely the tip of an iceberg. Beneath the surface there is an immense body of research material, at the core of which are several thousand CBA (Council for British Archaeology) industrial archaeology site record cards[5] covering all of Scotland, and a photographic collection comprising many tens of thousands of mostly black and white negatives, all of which have been meticulously indexed.

Since the mid-1980s, John Hume has been making this material available to the National Monuments Record of Scotland (NMRS) in an arrangement with its then Curator, Kitty Cruft, which has involved the printing of a substantial

Figure 1. Hayford Mills in 1974, a large former textile mill complex at Cambusbarron, Stirlingshire, **dating from the 1860s.** (John R Hume)

Figure 2. Dalwhinnie Distillery, Inverness-shire 1974 (H74/117/8). The whisky industry was considered worthy of special attention, resulting in the publication (with Michael Moss) of *The Making of Scotch Whisky* in 1981. (John R Hume)

Figure 3. View from the Arrol Collection (donated to RCAHMS in 1987) of the swing bridge over the Forth & Clyde Canal at Clydebank, next to the Singer Factory, taken in the 1930s (B 91746/PO). (Crown Copyright: RCAHMS)

portion of the negative archive, and the gift of the entire CBA Card collection. Although the early batches of photographs were carefully integrated into the collections, the great quantity of images involved resulted in the accumulation of many thousands of images awaiting cataloguing and assimilation into the NMRS collections.

Meanwhile, John Hume's work further contributed to the NMRS collections in a number of ways, not the least of which was the transfer of the Scottish Industrial Archaeology Survey's (SIAS) archive from Strathclyde University in 1985 (RCAHMS 1990).[6] Other important deposits of historical material with which he has been involved have included the Sir William Arrol Collection (see Figure 3),[7] which was donated by the company in 1987, and the Scottish Power Collection (see Figure 4).[8]

There can be few other individuals who have contributed so much important historical material to the NMRS. However, the quantity and complexity of the collection has itself posed challenges hitherto rarely if ever encountered by NMRS staff. The purpose of this paper is therefore to examine briefly the nature, importance and extent of these records, to review how they have been tackled so far, and to consider ways in which they may be made more accessible in the future.

The Importance of Industry

In spite of the kudos associated with the Industrial Revolution, manufacturing industry has never been particularly fashionable in Britain. Even the offspring of early successful entrepreneurs tended to gravitate towards more genteel activities and artistic social circles where possible, whilst the masses naturally aspired towards less gruelling and more lucrative work away from the squalor of rapid urbanisation and expanding mines and factories. British industry nevertheless prospered throughout the 18th and 19th centuries, and nowhere more so than in Scotland, where its success manifested itself in a complex, sophisticated and incredibly diverse industrial economy with important links across the globe (see Figure 5).

By the beginning of the twentieth century, Scotland was an intensely industrialised country,[9] particularly in the central Lowlands, but also further afield where advances in agriculture transformed rural landscapes and induced the development of new industries. Industry had become so much a part of life that it was taken for granted. The outbreak of the First World War in 1914 represented the beginning of the end of this period of expansion

and success, heralding the start of a prolonged period of decline for Scotland's traditional industries. The negative emotions associated with such change are inevitable, and the sequences of colliery, steelworks, shipyard and mill closures created immense social and economic upheaval, even where industries adapted, rationalised and re-generated.

In physical terms, the impetus created by decades of decline in these industries resulted in the unquestioned wholesale destruction of many of the industrial buildings and machines from which contemporary Scotland's wealth and culture were built (see Figure 6). Inevitably, much of this destruction occurred without any connection being made between national heritage and industry. There was simply a perceived need, often driven by local politics, to clear away symbols of recent industrial failure and to start afresh.

Figure 4. Aerial view from the Scottish Power Collection (donated to RCAHMS in 1992) of Barony Power Station and adjacent Colliery (from Barony Album No.7), not long after completion in 1956.

Figure 5. Stanley Mills, Perthshire, 1974. Founded in 1785 by George Dempster, Graham of Fintry, Richard Arkwright and others, it is one of three important surviving cotton mill complexes to be established in the late eighteenth century in Scotland (the others being New Lanark in 1784 and Deanston in 1785). (John R Hume)

Figure 6. Frances Colliery, Dysart, Fife was one of the last traditional coal mines to close, leaving Longannet as Scotland's only deep mine. In keeping with most coal mines, all surface buildings around the pithead were demolished after closure, although in this case, the headframe was spared because of listed-building status. (John R Hume)

It was against this background of destruction and economic transformation that an interest in the industrial period began to emerge in the 1960s and 1970s. In Scotland, there was no better place to conduct research into the historical importance of industry than the Department of Economic and Industrial History at the University of Strathclyde. With the encouragement of Professor Edgar Lythe,[10] his head of department, John Hume embarked upon important research which was augmented by the substantial contributions of colleagues, and by theses completed by undergraduate and postgraduate students at the Department.

The Power of Photography

The study of Scotland's industrial history at this time differed significantly from research normally encountered in an arts or social sciences faculty, where reliance on documentary (usually secondary) sources was the norm. Industry posed several challenges, not the least of which was the huge range of technologies, its often vast scale and geographical spread, the fact that it was disappearing rapidly, and a tendency for economic historians to ignore empirical and technological detail, much of which was beyond their personal experience. It was, however, the speed with which the physical evidence was disappearing that demonstrated the need for research which had its heart the collection of primary data through rapid recording programmes. Photography provided the only means by which this could be achieved (see Figures 7 and 8: Ettrick and Yarrow Mills).

In the late 1990s, many households are awash with unwanted photographs, and many local, regional and national libraries and archives regularly receive gifts of photographic collections that are of potential historical interest. Although some are useful and gratefully received, variable quality, repetitive and unreliable content and poor indexing sometimes render them of little or no value. Some might indeed argue that they clutter important collections, hindering browsing and diluting the value of archive holdings. Certainly, the quality of photography is vital if it is to be of lasting value. In contrast, some collections have become immensely important, constituting the only record of important people and places.

In the context of recording industry, photography proved to be the perfect medium. Until recently (and the advent of digital imaging, of which more is said below), photographs rarely lied. In competent hands, a camera can record huge amounts of data with one image that could take days of work (and subjective argument) to describe in text form, and many hours of drawing. Photographs can bring together elements of a complex site, emphasising functional relationships. They can capture people, machines, processes, and working conditions. They can be used to record both the ordinary and the exceptional. Perhaps most important of all, photography is efficient and flexible, permitting rapid recording where necessary, often with minimum intrusion.

With the support of his department and the Carnegie Trust for the Universities of Scotland, John Hume was able to build a formidable photographic collection. Several factors were important at this juncture, not the least of which was his understanding of industry, and the resulting appreciation of what was important, what was happening, and where and when it was happening. Perhaps most significant, however, was the fact that he has a good eye, and is a competent photographer. He equipped himself with excellent cameras, familiarised himself with the equipment, and established his own darkroom. He was also aware of the continuing uncertainties relating to the long-term stability of colour film, concentrating on black and white photography.

Just as important, however, was the attention paid to background research, physical organisation and the indexing of the photographs. The collections would have been worthless without the support of reliable identification and retrieval systems. This was achieved through the routine maintenance of handwritten indexed caption sheets (including map grid references), and by cross-referencing with a rapidly expanding collection of Council for British Archaeology (CBA) industrial archaeology site index cards. In most cases, the CBA cards included negative numbers, often also having a print or contact print

Figure 7. Ettrick Mill, Selkirk in 1974, a fine example of a Borders woollen mill. By the 1990s, it was disused and attempts were being made to find an alternative use for the buildings. (John R Hume)

Figure 8. Yarrow Mill, Selkirk, in 1974. After the closure of this mill, long-term survival proved to be impossible, despite listed-building status. Like many others in the Borders, most of its buildings have since disappeared. (John R Hume)

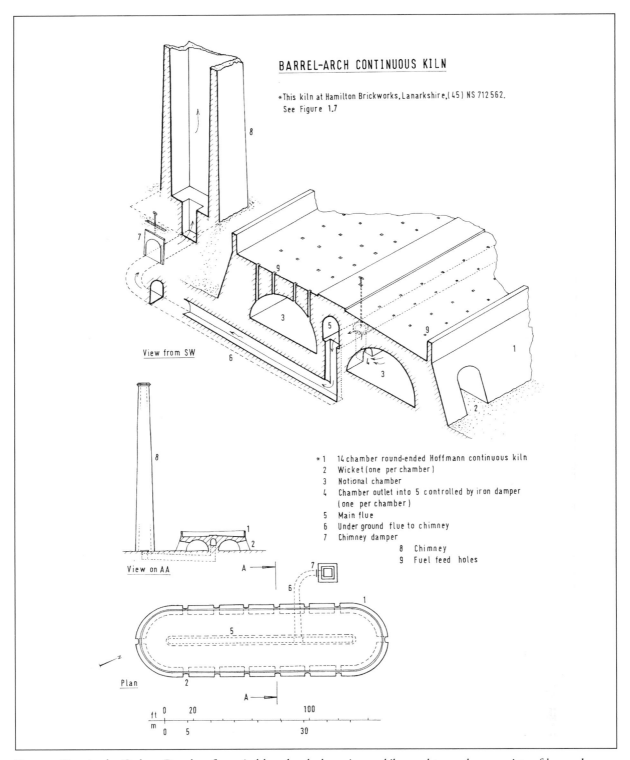

BARREL-ARCH CONTINUOUS KILN

*This kiln at Hamilton Brickworks, Lanarkshire, (45) NS 712 562.
See Figure 1.7

View from SW

View on AA

Plan

* 1 14 chamber round-ended Hoffmann continuous kiln
  2 Wicket (one per chamber)
  3 Notional chamber
  4 Chamber outlet into 5 controlled by iron damper
     (one per chamber)
  5 Main flue
  6 Under ground flue to chimney
  7 Chimney damper
  8 Chimney
  9 Fuel feed holes

ft 0   20   100
m   0   5   30

Figure 9. Drawing by Graham Douglas of a typical barrel-arched continuous kiln, used to produce a variety of heavy clay products (Scottish Industrial Archaeology Survey, 1992). Derived from record of Hamilton Brickworks.

attached or appended. The success of these systems allowed for the inclusion of many of these images in subsequent industrial archaeology publications both by John Hume, and where requested, by other authors too.

SIAS

Although photography provided many of the answers, it became clear during the 1970s that many industrial sites required more detailed attention. This resulted in a subtle and enlightened change in priorities, the intention being to devote resources towards the recording of extant structures. This was achieved by diverting funds provided by the then Ministry of Works (later the Scottish Development

Department) from rescue archaeology to allow the establishment of a specialised unit, the Scottish Industrial Archaeology Survey (SIAS).

The new unit was established at Strathclyde University under the directorship of John Hume. Graham J Douglas was appointed survey officer, and a new pattern of survey was established.

Survey priorities were determined with the assistance of a Panel made up of interested parties, such as Chris Tabraham of SDD Ancient Monuments. In addition to important threatened individual cases, thematic strands were developed which resulted in the systematic survey of, for example, wind and water mills, wind engines, threshing mills, hand-cranes, egg-end boilers, brick and tile works,

Figure 10. Continuous kiln operating at Gartliston Fireclay Works, Glenboig in 1980. This was one of many specialist refractory works in Scotland, all but three of which had disappeared by the early 1990s. (John R Hume)

boat yards, and a wide variety of bridges.[11] A number of publications resulted directly from this work, including books on windmills and the heavy ceramics industries.[12]

Graham Douglas pioneered the survey methodology, compiling annotated site sketches of buildings and machinery, sometimes producing scaled drawings, especially where publication was intended (see Figure 9). Detailed photography (see Figure 10), cartographic evidence, and documentary material were acquired at or near the site. Work in the field was also supported by a research assistant working from a small office situated in the heart of the History Department. Information from secondary sources and John Hume's own record collections was subsequently added to the primary data gathered in the field, all the material being assembled where possible into a single package. The concept of a single co-ordinated record package proved to be particularly popular with researchers who used the material.

Between 1979 and 1985, approximately 1500 packages were amassed, alongside other documentary material, a selection of artefacts (some of which were donated to the National Museums of Scotland) and several films of working industries made with the assistance of the University's Audio-visual Department. In 1982, responsibility for funding SIAS was transferred from SDD to RCAHMS, and three years later, the unit was itself transferred to RCAHMS in Edinburgh. Its two staff, Graham Douglas and Miles Oglethorpe, were incorporated into survey programmes, and the archive was to be catalogued and assimilated into the National Monuments Record of Scotland collections.

RCAHMS

The Royal Commission on the Ancient and Historical Monuments of Scotland (RCAHMS) was founded in 1908, its remit being to record the built heritage of Scotland.[13] From an industrial standpoint, it was born with the severe handicap of a remit which excluded any structure post-dating 1707. Industrial recording could not therefore emerge until after the embargo was lifted in 1948,

and the recording of industrial buildings gradually crept into survey programmes in the 1950s. By the time of the publication of the Stirlingshire Inventory in the 1960s, important early industrial structures were routinely included within inventory programmes.[14] Thereafter, they became a significant element within survey operations, particularly in relation to threatened buildings surveys, culminating in the publication in 1986 of Geoffrey Hay and Geoffrey Stell's book, *Monuments of Industry*.[15]

The arrival of SIAS at the Royal Commission eventually paved the way for the establishment of an Industrial Survey section which took its place in the newly created Buildings Division in 1991. Survey priorities began to shift accordingly, reflecting the Hume philosophy of concentrating on extant sites. Experience had shown that a more strategic approach to surveys created much fuller records. In contrast, waiting for notification of the imminent demise of buildings was less rewarding, most being already gutted and badly vandalised. In particular, the opportunity was taken to record working industries, and to co-ordinate recording activities with sister organisations such as museums, business and local archives, and libraries and universities.[16] Also significant was the fact that industrial surveys were able to draw upon the experience of established and highly experienced Drawing Office and Photographic Departments at RCAHMS, and continue to do so today.

Meanwhile, on the archive front, RCAHMS had been given responsibility for maintaining an archive of the built heritage of Scotland with the advent of the Scottish National Buildings Record (SNBR) and the subsequent creation of the National Monuments Record of Scotland (NMRS) in 1966. The principal task of the NMRS was to accommodate the needs of both the archaeological and architectural archives. In 1985, this task was further complicated by the arrival of the SIAS archive.

The major challenge proved to be the cataloguing and assimilation of the integrated record packages, which did not comply with the standard archiving practice of depositing drawings, photographs and manuscript material in separate areas, the requirement being for each to be stored in appropriate environmental conditions. A solution was found in which only photographic negatives were removed from the packages and catalogued normally before being deposited in the negative store with the main collections. The packages were otherwise retained intact, but site sketches were also given separate drawings collection catalogue slips and numbers. Much of the SIAS Archive is therefore stored within the Manuscript Collection (MS500), and users can continue to consult the packages as integrated records.

It was also in the mid-1980s that the NMRS Curator, Kitty Cruft, brokered the arrangement by which RCAHMS began printing copies of a major block of John Hume's photographic collections. The agreement resulted in the NMRS receiving prints, usually supplied in batches of 100 films, which was the equivalent of 1500 images per batch. This process continued until 1996, and the completion of all the medium-format negatives. As the batches arrived, the photographs were catalogued, and location data for every site was checked and upgraded. This involved imposing archaeology database standards, and included verifying names, plotting the sites on record maps, and providing eight-figure grid references. However, the quantity of the photographs involved, and huge number of sites to which they refer, has meant that the process of cataloguing and assimilation into the NMRS has not kept pace with the printing. It is estimated that in 1998, only one quarter of the collection has been incorporated into the collections. A brief examination of the quantities involved is illuminating.

The Hume Archives

In the first major phase of photography between 1966 and 1969, John Hume took 520 films using a medium-format Yashica camera. It is estimated that these amount to approximately 3000 images. Between 1974 and 1980, he converted to a Hasselblad (medium-format) camera, taking an average of 100 films a year. It is estimated that this period generated approximately 15,000 images. These are mostly industrial, but there was an increasing ecclesiastical tendency, sewing the seeds of a separate Churches collection. In addition, there is the added future

challenge of his collection of 35mm films. Between 1964 and 1979, he took an average of one hundred 36-exposure films each year, amounting (conservatively) to over 50,000 images.

Concentrating on the medium format material, John Hume generated an archive of at least 15,000 medium-format industrial images between 1966 and 1980, all of which have been printed, and most of which are awaiting cataloguing and assimilation into the NMRS collections. The problem is that these processes are time-consuming, requiring checking the index sheets against existing site records in the NMRS catalogue, checking names, providing unique site numbers and eight-figure grid references, and plotting on maps. Fortunately, the quality of the data is already very high, but the checking and cataloguing process is unavoidable, and takes time if it is to be done thoroughly and consistently. It also coincides with a period of increasing pressure on resources, with repeated years of reduced funding resulting in losses of staff. Dealing with the Hume Collection is therefore a major challenge, but recent developments may present a potential solution.

The Future

When in the mid-1980s the NMRS was originally presented with the SIAS archive and the first batches of Hume photographs, cataloguing and data retrieval was primarily a manual process, although the archaeology side was already beginning the process of computerisation. Since then, there has been an Information Technology revolution which has had major ramifications throughout RCAHMS. The first area of development related to databases, and with the assistance of Oracle software, it has been possible to build a computerised catalogue for archaeology. A data upgrade and input programme for the architecture side of the archive is now in place, and it is hoped that by 2000, the entire NMRS collection will be catalogued, and will be accessible via CANMORE [17] on the Internet.

At a lesser scale, the development of small database packages has revolutionised the way individual collections can be catalogued. John Hume was quick to embrace early databases such as Cardbox, the simple efficiency of which has yet to be matched by more powerful contemporary software. Cardbox was also used in the late 1980s to handle SIAS data, but since then, new packages such as dBase and Microsoft Access have provided the opportunity for more sophisticated applications which can feed directly into the NMRS Oracle database.

The availability of these database packages should permit a much more streamlined approach to cataloguing the Hume Collection. It is now possible for site data to be gathered systematically from each film's index sheet, and to be checked and augmented subsequently by NMRS staff, who may, for example, wish to deal with batches of sites by area or map sheet. This data can easily be cross-referenced with data gathered from the CBA cards, and from the NMRS Oracle database. The potential of these databases has been further enhanced by the development at RCAHMS of Geographic Information Systems (GIS) which allow for the use of digitised maps on computers, and by integration with the NMRS Oracle database.

Most recent of all has been the rapid development of digital imaging technology, which allows the scanning and storage of images by computers. In its infancy, digital imaging was troubled by technical problems, poor resolution, slow processing, the high cost of computer hardware (especially memory), unstable, ever-changing technology and standards, and poor public access to computers. By 1998, multimedia PCs were becoming household items, the teething technical problems appeared to be receding, and RCAHMS had embarked upon programmes to digitise selected images both for publication, and for use in education via the SCRAN [18] programme.

The potential for the application of digital imaging to large photographic collections has also become clear, and is already widely used by newspapers and specialist archive bodies. In particular, the ability of high-resolution flat-bed scanners to scan entire strips of films (i.e. 120 medium-format and 35mm films) at one time will be significant, as will accompanying integrated database software which allows for the efficient and reliable retrieval of images from digital archives. If this technology is applied successfully to the current batch of 15,000

Hume images, it is possible that it could also be used to capture and catalogue the additional 60,000 35mm-format images that he took between 1964 and 1979.

Currently, the ways in which the new digital-imaging technology can be adopted to assist with the cataloguing and assimilation of the Hume archives and other large image-based collections are under active discussion at RCAHMS. Much depends on the power, speed and flexibility of the new image scanners, and on the availability of external funding both to support the acquisition of the necessary software and hardware, and to pay for scanning and cataloguing staff.

It was for this reason that RCAHMS recently submitted a grant application to SCRAN. This was subsequently accepted, and RCAHMS will soon therefore begin the process of making the Hume images available to schools, libraries, museums and community centres throughout the country. This will allow a huge variety of historical images to be brought into the public domain, and in particular, made available to educational establishments throughout the country.

Conclusion

John Hume's contribution to the collections within the National Monuments Record of Scotland has been immense. The material that he has provided both directly and indirectly is of great importance, and demonstrates not only the great power and potential of photography, but also the importance of backing it up with sound research and organisation.

As the upgrade of the NMRS catalogue continues, the importance even of the small number of Hume photographs so far integrated into the system is becoming more evident (see Figure 11). When the Highlands were completed recently, for example, the new catalogue revealed that Hume photographs were the only surviving evidence of the existence of many buildings. This is certain to be the case in Glasgow, where large parts of the city were destroyed in the comprehensive re-development programmes and environmental 'improvements' of the 1960s, 1970s and 1980s.

With the SIAS archive already integrated, the

Figure 11. Achingale Mill, Caithness in 1974. This is one of several very fine and distinctive water-powered grain mills in Caithness. (John R Hume)

next challenge is to tackle the photographic archive of 15,000 images, and capture data both from the accompanying index sheets, and the CBA cards. Once this is achieved, and the data is integrated into the main NMRS catalogue, the full extent and value of the collection will become apparent. Most important, however, will be the use digital of imaging technology resulting from the new SCRAN funding. This represents the beginning of a new era in which new imaging technology radically enhances access to the collections within the National Monuments Record of Scotland.

NOTES

1. J R Hume, *The Industrial Archaeology of Scotland, Vol 1 – Lowlands and Borders*, and J R Hume, *The Industrial Archaeology of Scotland, Vol 2 – Highlands and Islands* (Batsford, London, 1976 and 1977). These two volumes constitute the only available published gazetteer of Scottish industrial archaeology.

2. J R Hume, *The Industrial Archaeology of Glasgow* (Blackie, Glasgow, 1974). A large proportion of the buildings included in this book have since disappeared.

3. Examples of Hume-Moss projects include books on engineering and shipbuilding, such as M S Moss and J R Hume, *Workshop of the British Empire: Engineering and Shipbuilding in the West of Scotland* (Heinemann, London, 1977), M S Moss and J R Hume, *The Making of Scotch Whisky: A History of the Scotch Whisky Industry* (James & James, Edinburgh, 1981)

4. J Butt (ed), *The Industrial Archaeology of Scotland* (David & Charles, Newton Abbot, 1967).

5. Council for British Archaeology (CBA) Cards were compiled for Scottish industrial sites by John Hume (with occasional assistance from others) over many years. They are organised by county and parish, and have been deposited in the NMRS, where they can be viewed by arrangement.

6. RCAHMS, *Scottish Industrial Archaeology Survey 1977–85: Catalogue of Records* (RCAHMS, Edinburgh, 1990). This is a catalogue of SIAS record material transferred to the NMRS in 1985.

7. RCAHMS, *The Sir William Arrol Collection: A guide to the Scottish material held in the National Monuments Record of Scotland* (RCAHMS, Edinburgh, 1998). Publication of a catalogue of the entire collection (relating to Scottish, British and overseas sites) is planned for the near future.

8. RCAHMS, *Catalogue of the Scottish Power Collections* (RCAHMS, Edinburgh, 1994).

9. The ascendancy of Scotland's industrial economy is well illustrated in, J R Hume and M K Oglethorpe, 'Engineering', in J Langton and R J Morris (eds), *Atlas of Industrialising Britain, 1780–1914* (Methuen, London, 1986) pp 136–9.

10. Edgar Lythe trained at the Dundee School of Economics, which pioneered studies in applied economics.

11. The wide range of SIAS recording activities is represented in the catalogue of its records produced by RCAHMS in 1990.

12. Publications emanating directly from SIAS work include, G J Douglas *et al*, *Scottish Windmills: A Survey* (SIAS, University of Strathclyde, Glasgow, 1984), G J Douglas *et al*, *A Survey of Scottish Brickmarks* (SIAS, University of Strathclyde, Glasgow, 1985), and G J Douglas, and M K Oglethorpe, *Brick, Tile and Fireclay Industries in Scotland* (RCAHMS, Edinburgh, 1993).

13. An excellent account of the history of RCAHMS is provided in, J G Dunbar, 'The Royal Commission on the Ancient and Historical Monuments of Scotland: the First 80 Years', *Transactions of the Ancient Monuments Society*, Vol 36, 1992, pp 13–77.

14. See RCAHMS, *Stirlingshire: An Inventory of the Ancient Monuments, Volume 2* (HMSO, Edinburgh, 1963).

15. see G D Hay and G P Stell, *Monuments of Industry* (RCAHMS/HMSO, Edinburgh, 1986).

16. Much of this activity was enhanced by the continued work and evolution of the Scottish Industrial Archaeology Panel (SIAP), which had been formed originally to oversee the work of SIAS

17. CANMORE is a computer application which provides internet access to the database of the National Monuments Record of Scotland. It is available at www.rcahms.gov.uk. Email enquiries can be made through nmrs@rcahms.gov.uk.

18. SCRAN (Scottish Cultural Resources Access Network) is a partnership founded in 1996 by the National Museums of Scotland, the Scottish Museums Council, and RCAHMS. Its purpose is to promote access (via computer multi-media facilities and the internet) to cultural resources throughout Scotland using a wide range of outlets, including schools, libraries, museums, community centres, tourist information offices, and even individual PCs in the home. SCRAN is oriented towards the needs of the national curriculum, and 50% of its funding is secured from the Millennium Commission.

3

JANE GEDDES and EDWINA PROUDFOOT

The Inventory of Scottish Church Heritage

The Planning Stages

Before the 1980s, the archaeological potential of historic churches, both above and below ground, had already become increasingly well-understood in England, where, from the early 1970s Rodwell and others had pioneered modern excavation below the floors and around the external foundations of early and medieval churches.[1] As a result, exciting new information had begun to emerge about their dating and origin and many churches were found to be much older and more complex than previous historical records had shown. Similar research was rare in Scotland at that time, although individual projects had shown the potential; for example, Radford (1950) had excavated at Whithorn in 1949[2] and Reece (1981) reported on 'Recent Work on Iona', but no comprehensive research or monitoring were being carried out.[3]

When the Council for Scottish Archaeology (CSA) Churches Committee was set up in 1985, under the chairmanship of Liz Thoms, its role was to address all aspects of church archaeology. The removal of church fittings and the effect of liturgical re-ordering of interiors became an early focus and, as a result, in association with the Church of Scotland, *Notes for guidance on the care of some church heritage items* (1987) were prepared. This leaflet primarily referred to portable items and fittings and was distributed to all Church of Scotland churches, together with *Care for your church* (1983), produced by the Church of Scotland General Trustees and the Advisory Committee on Artistic Matters. This booklet was a short but valuable compilation on various aspects of churches, graveyards, memorials,

planning law and archaeology and it informed Session Clerks of the plan to appoint Honorary Archaeological Advisers to each Presbytery. It was thought that teams of Honorary Archaeological Advisers (HAA) would increase the awareness of both archaeologists and the various denominations in the archaeological value of church property. A liaison role was envisaged for the HAAs, who were to pass archaeological information to the relevant church body as well as to the local authority whenever development proposals were first discussed. It was hoped that, by this means, a useful service relating to churches and sites of any date could be provided, to explain potential archaeological significance or answer queries about particular churches.

In due course the Church of Scotland and the Episcopal Church warmly welcomed this proposal and appointed HAAs throughout Scotland. In order to promote the importance of this collaboration the CSA Churches Committee organised two conferences in collaboration with the Church of Scotland – *Archaeology and the Church in Scotland* (1986) and *The Way Forward* (1988), bringing together archaeologists, historians, architects, other researchers, planners, presbytery clerks, church officers and other officials. The goodwill generated led to increased co-operation, but it also highlighted the lack of both archaeologists and of a central pool of accessible up-to-date information, suitable for rapid responses to presbyteries or planners, for example. The lack of individuals willing or able to become Advisers presented severe difficulties and meant that the HAA scheme could not be followed up fully at that time. However, in 1997 the present Churches Committee chairman, Derek Hall, set up a pilot project in Fife, in the belief that a comprehensive HAA team was feasible by this date.

A third conference, *Scottish Graveyards Yesterday and Today* was held in 1990, run jointly by CSA and Scottish Local History Forum, aiming to encourage wider interest in the recording of graveyards along with that of churches. While many graveyards have been surveyed, St Andrews, for example,[4] the co-ordination of these in relation to the *Inventory* which is the subject of this paper has been limited, although this information should be added to the database when the opportunity arises.

From the early 1980s the increasing numbers of unused churches, such as Dairsie, Fife, and of redundant churches being sold into secular use, such as St Leonard's Free Church, Perth (which became a bingo club), provided stimulus for archaeological debate. As the status of many church buildings changed, it became clear that remarkably little was known about the archaeological resource of churches and their sites in Scotland. Therefore, the Churches Committee targeted its discussions towards ways of improving knowledge of the archaeological importance of churches and ways of liaising with all the denominations and other bodies whose roles involved caring for churches. The object of this was to help them understand the archaeological and heritage significance of church buildings and sites, not only for the Church, but also as part of the historic landscape. Crucial to the success of this was the requirement for accessible information.

As the CSA had recognised an increasing need for valid archaeological data for development casework and for responses to church-related queries, particularly about the future of redundant churches, these items were to dominate the Churches Committee's deliberations at this early stage. Significantly, there proved to be no (available) records of church development proposals affecting the above or below ground archaeology of any church and there was a continuing lack of archaeological investigation during improvements to facilities at churches in use. However, there was at this junction neither a mechanism for providing archaeological information to individual churches nor for churches to report that they were proposing to carry out works that could

Figure 1. Restenneth Priory, Forfar, Angus. The tower of the earlier church sits off-centre within the remains of the thirteenth-century church of the Augustinian Priory. (Edwina Proudfoot)

Figure 2. Dalmeny Church, Edinburgh. The twentieth-century tower was added to the twelfth-century structure, which is a fine example of Norman architecture, with a carved porch as well as carved window surrounds. (Edwina Proudfoot)

Figure 3. St Clement's Church on the Isle of Lewis is a powerful landscape feature, set within a walled graveyard. Inside are an early sixteenth-century carved tomb, erected for Alexander MacLeod of Dunvegan, and two effigies, also sixteenth century. (Edwina Proudfoot)

affect archaeological remains, other than to their own central office. Nor was a comprehensive list or database available from which to provide information to the local authority planners or to churches, and so the idea developed for compiling an *Inventory* of Scottish Church Archaeology.

The fabric of a church building can be as important archaeologically as the below-ground remains, as, for example at Restenneth, Angus (see Figure 1), while in a majority of buildings the architecture might be the most important aspect of a church, as at Dalmeny, Edinburgh (see Figure 2), while St Clement's, Rodel, Lewis (see Figure 3) is also important for the monuments within the building. As more modern churches came to be recognised as being of importance too, the remit for the proposed *Inventory* widened, until eventually it became the *Inventory* of the Scottish Church Heritage. The intended focus was on any building used at any time, including the present, for any form of Christian worship. Although initially it was thought feasible to include every aspect of a church building, inside and out, above and below ground, together with internal fittings, it was finally decided by constraints of time to concentrate on the external and below ground features, leaving the sensitive interiors for a future project. By 1988, a detailed checklist of terms had been generated, covering every aspect of a church or site. This was designed to ensure that comparable data would be collected for every church or chapel, whether this was in use or the fragmentary remains of a long-destroyed early church.

As the word-list grew, the project expanded well beyond the capability of the CSA Churches Committee, although members represented all the main church bodies, as well as the National Monuments Record for Scotland and Historic Scotland. It became clear that plans for the *Inventory* would have to be modified.

Liz Thoms retired from the committee in 1988 and was succeeded by Professor Eric Fernie, until 1992, and then by Dr Richard Fawcett. They piloted the Committee through the difficult discussions about the way forward for the *Inventory* and how it could become a reality. Attention was directed to ways of developing the *Inventory* as a

directory, listing sources of information of every kind from archaeological, through historical to architectural, as well as including important local events. Basic data were required, but the focus remained on sources, rather than on incorporating illustrations or passages of text. The inclusion of at least one accessible reference was deemed to be important, particularly one that would provide relevant information about a church and its history.

The *Inventory* was designed to be all-inclusive, including meeting houses, burgher kirks and gospel halls, for example. While the majority of medieval churches, such as Kilmany (see Figure 4), and churches in use, belong to the Church of Scotland (*circa* two thousand), the Episcopal Church owns three hundred, the Roman Catholic five hundred, the Free Church and Free Presbyterian Churches, two hundred with another four hundred owned by the Baptist Church (see Figure 5), Methodist and Congregational Churches. Over and above this were archaeological sites of early churches as well as redundant and demolished buildings. No accurate estimate was available of the numbers of sites and buildings at this stage and the fact that the above figures were minimal became clear from the first weeks of the project.

Recognition of the fact that the probable number of churches was huge led to the then novel proposal to compile the *Inventory* on a computer, if funding could be secured for this. A Working Party refined methods and objectives of this massive collation exercise and prepared preliminary computer fields in anticipation of such an important innovation. After seeking advice, it was agreed that the program DBase3 © was the most suitable, since this was being used by various organisations for archaeological records and seemed to be good at handling data, while being claimed as 'user friendly'. At this early stage, no consensus had emerged about how the project might proceed, but, as portable computers gradually became available, with sufficient memory to handle a large database, their use appeared to provide the best way forward, not least in facilitating the amount of travel to libraries and field work envisaged as necessary by the Committee.

By 1988 discussions had turned to project costs

Figure 4. Kilmany Church, north Fife, is a typical example of a simple medieval rectangular church set on rising ground, so it can be seen easily from a distance. (Edwina Proudfoot)

Figure 5. The Baptist Church, Leslie, Fife, a large nineteenth-century building which occupies an edge-of-town site away from the centre of Leslie, where the redundant parish church has been converted to flats. (Edwina Proudfoot)

and how the research and in-putting were to be carried out. It was agreed that at least one researcher would be required initially, someone with an archaeological, or related, background and with some computer skills. There could be no further progress, however, since the Committee had no financial resources. Attention now focused on fund-raising and the co-writer, Edwina Proudfoot, as then President of CSA, was asked to develop a fund-raising strategy. A sub-committee was formed to identify and approach funding bodies. In-kind support was offered by Historic Scotland and the Royal Commission on the Ancient and Historical Monuments of Scotland, as well as by the Church of Scotland and the Episcopal Church. Applications were submitted to a number of Trusts and all were excited by this innovative project and were generous in offering funds over each of the planned three years of the initial project. The Graham Hunter Foundation (the Hunter Charitable Trust) of Restenneth Library, Forfar, offered approximately fifty percent of the estimated funding requirement, while the Russell Trust, The Hunter Archaeological Trust, the Binks Trust, The Dalrymple Trust, The Society of Antiquaries of Scotland, the Church of Scotland, the Episcopal Church and a number of individual donors, together contributed sufficient funding to enable the *Inventory* project to be set up and run for the proposed three years.[5]

The co-author, Jane Geddes, was duly appointed to initiate the research and in January 1990 the project was formally launched at Restenneth Library, the home of the Graham Hunter Foundation. Accommodation was made available for the project and its archive in this library, in particular for the church pamphlets and histories that were to be collected as part of the project, and for the necessary meetings. As a result, Restenneth Library and the National Monuments Record of Scotland (NMRS) would be the main bases for the project, although it was anticipated that the Project Officer would travel to visit archives and other organisations.

How the *Inventory* was made

The brief drawn up by the Churches Committee of the CSA in June 1988 was an ambitious challenge.

It set out to locate and record all known church sites in Scotland 'within one year' or 'in any case not longer than two years' and thereafter run on to listing furnishings, architecture, tombs and reading material. The project got off the ground, with all the necessary funds in place for a three-year project, in January 1990. Two features made the project unique: all the information was to be stored in a uniform fashion on a computer database; and the *Inventory* was to cover all material remains of the church in Scotland, regardless of age, quality or denomination.

Technology has moved so fast since then that it is hard to recall its primitive state in 1990. The project's 'wizard' new computer had 20MB memory. The immense primary source of the National Monuments Record of Scotland was already on computer, on the expensive but unfriendly Stairs program but this could not be accessed by a normal computer and it could not be translated into the DBase© program chosen for the *Inventory*. The only way to create the core of our database was to copy manually large amounts of Stairs printout – there were about four thousand items. Scheduled churches were also on a computer list but had to be copied manually. Listed buildings were then even more intractable, recorded on paper with only a typed index to indicate where they were. The basic criteria provided for listed buildings were quite different from those of the Scheduled items held by the National Monuments Record, in particular in not requiring an eight-figure grid reference. Sites and Monuments Records from the Regions, again all presented in different ways, were logged. Then came all the denominational handbooks recording the level of ecclesiastical activity but far from precise about the location of their buildings. Out of all these compendious archives, only one could be electronically transferred in an instant. It contained all the location data of the NMRS, the architectural information of the Statutory List, the denominational information of the year books. This was the personal record of one thousand churches in Strathclyde made by John Hume.

By the end of the first year a core list of about 8500 sites, assembled from official sources, was logged.[6] To standardise the data, research assistants were employed to find or check the eight-figure grid references on Ordnance Survey maps. At this point, the CSA came into its own. The Council was able to provide a nation-wide network of contacts, people who were prepared to check the lists of churches in the field, reporting on the condition and other details about sites. It was important to provide the volunteers with an appropriate level of research. They were sent a print-out of the existing sites known in their locality, a short questionnaire asking purely visual questions about condition and use, plus a request for any local printed information and any additional sites provided by local knowledge.

The results obtained by 'foot slogging' were often spectacular. George Watson, exploring Caithness, produced a sixty percent increase on nationally recorded sites. Specific field studies were carried out by the Project Officer in Forfar and Inverness. Here archives were trawled and old maps used to locate defunct churches, a depth of information not required from the other fieldworkers. Even in these well-recorded towns, an archive search produced a thirty percent increase on the national figure. About three thousand sites were explored in two hundred and thirty (out of about nine hundred) parishes. This up-to-date survey was of a type never attempted before, giving equal weight to archaeological traces, outstanding architecture and minor sectarian buildings. At the same time as the fieldwork data were coming in, the bibliography began. This was intended to focus on the major church histories, in particular providing dates and architects for Church of Scotland buildings.

Funding for the project ceased in 1993, leaving an interesting product and useful tool. Its main home is in the Restenneth Library, Forfar, where the large collection of church guide books sent in by fieldworkers also resides. On disc, the database has been updated and is now on Microsoft Access©. It can be interrogated in numerous ways, not only by map references or denomination but also by church name, monastic order, period and condition. It also highlights the peculiarly intractable nature of Scottish church history with its numerous schisms and reconciliations. It shows how even the poorest communities were prepared to build their own house of worship, just to avoid sitting in the same service as their neighbours. It shows how today, all these schisms become irrelevant as the church drifts away from the centre of Scottish communal life. As congregations disperse and the buildings become an increasing burden, an *Inventory* becomes increasingly important.

Conclusion

When the initial project came to an end in January 1993, although much remained outstanding, a huge amount of data had been collected and systematised into a basic computerised *Inventory*. A formal launch, held in the former Glasite Church, Barony Street, Edinburgh, included a computer demonstration of the data. Support for the project had been overwhelming and it had been abundantly clear throughout the three-year period that a great many potential users recognised that this database was necessary and were anticipating its completion and distribution. In three years as Project Officer, the co-author had created the first phase of a database of over ten thousand churches and sites. Although few entries were complete in every detail this was an impressive compilation, capable of easy updating. However, little funding had been secured for further work and so the *Inventory* had only in part fulfilled its initial promise.

A computer database of this type is, above all, a living tool, only as accurate as the latest entry. From 1994 to 1997 the computer software was upgraded to improve access to the data. Mike Heyworth, of the Council for British Archaeology (CBA), Jeremy Huggitt of Glasgow University and Jill Harden, the Director of CSA improved the database itself, compressing it and making it more 'user friendly'. When limited funds became available in 1996, a new part-time Project Officer, Morag Cross, was contracted to complete the checking of outstanding fieldworkers' reports, and to establish which parishes had been recorded, and those which were incomplete or untouched. She has redesigned the field workers forms and has also run a pilot project to gather field data with the help of a team of voluntary helpers, although so far this new information has not been added to the database.

Without further funding it was obvious that the *Inventory* could not be brought to the stage where the initial *directory* would be complete for each record currently in the database. A Working Party was set up early in 1998 to examine the future of the *Inventory*. However, a preliminary application to the National Museums of Scotland Scottish Cultural Resources Network (SCRAN) had been successful. The application was by the Hunter Charitable Trust, with in-kind support from NMRS, Historic Scotland and the CSA. The co-writer, Edwina Proudfoot, was made Manager of the project and one short-contract researcher was appointed to prepare the data for SCRAN use. It is an *internet* project, aimed at schools. It makes use of the *Inventory* but new information is being gathered in addition, which should benefit the *Inventory* in due course. A thousand records have been adapted for SCRAN, seven hundred and fifty basic and two hundred and fifty in more detail and supported by digitised illustrations.

Some two hundred of these records are photographs generously provided by John Hume, since photographs had not been collected for the *Inventory*. Among these were many nineteenth and twentieth-churches previously omitted, but now seen as an important aspect of the *Inventory*. Among the many names connected with the project, John Hume's was particularly prominent although he had not been involved in the formative stages of devising the *Inventory*. Co-author, Jane Geddes, frequently commented during her period as Project Officer, on Hume's detailed and immaculate records of churches which he made freely available to the project.[7]

Because Scottish church history has been so fragmented, no single body had ever before had an interest in recording the whole picture. This *Inventory* has pulled together all the strands, tying Scotland together in its past, at a time when the relevance of the contemporary church is increasingly questioned.

NOTES

1. W Rodwell, *Church Archaeology* (Batsford and English Heritage, 1989), chp 7, pp 114–42.
2. C A R Radford, 'Excavations at Whithorn ... 1949', *Transactions of the Dumfries and Galloway Natural History and Antiquarian Society*, Vol 27, pp 85–126.
3. R Reece, 'Recent Work on Iona, 1964–74', Institute of Archaeology, University of London, Occasional Paper 5 (London, 1981).
4. E Proudfoot with C Denholm and A Nickell, 'St Andrews Cathedral Graveyard Survey', *Tayside and Fife Archaeological Journal*, No 4 (1998), pp 248–59.
5. Support for the *Inventory* was immediate. The Graham Hunter Foundation (The Hunter Charitable Trust) main Sponsor, The Society of Antiquaries of Scotland, The Russell Trust, The Hunter Archaeological Trust (Falkirk), The Binks Trust, The General Trustees of the Church of Scotland and two Anonymous donors, committed the finance for the full three years of the project. The National Monuments Record, Historic Scotland, the main denominations of the Church, other church organisations, Local Authorities, many presbyteries, local churches and numerous individuals all contributed a great deal of help in kind and many individuals took part in the fieldwork. To all of these an enormous debt is owed, and our thanks are offered for all the generous assistance and support for the project.
6. The fields of the computer database for which information is entered, where possible, are as follows: ADDRESS: Site Name. Dedication. Address. Civil parish/burgh. In Use? County. Postcode. District. Region. CLASSIFICATION: Inventory No. NMRS No. Maps. Map Checked? OS Grid Ref. HS status- Bdg B. Type. Monastic Order. Checked on Ground. New Site? Are there paper references or paper records? DENOMINATION: Original denomination. Present denomination. Ecclesiastical parish. RC no. Ecclesiastical administrative area. SITE: Topography. Archaeological potential. Association. Present use. Structure. Concern? Walls. Roof. Style. PERIOD: Early Christian. Medieval. Post Reformation. 19th-century. 20th-century. Date. Associated with. Date. Associated with. BIBLIOGRAPHY: printed/archive/ correspondence. Subject. The report options comprise: Print Full Record. Print Summary Report. Print Report by Parish.
7. This brief outline of the development of both the *Inventory* and the SCRAN projects is offered here in recognition of John's undoubted enthusiasm for churches and of his generosity, help and encouragement to the Churches Committee and its *Inventory* – and to both authors – always with a touch of humour and a quiet smile.

4

GORDON JACKSON

In-Ports and Ex-Ports:
The Problems and Promises of Constant Change

THE ROMANS thought Britain economically attractive, and so did the Saxons and Danes. Above all, the alien Norman rulers of this offshore colony of France, with its abundance of wool and lead, but no wine, found traffic with the homeland necessary for their economic, social and political ambitions. French monks planted sheep runs through the grass lands, though real wealth accumulated as their successors turned wool into rough cloth for the export trade. A wide scattering of clothiers is marked by 'Wool Churches' from Yorkshire round to Wales, and by an equally extensive scattering of ports, each dealing with a hinterland constrained by the poverty of inland transport.[1]

The siting of ports was not, however, haphazard. Shipping places required above-average links with sheep runs and lead mines, and that meant collection and distribution by navigable rivers. Moreover, their seaward aspect must offer an easy route to France, the Low Countries and Hanse Towns through which the fairs and markets of Western and Central Europe were reached. From Roman Rutupiae to Mediaeval Cinque Ports, trade thrived in the South East, and only the most favoured places flourished along the distant coast to the Humber and westward to the Severn.

These early ports answered in varying degrees a question which still remains: where should ports be sited? Clearly they needed safe and sizeable harbours, good sea lanes, favourable prevailing winds and, generally, room to manoeuvre without damaging rigging, and – since almost all harbours were tidal and shallow – they required a mud or shingle base on which ships settled at low tide.[2] 'Port facilities' for handling cargo must also be appropriate. Finally there must be a favourable human concatenation: merchants thrived on connections, and trade attracted trade where a fairground of buyers and sellers found warehouses, shipping and credit.

The tiny size of early vessels encouraged the siting of ports upriver from the coast, offering safety and a deeper penetration of the hinterland. The major In-ports were York, Lincoln, Norwich, London, Exeter, Bristol, Gloucester, Chester and so on: none renowned for its seaside air! However, a number of definite trends were apparent by the fifteenth century. Firstly, a growth in the size of vessels, and in the volume and complexity of trade, diminished the appeal of the riverine ports and started the move to the estuaries. York, with much kicking and screaming, gave way to Hull, Lincoln to Boston, Norwich to Yarmouth. 'We have no ships nor mariners belonging the City of York,' the Corporation complained in 1554, 'but only lighters that carry our merchandise duly between Hull and York.'[3] Except for London, the chief In-ports became very much the Ex-ports! There is no permanence in port history.

Secondly, many ports declined for physical reasons. Those on the coast or on silty rivers were choked to death: 'the merchants', it was said of Chester (whose trade was with Ireland rather than the Continent), 'cannot freight any ship beyond the seas to arrive in this port but at extra-ordinary rates by reason of the danger of the river ...'[4] Others were cut off by shifting sands. On the north Norfolk coast Wells-next-the-Sea was a living lie, while the sea, Defoe wrote of Orford, 'was resolved to disown the place, and that it should be a seaport no longer'.[5] Grimsby's river Freshney cut a new channel to the sea, but Wisbech deserved to survive since it appeared itself to be at sea: starting in the Middle Ages on the river Ouse four miles from the Wash, it found itself eventually on the river Nene eleven miles from the Wash.

Such unfortunate peculiarities affected the ability of ports to handle trade passing through them, but the third and perhaps most damaging trend was the shift of trade itself for exogenous reasons. The substitution of cloth for wool was particularly upsetting, since the same places were not necessarily involved. Hull, for instance, shipped around sixty thousand sacks of wool annually *circa* 1300, and four thousand by 1500. Some places suffered on all accounts: the sinking of the Cinque ports in a sea of mud and sand was hardly more dramatic than the failure of their trade.

This last point raises the most important trend, and, indeed, one of the most important recurring themes of British trade and shipping. The tendency for activity to concentrate in narrow lanes is clearly revealed in the history of the cloth trade. Bristol traditionally had a large share of it, but her exports were, literally, decimated in the early sixteenth century; her wine imports also diminished as she shared the troubles of the English economy.[6] The short crossing from the shelter of the Thames to the Low Countries – initially to Antwerp – was preferred for valuable cargoes, and reinforced by mercantile monopolies of Germanic Hansards or English Merchant Adventurers who drew trade into London to the cost of the Out-ports. If we add its own intensive market it is obvious why London, more than any other port, developed a highly sophisticated trading system that was poised to expand when new opportunities offered. For decades the Outports complained of London's success, though that might have owed as much to London's superior cloth market as to its geographical position.[7]

In fact distress in the out-ports sprang partly from a general malaise of the economy from around 1500

to 1660 during which British trade marked time with a European economy deeply upset by recurring wars, plagues and religious persecutions. The way out for the British was to exploit favourable factor endowments and raise the stock of land, labour and capital. Such enterprise was inherently related to overseas trade and produced immense consequence and opportunities for British ports as merchants and pirates followed the European exploration of the world. The growth in value and volume of trade was less notable than initiatives of small size but great potential in what might loosely be called 'imperial' activity, leading into the Commercial Revolution *circa* 1660–1740, which in turn stimulated Britain's Industrial Revolution.[8]

Though not first in time or size, the English East India Company (established in 1601), imported Indian and Chinese silks, muslins, saltpetre, pepper, spices and tea which could be sold into Europe to purchase imports to make profits whose multiplier effects were an important stimulant to the economy. However, while fixing the monopoly (like the Russia, Whaling and Levant monopolies) in London increased commercial activity there, neither the trade nor the large East India-men stimulated experiments in port facilities and shipbuilding in the provinces. A more crucial initiative for the other ports was the establishment of America which turned the face of British trade and was the main prop of the Commercial Revolution. British capital and labour produced oil, fish, and timber on land in the Northern colonies, and, further south, the tobacco which produced great wealth in the early days and cotton which subsequently maintained Britain's greatest industry. In the West Indies, bereft of settlers, agents employed British capital to set African labour to work producing sugar, rum and spices. Whatever the factor inputs, the result was the same: an immensely valuable and wide ranging mixture of goods for re-export to Europe, with or without value added.

Colonial consumption was also important in stimulating industrialisation. Emigrants demanded the things distinguishing them from 'savages'. When Edward Hyrne bought his Carolina plantation in 1701 he imported 'goods proper for South

Carolina', chiefly light cloth for the summer, and heavy cloth and duffels 'proper for ye winter'. He also wanted buttons, lace, writing paper, tools, gunpowder, bullets and shot.[9] Gunpowder was thought an appropriate birthday present from the homeland.[10] The Scottish stores system in Virginia helped Glasgow to dominate the tobacco trade.[11] The West Indies demanded slave cloth – a mixture of rough flax and hemp – and slave irons as well as the slaves which stimulated other areas of shipping and economic activity. And long before the independence of Latin America one Jamaica merchant told his English contacts: 'If you would send us over goods proper for ye Spanish trade, and give us leave to send them out, ... we could make you returns speedier than for goods sold in [Jamaica]; and in weighty money; and ye risk is nothing.'[12] Compared with the East India trade, the ramifications of transatlantic trade were widespread. Dundee linen producers and Sheffield cutlers responded to colonial demand; Sugar Houses on the Clyde, Avon and Thames responded to supply, as did the best of all examples, cotton manufacture in Lancashire and Lanarkshire.

There was nothing to stop a port from adventuring westwards. Aberdeen shipped linens, Montrose dabbled in slavery, Hull shipped cutlery outwards and whale oil inwards, Whitehaven was rich for a time on exported coal and imported tobacco, and Dumfries, across the Solway had its finger in the colonial pie. But since the voyage round the north and east coasts of Britain was dangerous and time-consuming, transatlantic influence was felt chiefly on the west coast where the rise of the new In-Ports and the development of their coal-bearing, metal-working and damp hinterlands were inter-locked. In fact the most revealing thing about the important western ports in the eighteenth century was their small number. If Bristol was favoured when her narrow southern European wine trade was overtaken by complex transatlantic interests which 'created a centre of early modern capitalism out of a mediaeval commercial town',[13] it was chiefly because her hinterland encompassed the pioneering industrial region around Coalbrookdale. When that region was by-passed by industrialisation in central

England and Scotland, Bristol remained an 'In-port', but by 1800 was, comparatively, past its best.[14]

Ports were not slow to inspire their hinterland, and none rivalled the meteoric rise of the two giants, Liverpool and Glasgow, which also became manufacturing as well as collection and distribution centres.[15] They dominated foreign trade outside London because they were effective links in a chain of transatlantic supply and demand deeply embedded in the two major industrial regions. Their ability to respond to new challenges would appear to lie in an appropriate mixture of mercantile and maritime expertise and enterprise that penetrated markets in most parts of the world, good port facilities and inland communications, and exceptional hinterlands. Indeed, so great were the factor endowments and entrepreneurial skills on the Clyde itself that Glasgow ultimately became a sort of Liverpool and Manchester combined, the 'second city of the empire'.[16]

In a Britain mesmerised by empire the importance of European trade is oft-forgotten. In the early eighteenth century a huge variety of European manufactures and raw materials flowed into Britain. The assumption that Britain could have managed without Europe is dispelled by a glance at the Customs ledgers. Most British ships operated in European waters and carried pit props and crib wood on which coal mining depended; uffers and double uffers which – literally – supported the building and shipbuilding industries; timber for general construction (Arkwright's cotton mills used timber from Russia); flax for the linen industry; bar iron from Sweden and Russia; and so on.[17] The Industrial Revolution was founded at least partly on younger sons from British ports searching the northern seas for new resources. Sometime around mid-century the flow of manufactures was reversed, but Europe remained more significant as a source of goods than as a volume market until the expansion of the coal trade in the nineteenth century. There were, of course, other items of interest. The Iberian and French wine trades went on regardless of other developments, and fruit came from the south and from Holland, which also sent vast quantities of its cheeses and seeds. How much more would have come had Britain not maintained a vigorous protectionist policy is difficult to assess. French trade was restricted until the mid-nineteenth century, and Russian and German markets were constrained by local hostility towards British goods because of British taxes on their goods, especially corn and timber.[18]

We would not expect London to lose the leadership in European trade which it had had since the rise of cloth exports, because the great flow of miscellaneous goods, of foodstuffs and wines, continued to go through the capital which was the richest and largest consuming region in the country. Moreover, London was, beyond doubt, the most important shipper to Europe of colonial goods, and this meant that a very considerable volume of shipping left London for European ports and tended therefore to offer suitable freights to Britain even if not to the right British port. The other major east ports – Aberdeen, Leith, Newcastle, Hull and Yarmouth – remained the same, but they did not have the colonial traffic and so always had trouble with ballasting; even where they had large trade flows – as in flax or timber – they tended to be in only one direction. What is important is that the ports of the Forth, Tyne and Humber dealt with the major industrialising regions of Britain, and in consequence they grew strongly and maintained an 'IN'-Port status while many of the other eastern ports stagnated and many more became 'EX'-ports – Scarborough and Grimsby, for instance – on the basis of ruined facilities or stagnant hinterlands.

Although much is written about foreign trade, the traffic of most ports was a compromise between the economy and convenience of direct versus coastwise shipments. Anything might be had from London, so that foreign trade statistics do not reveal the full picture. Hull in particular was a huge coastwise importer, chiefly because her imperial goods came from London, and imperial exports commonly went there until the mid nineteenth century.[19] The same was true of Dundee's linen exports, which went through the Forth & Clyde Ship Canal and out through Glasgow or Liverpool, or down the coast to London, and her subsequent imports of Indian jute arrived, initially, via London.[20]

However, coastal trade was no mere adjunct to foreign trade. With regional specialisation in food and fuel production, in manufactures and in the provision of building materials, coasters were constantly on the move, especially to and from London. Indeed, the opening of coal mines, slate quarries, lime kilns and brick pits owed something to the nearness of navigable water. The coastal coal trade was a major employer of shipping throughout the modern period, and if vessels involved in interregional distribution are added to those moving foreign trade goods, there is justification for a recent statement that 'from 1760 to 1830, it is clear that coastal shipping tonnage rose at a faster rate than the general level of economic activity'.[21] As so often happens in port history, influences are more widely disseminated than might at first be supposed.

Only ports with the necessary connections, expertise and facilities could benefit from new opportunities, yet many showed a complete disregard for this simple truth. The basic premises for discussing port facilities are that they always lagged behind need, were built only after great debate and opposition, and were out of date before they opened. They were also frequently built in the wrong place. These shortcomings did not always spring from cupidity or stupidity, though both play a role in transport history. The basic problem was recognising need. Generally speaking the irregular nature of trade required a sort of average harbour capacity of adequate depth and safety to cater for loading and unloading and for laying up the fleet in winter. Unfortunately as trade boomed in the eighteenth century, harbours failed to cope with either of these problems, though not necessarily together. Most ports were troubled first by the need to park 'light' ships, though there were various ways round the problem; colliers, for instance, were commonly laid up in minor ports with good harbours such as Whitby, Scarborough and Ipswich.

Thriving ports began substantial improvements around 1700 in what might be called the first phase of development, lasting until the 1830s. Exeter's sea connections were improved in the 1690s.[22] The 'new' port of Glasgow took the opposite line and moved her trade down river to Port Glasgow and

Greenock at the turn of the century. On the Thames the Howland Dock was opened around 1700 for 'light' ships and dry-docking, and one on the Avon around 1710; neither catered for trade. It was another 'new' port, Liverpool, with no proper quay, that introduced the first commercial dock in Britain around 1715, with others following in a fairly regular succession for the next two centuries. Hull, under great pressure from coasters, 'light' vessels and floating timber, was the first port to open a generously sized modern dock in the 1770s. Here, too, there followed other docks, and Leith and Bristol undertook work around the end of the century, but very few other places spent much money on major construction; it was, as yet, unnecessary even for 'In-ports'.

In order to gain revenue docks were monopolies owned – except in Hull – by public trusts. All ships entering a port paid dock dues even if they did not enter the dock, since all gained from its existence. London's problem was that her shortcomings by 1800 were so great that she needed a whole series of docks, but they would still be no more than additional to her good river system. Moreover, the West India merchants, who led the way, were chiefly inspired by pilfering, which could cost a ship half-a-ton of sugar a day. They pressed for a dock which was more akin to a fortress than a harbour work, and since this was not appropriate for all trades, the West India, East India, London, Commercial, Baltic and East Country Dock Companies were formed, each with rights over specified ships or cargoes. It is difficult to imagine how London's trade expansion could have continued without them.[23] These works were magnificent in conception and engineering, but there was soon a paradox. As part of the Free Trade movement of 1820 Thomas Tooke became chairman of a predatory company expected to reduce port costs. The contribution to the provision of London facilities by the resultant St Katharine's Dock could be described as ludicrous were it not for the fact that its mummified corpse is so attractive. Practically everything about St Katharine's was wrong. The water area was too small, the river site was inappropriate, she had inadequate quay space and could not tie up large coastal steamers at its so-called steamship quay. But the dock survived because of those magnificent warehouses which were built to attract valuable cargoes from other docks.

It is, perhaps, worth adding a note about *public* warehouses, since they figure so prominently in modern approaches to dockland refurbishment. Of relatively slight significance until quite modern times, they came into their own for seasonal colonial produce, while the high value of goods and the introduction of Customs bonds (for Indian goods in 1700, tobacco in 1751, reinforced by general Warehousing Acts of 1799–1805) demanded secure warehouses.[24] But bulky, low-value cargoes required open quays for rapid handling or timber storage. So, while London, with its particular needs, built huge public warehouses, and Liverpool had its Goree range, the general pattern was for private warehouses away from docks (as, indeed, were London's private wharves). It made for greater manhandling, but caused less immediate congestion and was therefore cheaper.

While London and the major ports built large expensive docks benefiting from advanced engineering skills, most small ports endeavoured to manage with rebuilding existing harbours which catered for moderate trade while precluding serious expansion and, particularly, investment in the all-important 'liner' shipping which bound trade to specific ports. Lancaster was the only minor port to produce a dock in this first phase of building. On the other hand several new ports emerged as part of the canal system. For example, the Duke of Bridgewater built Runcorn between 1773 and 1800 as the terminus of his Manchester-Liverpool canal and Bowling and Grangemouth were built at either end of the Forth & Clyde canal. But the two most important 'canal ports' were certainly Goole, built by the Aire & Calder Canal Company to tranship goods between barge and ship on the Humber, and Gloucester by the Gloucester & Berkeley Canal Company to serve barge traffic on the upper Severn.

It was fairly obvious that if docks were only to be built in existing ports, there could be no competition from new ports established outside existing trade patterns. It was assumed that early dock companies over-charged, and to be fair, some probably did, Hull Dock – the first private enterprise dock – obscenely so. Inevitably some misguided – or plain greedy – merchants and shipowners argued that facilities could always be made cheaper by introducing competition, and speculators were quick to agree. Was anything easier than building a port? Grimsby dock, *circa* 1800, was therefore important as the first serious speculation intended to create a major 'In-port' by seizing trade from a natural one: Hull. Compared with Goole, it failed for lack of a hinterland and overseas or coastal connections.[25] Nevertheless it was a precednet followed by railway companies and others in the nineteenth century, and sadly port history is littered with the remains of ports pandering to local pride – or greed – and lacking economic justification. Almost anything was easier than building a port!

By the early nineteenth century it looks as if the 'In-ports', the major ports and those well established but less well connected, were firmly on the map. The problems facing the port system were over-all growth rather than novel shifts in direction of trade. Transatlantic and imperial trade continued to benefit Glasgow, Liverpool, Bristol and London. So, too, did European trade, to the benefit of eastern ports. But huge advances in the volume of trade, especially the bulk trades, relied on inter-active symbiotic advances in shipping and port technology with the application of steam and hydraulic power. Eighteenth-century docks built on valuable city-centre land (encouraging minimum quay space), assuming three hundred to three hundred and fifty ton vessels and hedged around with warehouses, were not appropriate for nineteenth-century initiatives.

Large, locked basins with small quays could not cope with steamships. Early river steamers thrived on rapid turn-round at open quays or piers, and by the 1830s, when steamers entered coastal and then long-haul trade, they were too big for the biggest locks. Several ports built ephemeral 'Steamship harbours' or 'Steamship docks' in the 1830s and 1840s, not least because steamers were fire hazards. But such works did not answer the other problems. While steamers were ramming the front gates, railways attacked from the rear. The latter demanded open access and wide quays and by mid century a second port revolution was under way as the 'In-ports' responded by building docks with wide locks, piers or quays for rapid transit steamers, reasonable railway access and modern handling devices based on hydraulic power, first introduced, it is said, at Grimsby. Both Hull and London built Victoria docks, while Liverpool, facing a fantastic expansion of transatlantic trade, built ten docks between the opening of Albert Dock as its first integrated warehouse dock in 1845 and Canada dock, with its 100 ft-wide lock for the largest transatlantic steamers, in 1859. There was a clear relationship between the rapid expansion of the leading ports and the adoption of the most advanced technology on land and afloat. No port could remain in the first rank without it.

The re-building of old docks might just have been possible, but was rejected because there was plenty of traditional short-haul traffic to fill them. Moreover, temporary closures were expensive and might cause walls to collapse. So ports acquired a variety of depths and facilities ranging from advanced hydraulic coal hoists and ever-stronger cranes to antique cranes serving the traditional vessels found in all ports, more, in fact, in the great ports than in the small. Normally, nothing was ever thrown away or built over, though it might be rebuilt or propped up: the Engineer's department was for ever active in busy ports.

Integration of railways, docks and shipping in the 'In-ports' confirmed their position, but also posed a novel threat. Railways gradually replaced waterways between hinterland and port, and old or new economic activities could be linked either to old ports or new. The first steam railway carried coal from Darlington to 'Port Darlington', a new quay outside Stockton, while one of the last was built by the Hull & Barnsley Railway and Dock Company in the 1880s to carry the newly exploited South Yorkshire coal to Hull.

Influences worked both ways. While most railway companies preferred established ports, some sought to attract business from them with purpose-built facilities offering plentiful land, equipment and suitable water. The North Eastern Railway (NER), for instance, built West Hartlepool to increase its domination of the northern coalfields and later used it to rival Hull (which was also an NER-dominated port) because that was cheaper than increasing rails to Hull; it was not a great success. The Manchester, Sheffield and Great Grimsby Junction Railway was built by industrialists eager to profit from a route to the Continent independent of Hull and the NER lines, and after a shaky start it became an 'In-port', with a very extensive trade in machinery.[26] By contrast, Birkenhead, intended by the Birkenhead, Lancashire and Cheshire railway to by-pass Liverpool, only survived because it was rescued from disaster by Thomas Brassey, a local lad, and acquired by the Mersey Docks and Harbour Board (thus defeating the intention of its projectors).[27] Southampton, after an encouraging start in the 1840s, was virtually bankrupt by 1870 because it had no significant hinterland, and was only saved (by London and South Western Railway) because its deep water suited transatlantic liners. A rash of lesser developments occurred around the coasts from *circa* 1870 under the influence or direction of railways. The Cumbrian and Scottish coal and industrial ports and the general ports of East Anglia – especially King's Lynn – depended heavily on railway initiatives or connections.[28] Most of them – Boston and Lowestoft, for instance – were important regionally though remaining small.

In fact most successful *new* railway ports were mineral ventures, some built by railway companies and some by coal owners, with the Marquis of Bute's Cardiff leading the way. Coal staithes were not new: the development of the coalfields from Tudor times depended on easy access to coastal or river staithes, with waggonways and railways from an early date. The ports of the Forth, Clyde, Tyne and Severn relied heavily on coal, and stimulated railways in the first place, while Whitehaven had had the largest tonnage of ships clearing Britain for a time in the eighteenth century on the basis of coal exports to the colonies and complementary imports of tobacco. But coal ports were very special places, relying on rapid through-put, and though the largest – Newcastle and Cardiff – handled other goods, they were really specialists, with no certainty that

their livelihood would survive that of the coalfield they served. The same was true of dozens of tiny ports supplying ores, clays, slates and other goods to the industrial regions. Their distinguishing feature was, perhaps, their lack of uniformity, ranging from full-scale docks with hydraulic hoists, to old-fashioned mineral staiths; several ports were constructed of slates; one tiny Humberside 'dock' was made of the tiles that were its only shipment. The birth and death of coal ports in particular was locked into the exigencies of supply and the more fickle impact of demand. Their hey-day was surprisingly short, starting with the surge of steam transport in the 1870s and mortally wounded by the First World War.

Fishing ports (as opposed to fishing hamlets) were also new, created to answer market opportunities served initially by 'fleeting' fish by sloop to London, but chiefly by railway fish trains clanking from the new fish docks along the coast to the fish and chip shops of industrial regions. Some were new – as at Fleetwood – but most were grafted onto existing ports such as Aberdeen, Hull, Grimsby and Lowestoft (built initially to link Norwich to the sea and by-pass Yarmouth). Railways made them 'In-ports' in the 1850s and their rather reckless over-fishing made them 'Ex-ports' a century later. Easily built, they shared an unhappy life-cycle with the coal ports, but few other ports were so meteoric in birth, so single-minded in life, and consequently so hapless in decay.

More significant for the future was another set of ports made or boosted by steam power. The 'Penny Black' and easy, cheaper travel enhanced business traffic at such Irish and American packet ports as Stranraer, Heysham, Holyhead and Plymouth. The south-eastern packet ports in particular gained from expanding commercial and social contacts with Europe. Steamers and two railways transformed Dover (where the State also spent huge sums from 1847 on a grand naval harbour which was never used by the navy). Other railways went to Folkestone (for Boulogne) and Newhaven (for Dieppe), while the Dutch and Belgian ferries regularly went from Harwich from the 1860s. Steam brought Europe nearer, and movement towards European trading integration brought increasing prosperity to the eastern ports.

The 1870s mark the start of the third phase of port development. The rise of the international economy, with worldwide investment in primary production, created an unprecedented rise in the volume of exported manufactures and imported bulk foodstuffs and raw materials, particularly timber, cotton, wool and oil. With reductions in freight rates, net tonnage of shipping entering Britain rose by one hundred and fifty-seven percent between 1870–74 and 1910–13, from seventeen to forty-five million tons.[29] Ships clearing rose from nineteen to sixty-two million tons. Such growth depended on massive dock extensions in the major ports, particularly the coal giants since coal was, by 1910–13 running at sixty-six million tons per annum, and fifty-one percent of the increase in ships' tonnage between 1870–74 and 1910–13 was attributable to the coal ports. It is difficult to exaggerate the importance of coal sent to Europe from the eastern ports, and worth remembering that many of the major ports were also largely involved in coastal shipments: Glasgow, Hull and Grimsby had dedicated coal docks, and Liverpool was also heavily involved. Coal docks in general handled more than their proportional share of increased traffic because of the great efficiency of hydraulic – and electric – coal hoists.

For the port system there were three distinct problems. The first was the crush of coasters, which did not peak until the 1920s, and comparatively small vessels in flourishing 'Nearby-European' trades in foodstuffs and manufactures. This required more space but it could be 'hand-me-downs' facilities at relatively small cost, or dedicated piers or river quays. The second was the introduction in the 1880s of long-haul steel cargo vessels of *circa* three thousand tons, which required thirty foot of water and longer, wider locks. The third was the huge oceanic passenger liners which required revolutionary facilities. In 1885 there were only thirty-two British steamers over three thousand tons and the average was one thousand and thirty-two tons; by 1910 there were two thousand, five hundred and seventy-seven over three thousand tons, the average

was two thousand three hundred and the largest, the liner *Olympic*, was forty-six thousand tons.[30] Such liners were enviable evidence of Britain's technical prowess and economic greatness which captured the popular imagination, not least for the carriage of European emigrants and American heiresses, but there was agonising debate over their accommodation. Owners of medium-sized cargo-liners demanded more consideration and resented subsidising these atypical status symbols which required extraordinary depth and space but did not pay proportional dues.[31] One compromise was to build piers into deeper water, and a major reason for the eventual success of Southampton was the use of river quays rather than deep docks, which were vastly more difficult and expensive to build.

This attention to deep-water facilities and operational procedures tied the largest liners literally to a handful of ports and was a foretaste of future patterns as economies of scale were realized. Technological developments also changed the topography of ports by forcing a 'down-river' movement towards open space and deeper water, which in turn led to traffic problems within ports, and not least to difficulties for dockers getting to work. Both Hull and Grimsby built several miles from their centre. London built at Tilbury to avoid the long passage up-river, but still lost the transatlantic passenger trade to Southampton because ships starting from European ports avoided the Thames. Glasgow, by contrast, canalised the Clyde to avoid this desertion by large vessels. In fact, liner companies became so necessary to major port operations that they could dictate terms, demand dedicated berths and machinery and, if thwarted, scupper a port by withdrawing their vessels.

At a lower level, ports were also under pressure to provide specialist facilities for an increasing number of commodities. Grapes, bananas, meat and butter required freezing or chilling warehouses; railway engines required 150-ton cranes, and medium sized cranes of 20 tons were required for shipping machinery. The grain trade required large silos and pumping machinery, while the importation of live animals requires lairages. The importation of iron ore required grabs and, in the final stages, conveyor belts. Nothing was simple any more in the life of ports.

By 1914 the port system appeared to be adequately diverse and permanent in structure. Over half a century the interaction of entrepreneurs and engineers had produced a stupendous maritime achievement, creating trade, stimulating production, securing raw materials, 'modernising' shipping and building physical infrastructures. British ports were the nodes of world-wide networks, based on traditional divisions of labour, but with significant developments in the coal ports, and in one or two new ports for general commerce, of which Manchester (another futile attempt to cheapen transport by creating rival capacity!) was the chief. Although the great ports handled the bulk of foreign trade, almost all ports played their part in the system. There were, of course, the dead and dying, the mediaeval survivors turned seaside resorts or scraping a living in coastal trade, but by and large the British ports in 1914 were all, in their varying ways, 'In-ports'. Within four years the port system was in disarray and would never fully recover.

Paradoxically, after traditionally lagging behind demand, port authorities were sufficiently encouraged by unprecedented trade growth in the period 1890–1907, gingered-up by increasing competition, to anticipate its continuance. Hindsight finds them naive. Almost every major port was expanding facilities on the eve of the Great War, and even without the war it seems likely that over-supply of facilities would result. Moreover, whatever merchants and shipowners might think of 'imperialists' advocating colonial preference and tariffs,[32] and warmongers who wanted to fight – or warned of the threat from – their major trading partners,[33] it is a pity they did not also anticipate the likely results by tempering their dock building. Optimism in the sea air obscured the fog of hysteria blanketing Europe. But it was political rather than maritime incompetence which lumbered ports with facilities that would not pay their way for years to come, and sometimes never.

The Great War and its aftermath brought local disaster to many ports closed to eliminate railway inefficiencies, rationalise shipping movements and facilitate sea defences and convoy protection. Once concentrated in more cost-effective environments trade was not easily attracted back to old paths. Grimsby and Goole, for instance, never fully recovered from loss of trade to Hull and many minor ports lost status. For the first time since the early eighteenth century there was a serious decline in a significant area of activity as European trades collapsed. Germany had been a major trading partner, with Russia not far behind. The coal trade, for which many of the latest docks were designed, was halved. Methil in Scotland was never fully commissioned; Immingham dock lay empty. But war also emphasised imperial connections and financial chaos encouraged 'sterling area' trading. At the same time coastal trade was less dynamic, and the demand for low-grade harbour room diminished. But to some extent the eastern ports' loss was the western ports' gain. Liverpool, Glasgow and London, with close imperial connections, reached the height of their trading experience. This was the period when the greatest port facilities were introduced for passenger trades: Liverpool's Gladstone dock, London's George V, and works at Southampton and Hull, with lesser but very important developments at Harwich, Dover and Folkestone which began, gradually, to filter goods – as well as passenger – traffic away from more northerly ports. Few of the eastern places could now be described as 'In-ports', and even the larger ones suffered a lengthy government ban on 'communist' timber. With such diversity in experience the problem was how, rather late in the day, to rationalise the port system. Du Plat Taylor, a leading docks consultant, recommended nationalisation as the only way to get systematic planning and eliminate local interests. In fact nothing was done and the system in general decayed. Politics was not good for 'free' markets. The Second World War again concentrated trade in western ports, while the eastern ports suffered from serious bombing and continued to decay.

There were two powerful trends after 1945 when the port system was effectively destabilised. The first was the peak of imperialism and costly peacetime military activity, upsetting the Americans and causing balance of payments problems and trade restrictions. Imperial preference was preferred to 'multi-lateralism' while Europe was still in economic chaos; well over half of exports went to North and South America and the empire. Again the western ports and London were obvious beneficiaries. But the second trend was towards European trade, rejected for a decade because the weaker European economies initially offered little to a country exporting as much as the rest of Europe put together. By the 1950s the relative decline of the British economy and empire, and Cold War realities, increased the attractiveness of Europe. Trade was turning towards the Continent long before Britain joined the EEC in 1972, and by the 1980s most of Britain's trade was with the EEC.[34] The consequences were probably the most significant upset to the port system since the rise of the American colonies in the early eighteenth century. In a nutshell, many south eastern ports boomed while most of the western ones died. One can play 'hunt the dock' in Liverpool and Bristol, or 'hunt the port' in Maryport, Troon and (on the east coast) Hartlepool. An exaggeration perhaps, but the survival of small-scale activity cannot hide the massive concentration of large-scale activity in very few places.

The violence of the changes were not a symptom of shifts in the direction of trade alone. The Common Market coincided with technical changes at sea which turned the whole world of commerce upside down and made and unmade ports or parts of ports. The application of thought to transport (which apparently only occurs in wartime) led to experimentation with palletisation, 'roll on – roll off' and containerisation, all of which revolutionised handling methods and eliminated the need for large scale storage in ports and for large workforces. Much traffic moved from cargo vessels in docks to ferries at piers, and since owners of very expensive new vessels wanted short crossings and speedy turn round, trade homed-in on the old packet ports of the south east. Huge quantities of material could be handled with clockwork precision, through very small areas of deep water docks and piers, The trade of London deserted to Dover, Felixstow and Harwich; that of the Midlands to Hull. So did much of the trade of northern Britain, since the

economics of large ships makes it more desirable to have short sea-crossing and long land routes. It was many years before anyone in Britain became concerned at the lack of roads to the new ports! The fact that railways were not built for the new 'In ports' was either stupidity of the sort always found in transport policy, or (as rumour suggested) a response to the activity of certain lobby groups. But if not railways, why not decent roads?

To be fair, the great days of shallow ports were already numbered because of very large ships for bulk carriage, particularly of oil, minerals and grain. Already oil tankers were seeking deep-water piers with space for storage and oil refineries. The subsequent globalisation of shipping, involving fleets of very large container vessels breaking bulk at few ports world-wide, by-passed Britain; Rotterdam monopolised European container business. Glasgow, Liverpool, Southampton, Felixstowe and Hull lost the largest vessels and became secondary hubs handling bulk carriers or Ro/Ro vessels, or individual containers transferred from Rotterdam by large ferries. So far as exports were concerned coal was concentrated on ports such as Immingham (Grimsby) and iron ore imports were similarly concentrated (at Hunterston Quay, for instance) until the steel industry itself went into serious decline.

Paradoxically, while the largest vessels no longer came to British ports, many of the east coast ports were re-born as servers. Moreover, smaller bulk carriers could now anchor in or off ports that were ports only in name: the old Cinque port of Sandwich, for instance, now received Ro/Ro vessels with imported cars. Indeed, a cheaper option was to ignore established ports altogether and go for up-river landing stages with no traditions – or, like Sandwich, decent roads. Small vessels up the Trent land timber at river quays no bigger than the juggernauts that thunder around the country lanes of Lincolnshire. The ancient port of King's Lynn with no decent roads into the docks or out of the town, is a grand example of small-minded planning in transport. But these places are, one presumes, cheap so long as one does not examine the true economic and social costs of allowing shippers to choose this week's cheap offer. In the current system's assessment of values, the life of a small 'In-port' can be very short indeed, nowhere more obviously than in some of the oil-related ports where investment is encouraged and is hardly productive before the industry moves on!

Change in the port system since 1945 has been rapid, and its diversity exceeds that of any previous similar period. There had been substantial breaks in trend before, and minor ports had fallen by the seaside, but for two centuries or more the pattern in general trade (as opposed to the rise and fall of mineral harbours) was for small-to-medium places to mind their own business while the major ports grew from strength to strength. They handled the bulk of foreign and coastal traffic; they made the great investment in facilities and ships. Their merchants facilitated industrial growth by creating a symbiotic trading system in which imperial trade and European trade were linked. In the process the work of the eastern and western ports became complementary. In recent decades the rise of the eastern ports has not stimulated the western ones, and most of the mineral ports are derelict. Outside the major ports, balancing importation and exportation is difficult, and shipping arrives with the regularity of exogenous arrangements. Few foreign ships tramp down the coast with cargoes of apples, wood, or fish.

There have been other changes. Ports were once places where merchants grew rich. Others observe that dockers grew poor. Either way, there was wealth and employment. Just how much wealth and employment was determined by the principal trades pursued. Mineral ports were not the richest, and mechanisation meant that their population might be small; agents acted for coal owners, and the bulk of the wealth created lay in the hands of the latter and of shipowners. General commercial ports where merchants pushed trade were the wealthiest, but even here the great merchant houses were in decline in the export trades by *circa* 1800 and with regular shipping movements agency houses tended to replace merchants. By the middle of the nineteenth century the rich men in ports were the shipowners, and the general population was tending towards poverty except in times of good trade. In fact some

of the hardship suffered by dockers was inherent in dealing with irregular shipping, and it is doubtful if their hardship, and that of the wider port community, owed more in the long run to inadequacies in the maritime world than to the constant political intervention in matters of trade which so annoyed Adam Smith. The shifts between ports was initially driven by the ports themselves. By the late nineteenth century it was driven by governments looking for enemies, forcing trade into politically advantageous routes, re-imposing tariffs, and at best abstaining in the present century when port authorities and workers conspired to ruin their comparative advantages. Above all, the complete lack of an integrated transport policy has meant that there is no sensible control over rapid shifts in internal transport systems which has made the port system as a whole volatile because the true costs of operation are obscured by the building of motorways or subsidising of railways. In fact the *Rochdale Committee of Inquiry into the Major Ports of Great Britain* (HMSO, 1962) suggested closures and integration, but nothing happened. So ports collapse in the 'provinces', and juggernauts do their work. One final irony for 'Ex-ports' is that the private companies to which they were assigned some years ago are now more wealthy from the sale or leasing of their land than they are from operating their ports.

The deliberate destruction of ports, or their use as office, shop and living space, assumes two things. Firstly that decline in the form it took was inevitable; and secondly that there will be no reversals. But the concentration of people and economic activity in the south of England may become politically and financially unacceptable, and concentration of shipping on southern ports which are cheap and cheerful may not outlast an examination of the real economic and social costs of long-distance internal transport. Concerns about motor transport are farcical without attention to the siting of major ports. Similarly, the encouragement of small ports without adequate distribution lines has been a catastrophic environmental failure. When the Victorians wanted an economy to move they built an integrated transport system. If ever we decide to do the same the role of major as well as minor ports may well change. Dover is in any case frightened by the Channel Tunnel, though the apparent inability to link the tunnel effectively to the heartland of Britain may produce a stay of execution. If Dover and the other duty-free havens become Ex-ports, there may well be room for a revival of some of the older In-ports once favoured by the railways. All precedents suggest that it is dangerous to build or close ports on the assumption that current economic and political demands will be permanent.

NOTES

1. A general survey of the development of British ports may be found in Gordon Jackson, *The History and Archaeology of Ports* (Tadworth, 1983).

2. The word dock originally meant the hollow into which a ship settled between tides.

3. Quoted in B F Duckham, *The Yorkshire Ouse* (Newton Abbot, 1967), p 40.

4. Quoted in J Thirsk (ed), *Seventeenth Century Economic Documents* (Oxford, 1972), p 330.

5. D Defoe, *Tour through England and Wales* (Everyman edition, 1928), Vol I, p 54.

6. D H Sacks, *The Widening Gate: Bristol and the Atlantic Economy, 1450–1700* (Oxford, 1991), pp 24–9.

7. See, for instance, Sacks, p 32.

8. Trends in trade were summarised in R Davis, *The Rise of the English Shipping Industry* (London, 1962), 'English Foreign trade, 1660–1700, *Economic History Review*, Vol VII and 'English Foreign Trade 1700–1774', *Economic History Review*, Vol XV, and more recently, in relation to port development, by G Jackson, *Ports, passim*, and 'The Ports', in D H Aldcroft & M J Freeman (eds), *Transport in the Industrial Revolution* (Manchester, 1983). The relationship between internal and overseas activity is discussed most recently by P K O'Brien, 'Inseparable Connections, Trade, Economy and Fiscal State, and the Expansion of Empire, 1688–1815' and J M Price, 'The Imperial Economy, 1700–1776', both in P J Marshall (ed), *Oxford History of the British Empire, Vol 2: The Eighteenth Century* (Oxford, 1998).

9. Lincolnshire Archive Office, Massingberd 21/20, E Hyrne to C Fowler, 17 July 1705.

10. L A O, Massingberd 21/22/2, B Massingberd to E Hyrnes, 25 Feb 1705.

11. T M Devine, *The Tobacco Lords* (Edinburgh, 1975) Ch. 4.

12. L A O Monson 28/B/5/4, W Parkes, Kingston, Jamaica, to J & T Eyres, 11 June 1705.

13. Sacks, *Widening Gate*.

14. K Morgan, *Bristol and the Atlantic Trade in the Eighteenth Century*, (Cambridge, 1993), p 220.

15. G Jackson, 'Glasgow in Transition', in T M Devine & G Jackson, *Glasgow, Vol I: Beginnings to 1830* (Manchester, 1995), pp 78–85; and R H Campbell, 'The Making of the Industrial City' and G Jackson, 'New Horizons in Trade', in *Glasgow*; Morgan, *Bristol*, pp 93–107.

16. J Butt, 'The Industries of Glasgow' and G Jackson, 'Trade, Commerce and Finance', in W H Fraser & I Maver (eds), *Glasgow, Vol II: 1830–1912* (Manchester, 1996). Tracing the ultimate ramifications of this imperial stimulus was one of John Hume's major achievements, in M S Moss and J R Hume, *Workshop of the British Empire* (London, 1976).

17. The importance of this European connection is emphasised in G Jackson, *Hull in the Eighteenth Century* (London, 1971) and 'Anglo-Dutch Trade', in C Wilson & D Proctor (eds), *1688: The Seaborne Alliance and Diplomatic Revolution* (London, 1989), pp 75–88.

18. See, for instance, J B Williams, *British Commercial Policy and Trade Expansion, 1750–1850* (Oxford, 1972), p 175 for Russian attitudes, and pp 198–208 for German.

19. G Jackson, *Hull*, Ch. IV.

20. G Jackson, *Trade and Shipping of Dundee, 1780–1850* (Abertay Historical Society, Dundee, 1991), Ch. 4.

21. Armstrong & P Bagwell, 'Coastal Shipping', in Aldcroft & Freeman (eds), *Transport in the Industrial Revolution* p 147.

22. E A G Clark, *The Ports of the Exe Estuary, 1660–1860* (Exeter, 1960), Ch. II.

23. For a brief introduction, see J Pudney, *London's Docks* (London, 1975).

24. E E Hoon, *The Organisation of the English Customs System, 1696–1786* (1938, reprinted Greenwood Press, New York, 1968), pp 150–6, 262–4; Warehousing Acts 39 Geo III, cap 59, 43 Geo III, cap 132, 45 Geo III, cap 87.

25. See G Jackson, *The Grimsby Haven Company, 1786–1846* (Grimsby, 1971).

26. See G Jackson, 'Do Docks make trade?: The Case of the Port of Great Grimsby', in L R Fischer (ed), *From Wheel House to Counting House: Essays in Maritime Business History in Honour of Professor Peter Neville Davies* (Research In Maritime History No 2; International Maritime History Association, 1992), pp 17–41.

27. F E Hyde, *Liverpool and the Mersey: an Economic History of a Port* (Newton Abbot, 1971), Ch. 5.

28. For a brief summary, see *Ports*, pp 136–8.

29. Jackson, *Ports*, pp 114–15. Percentage based on actual formuales; allowance must be made for rounding.

30. For changes in shipping and ports in general, see G Jackson, 'The Ports' and 'Shipping', in Aldcroft & Freeman (eds), *Transport in Victorian Britain* (Manchester, 1988).

31. The difference between gross tonnage (which took dock

space) and net earning tonnage (on which dock dues were paid) was excessive for large liners, which were consequently subsidised by smaller vessels. For the debate between liners and cargo liners in Liverpool, see Hyde, *Liverpool and the Mersey*, pp 121–8, and Mountfield.

32. For example, E Burgis [and W V Jackson], *Perils to British Trade* (London, 1895).

33. For example, A White, *Efficiency and Empire* (London, 1901, reprinted Brighton, 1973), and J A Cramb, *Germany and England* (London, 1914).

34. The immediate post-war relations with Europe are discussed in A Cairncross, *Years of Recovery, British Economic Policy, 1945–51* (London, 1985), Ch. 10; for the political side of shifts in trade see J D Tomlinson, *Public Policy and the Economy since 1900* (Oxford, 1990), *passim*.

5

W HAMISH FRASER

Remembering Work

WE LIVE in a time when there is considerable debate about the present and future of work. Undoubtedly the past twenty years have seen an extraordinary change in the nature of work for the bulk of the population. Whole areas of manufacturing and extractive industries have largely disappeared. The heavy industries of iron, steel, engineering and shipbuilding which, for a century and a half and more, provided work for a large proportion of central Scotland's workforce, are largely gone. The textile industries which led Scotland into its industrial revolution in the late eighteenth century are a mere shadow of what they once were. Even farming has become largely a one-man operation with a machine. The crowded fields of haymaking, harvesting and potato-picking are all things of the past. The new industries are, to a large extent, assembly plants for components often made half across the world and produced largely by machine tools rather than by manual labour. For most of the population work means a service industry not a manufacturing one. There are now more people in Britain employed in tourist-related industries than there are in coal mining and car manufacture combined. It is also a world where women make up a greater part of the labour force than ever before, or certainly than they have for three centuries.

For a younger generation then, the world of work, as it existed from about the 1780s until the 1980s, is increasingly the stuff of grandparents' memory and of heritage sites, whether the drift mine of Summerlee or the spinning mules of New Lanark. Industrially depressed areas are to be revived by 'recapturing the past'. The redundant mill, the closed factory, the derelict site where hundreds once worked becomes a place where hundreds now come, not to understand the reality of decay, but presumably to get some sense of what it was like once to work there. Not surprisingly some of the numerous critics of the burgeoning heritage industry have seen it as 'part of the self-fulfilling culture of national decline' while others see a Britain where a new museum for a time was opening every fortnight 'becoming a museum itself'.[1] It is, of course, a very different past from that which bodies such as the National Trust and the National Trust for Scotland originally set out to capture, the past of monarchs, princes and landed gentry amid the fine elegance of the country house.[2] Now it is the past of 'ordinary' people which is being regained. Not that it is necessarily a real past. Some of it, such as the Annie MacLeod experience at New Lanark, is about creating an imaginary past, creating a world which never existed in order to get across some points about the past. But, as post-modernists have been trying to convince us, traditional historians have always been doing something not so very different when they too have tried to re-create the past. The late Raphael Samuel has lamented the hostility which historians have shown to heritage, pointing out that 'Interpretation, the privilege of the archive-based historian, and "re-creation", the ambition of heritage, also share a common conceit; the belief that scrupulous attention to detail will bring the dead to life'. And, he concludes, 'the pleasures of the gaze – scopophilia as it is disparagingly called – are different in kind from those of the written word but not necessarily less taxing on historical reflection and thought'.[3]

A central part of regaining the past of ordinary

Figure 1. A scene at J & P Coats' Ferguslie Mills, Paisley, *circa* 1887, illustrating working conditions in the Old Turning Shop. Even this view and others like it cannot capture fully the noise, smell, dirt and conflict of the workplace. (Crown Copyright: RCAHMS)

people is to try to give some flavour of industrial labour. Yet the world of work is not an easy one to capture. Not many photographs actually existed of people working in the nineteenth and early twentieth centuries. We have plenty of photographs of posed groups: men with their arms folded, foremen with their bowler hats on, looking proud and dignified, perhaps beside some artefact of their trade but few of them actually working. The world of work has to be recreated, therefore, from memory and imagination. Displays of technology create some sense of the scale of operations, although there is often a bizarre eclecticism in the bits and pieces of machinery from different sites and different countries. Working machinery with their whirring belts and

pulleys and recordings give an impression of the noise of the machine shop or the factory. They are intended to awe with their size and their power. But even with them all in operation it is doubtful if they can ever come anywhere near the noise, the smell, the dust of a factory or an engineering workshop without risking litigation or closure by health and safety inspectors. It is barely possible to convey the arduousness of much of the work or of the hazards from sparks and flames and moving belts (see Figure 1). Nor can any site recreate the bustle generated by the numbers of people working. What they convey are mere shadows of the experience of work. They produce a sanitised version of the workplace, just as the rows of houses produce an often mythological version of the home: cleaner, less noisy, less cluttered, less crowded, more tranquil than was ever the case.

But at the same time such displays are not neutral. They involve particular interpretations of the past. In some cases they are just as much about extolling the 'nobility' of manual labour or the 'wonders' of technology as the posed photograph was. There is also an implicit desire to show progress from an apparently poverty-stricken, harsh past to a prosperous, kinder present. Again, neither the past projected in the static tableaux nor the present as assumed tell us much about the actuality of peoples' lives. How something nearer to the realities of the world of work can be captured in heritage centres is not something which this piece will attempt and indeed is beyond the competence of the writer. Rather it will limit itself to discussing how nineteenth and early twentieth-century manual workers who have left autobiographical material remembered their experience of work. There are dangers, of course, that such accounts can be equally sanitised and mythologised. The experience of work is just as capable of being viewed through rose-tinted spectacles as are the endless sunshine days of childhood summer or the wonderful taste and quality of the bread and jam.

We have many autobiographical accounts of working people from the eighteenth until the twentieth centuries. Written accounts of the more modern period have been supplemented by oral historians, who have been particularly active in unearthing the world of working women. In some ways the most surprising thing about most of the written autobiographies, particularly those written by men, is the limited amount of attention which they give to their work experience. Partly, this reflects those who left behind autobiographies. Many were concerned to tell a rags-to-riches story or a tale of triumph over adversity, although such life histories were in reality few and far between and decline and fall is more common than upward mobility.[4] Yet others were concerned to show the road to salvation, usually from drink to sobriety or from unbelief to belief. Some saw the central part of their lives as being in their association with organisations such as

friendly societies, trade unions or in political campaigns from parliamentary reform movements to socialism. The absence of much comment on their work experience is perhaps an indication that work was seen as a necessity, the means of survival, and certainly something that contributed to an individual's place in the world, but it was not, as sometimes is implied by historians, the centre of people's lives. That was the world outside work. The recently published diary of a Dundee millwright, John Sturrock, covering a couple of years in the 1860s, is full of brief notes like 'wrought until ten o'clock', 'commenced at five o'clock at Mill today and wrought till ten again', but the extensive comments are on Sunday jaunts, church attendance, visiting family and friends, self-improving outings.[5] Work was something which had to be borne but which one could do very little to control.

For many the world of childhood faded imperceptibly into the world of work at an early age. A handloom weaver remembered winding bobbins at the age of seven in 1829 and then at nine being 'put to the loom'.[6] The son of a reasonably well-paid millwright in Markinch recalled how he was put to work in a spinning mill at the age of eight from six in the morning until six at night. From there there was a period as baker's boy carrying bread trays on his head, something which regularly produced disfigurement of the neck.[7] Yet another recalled starting in a coal mine at the age of nine pushing a coal hutch.[8] Most people are familiar with the accounts of the brutalities against factory children which the investigations of factory conditions by Oastler, Shaftesbury and others in the 1830s and 1840s brought out. But half-timing in textile mills continued into this century and the exploitation of the young remains a well-entrenched feature of capitalism, albeit now on a global scale. Toward the end of the century the future 'Red Clydesider' MP, David Kirkwood, and the future West Fife Communist MP Willie Gallacher suffered as grocer's boys. Working as a message boy for a Dennistoun grocer, Kirkwood had to pull a two-wheeled porter's barrow laden with provisions three miles to Springburn, often uphill. 'I cannot remember any occasion when anybody gave me a hand with my barrow, though sometimes I have stopped in the middle of the hill, dead-beat and weeping.'[9] An apprentice joiner in Dundee remembered the effort required to push a barrow load of timber the mile from the yard to the docks, heat or snow.[10] Various accounts recall the exploitation experienced at the hands of small employers struggling to make a living.

But the real struggles in the workplace were not generally with employers. What many of the autobiographies bring out strongly is the brutality of fellow workers. A young miner in the early nineteenth century recalled the bullying, the teasing, the beatings, the petty tyrannies employed against him by the other apprentices and by the older men. A letterpress printer recalled the customary, unwritten rules of his workshop for which boys could be fined for breaking even if they knew nothing about them, the fines going to pay for drink for the men.[11] The tales of the humiliation of new apprentices are legion: being sent in search of non-existent items; having their work sabotaged; numerous tormenting pranks.[12] There are few memories of the older experienced man passing on his expertise to the boy. Most apprenticeship seems to have involved little training and much bullying. Most recall the dreadful monotony of the work which they were given. J D Burn, whose *Autobiography of a Beggar Boy of 1855* triggered off a vogue for working-class reminiscences, recalled the drudgery, the 'unvaried and monotonous' existence of a hatter's apprentice in the 1820s 'the common lot of all the apprentices in the trade'.[13] A century later an engineer on the Clyde remembered the terrible monotony of a year making bolts and studs on a turning lathe and realising that at the end of it, he 'knew no more about engineering than when I started'.[14] Edwin Muir, starting as an office-boy in a Glasgow law firm, felt the boredom of 'copying letters, addressing and stamping and delivering letters' like the 'beginning of a term of imprisonment'.[15]

Once out of apprenticeship, the search for work and the perpetual insecurity of work is what most workers remembered. In 1855, the recorded life of a Dundee factory boy concluded that 'The great mass of men and women are like corks on the surface of a mountain river, carried hither and thither as the torrent may lead them'.[16] A tramp of fourteen hundred miles that J D Burn undertook in search of work in 1830 was not uncommon among skilled artisans in the first half of the nineteenth century. Others recall the humiliation of standing around the gates of yards morning and dinner-time with hundreds of others, hoping that the foreman would appear looking for workers. They remember too the perfunctory way in which they would be treated:

> In most cases he [the foreman] did not appear, but if he did he would walk down the line of waiting men and then turn on his heel and go back inside the gates with a grunt of 'Nothing today', or sometimes even not a word.

Others might find themselves secretly blacklisted for having spoken up to a previous employer or because of their politics.[17] Short-time and redundancy were a constant threat and sometimes arbitrary. Muir recalled a new employer taking over the works and randomly ticking names on the list of those who were to be given a week's notice.[18]

What is often forgotten is that much of the time a high proportion of workers were incomers: incomers into a firm, incomers into the district, often from a rural or small town background, and relative novices at their trade. The stable workman, forty years with the same employer, was a rarity. While the unskilled were no doubt more vulnerable, few skilled men worked a full year with the same employer without facing redundancy or short-time at some point. The Dalkeith tailor, Mansie Wauch, whose memories created a sensation in Blackwoods' *Magazine* in the 1820s, heading for Edinburgh to work for the first time, comments on not knowing anyone and on 'the awful and insignificant sense of being a lonely stranger in a foreign land'.[19] The future Labour Minister, Emanuel Shinwell, worked for a dozen different employers as a tailor from the age of twelve until the age of twenty-five. Not until he got a job at the Scottish Co-operative Wholesale Society did he become fully employed.[20] As new arrivals they were frequently subjected to all the prejudices against the newcomer for religion or accent or work style. A Belfast cotton spinner coming to a mill in Glasgow's Woodside in the 1820s found himself 'surrounded with scoffing infidels, and many characters of the lowest description, drunkenness, dissipation and obscenity'.[21] A young Edzell blacksmith arriving in Dundee in 1844 fell among 'the most drunken and depraved characters that could well be conceived'.[22] Partly it may have been a deliberate desire to shock or from an embarrassment in social relationships. Although Parkheadborn, David Kirkwood found the labourers at D Y Stewart's of St Rollox rougher than anywhere he had been and wondered how outsiders would perceive them. He suggested, however, that part of it was affectation: 'Even in their friendly chaff, they seem as if at any moment they would exchange fun for fists. It is a convention to appear crude, to adopt a sort of "plain fact and no nonsense" attitude'.[23]

Even the most authentic piped noise and bottled smells can not come anywhere near the unpleasantness and brutalism of such workplaces. Drink consumption in the workplace was widespread and although there seems little doubt that the temperance movement did gradually begin to have its effects, together with an awareness of the dangers that drink combined with fast moving machines could have, it persisted in many places. It is too easy perhaps to write off the warnings against the demon drink as the mantra which allowed the middle classes to ignore the plethora of other social issues which capitalism created. But the fact remains that the majority of the members of Rechabites and Good Templars were working-class people who recognised that drinking was a destructive part of many working lives. Early in the nineteenth century almost all the rituals of the workplace were firmly associated with drink. Every stage of an apprentice's career, every social event would be the occasion for celebration in the workshop with drink and this pattern of drinking was carried into the early factories. James McCurrey, a carpenter turned temperance missionary recalled that, as the youngest in the workshop in about 1814, one of his tasks was 'to fetch the drink in for the men, and my reward was to have a "sup for mysel"'.[24] Early in this century, Edwin Muir remembered the horse-lorry delivery men in the bottling plant in which he worked arriving back tipsy 'for it was good business

to have a drink with the public-house keepers'.[25] According to Bob Stewart, working on the railway in Dundee, the railwaymen always had a barrel of whisky sunk into the ground on the loading pay from which 'anyone could drink as much as they wanted'. It was kept topped up by boring into the whisky casks loaded on the railway wagons.[26]

One danger of the heritage site, with its focus on technology and on the building of great machines, is that it over-emphasises the role of the minority who were skilled workers. Most workers had limited skills. J F C Harrison notes that most jobs involved brute force without much mechanical assistance: 'wheeling, dragging, hoisting, carrying, lifting, digging, tunnelling, draining, trenching, hedging, embanking, blasting, breaking, scouring, sawing, felling, reaping, mowing, picking, sifting and threshing'.[27] Most had to earn a living labouring, in many cases dependent on skilled workers rather than employers for their pay. They tended to be treated with scant respect; 'the labourer is the servant of every journeyman in the place; nay, mere boys presume, with impunity, to come and rate him as they please ... To this specious [sic] of tyranny there are honourable exceptions, no doubt, but to lord it over labourers is the rule.'[28] The future president of the Miners' Federation of Great Britain, Robert Smillie, worked as a plater's helper in a boiler-making workshop. He and his fellow helpers had to turn up every day, but, if their hammerman did not turn up then they were sent home unpaid.[29] Being paid by the skilled man or as part of a work gang strengthened the hierarchical nature of much industrial organisation. In the steel firms of Lanarkshire in the 1880s John Hodge and others battled against the subcontracting system by which workers were employed as a gang paid by the contractor, just as in mining there was resistance to the buttysystem.[30] Once again the struggles of the workplace are remembered as as much with fellow workers as with employers.

Perhaps an even greater danger, however, is the under-representation of the role of women. Women tend barely to feature. If they do it is in the home or in the kitchen. In white aprons and white mop caps the world of domestic service is generally portrayed within the world of the great house of 'Upstairs, Downstairs'. The photographic images we have are of the serried, hierarchical ranks of servants in the big house. But the reality of domestic service for most was very different, with the single servant in the petty-bourgeois household which required the servant for status but could barely afford it. There is little doubt that many young country girls coming into the cities to work suffered exploitation, harassment and assault at the hands of employing families. On farms and in small towns the exploit-ation of and the brutality against the all-purpose skivvy or 'kitchen deem' may have been even worse with even less prospect of escape. For many a cap and apron and being at the employer's beck and call all the time was 'the badge of servitude'. A young Stirling woman recalled that 'when I used to come home it used to break my heart 'cause I was going back – I didnae like it'.[31] It is no surprise that when other opportunities for women presented themselves from the First World War onwards, they seized them and abandoned domestic service in droves. Picking stones from coal at the pithead seemed more attractive than service and many times better paid.[32]

By presenting women in the context of domestic service, the whole effect can be to exaggerate the – often already exaggerated – idea of 'separate spheres' in which men and women reputedly operated. There is evidence that 'separate spheres' was some distance from the reality of most working-people's lives, and that historians have tended to marginalise the place of work in women's lives. Although, on the whole, married women in Scotland did not go out to work this did not mean that they were not involved in paid labour. Many of them were en-gaged in the sweated labour of sewing, box making, Christmas-cracker making, interspersed with end-less washing and cleaning. Few of the trim interiors displayed in heritage sites capture the world of home working.

Working women have left very few autobio-graphies and we depend to an even larger extent than with men on oral history. Even there, however, getting women to talk about their work rather than their husband's, from which they felt their status

came, required some prompting from the inter-viewers. There is evidence from such oral history, however, that women, probably more than men, actually enjoyed work outside the home and found that it gave their life a significance. Callum Brown and Jane Stephenson's oral history work among elderly Stirling women discovered fond memories of work among many of them. What emerged was that despite the fact that they were generally poorly paid and their work given low status, they wel-comed the independence which it gave them and they remembered the camaraderie, the singing and the jokes as much as the hard work.[33] This was particularly so at the pit-head and in the factory. A Stirling carpet factory-worker recalled the oppor-tunities for a 'wee blether' and the assistance which women gave to one another. The contrast with men's often-bitter recollections of work is striking. The same respondent claimed that 'there were people from Cowie, Bannockburn, St Ninian's, Plean and Stirling. You got on with every one of them ...', and she remembered the singing:

> You used to sing the whole day, all the songs, everybody. One started and everybody joined in. It was grand company.
>
> There was one girl from Bannockburn, she used to sing the football songs. I cannae remember what, but we all joined in and of course, we always ended up with a hymn.'[34]

If it is difficult in a heritage environment to cap-ture the social and emotional experience of work, it is just as difficult to come anywhere near re-creating the physical experience: the 'never-to-be-forgotten waugh smell' of the weaving shed; the dust of lint mills and cotton factories and the dampness to keep the threads supple which had a lethal effect on health.[35] In tanneries, early summer was the bone dust season when an impenetrable dust hovered everywhere and 'a succession of headaches [was] all but inevitable'.[36] The dangers and dust of the coal mine remained despite the many changes in work method. The impact of asbestos dust on the shipyard workers is only gradually being recog-nised. How would modern noses, highly sensitised to the odour of sweat, have coped with years in a bone factory where animal bones were reduced to charcoal for use in sugar refining:

> the grease of the bones worked into their clothes, their skin, their hair, and under their nails. They carried about with them everywhere the smell of sour fat.[37]

The working environment for many was then often one of discomfort and pain; too hot, too cold, always noisy and often smelly, generally unhealthy and frequently dangerous.

When industrial heritage sites first began to develop they were about capturing the cultural heritage to contemporary technological advance. They were linked to the search for Harold Wilson's 'white-heat of the technological revolution' which was to transform Britain. Now they are much more about preserving fast-disappearing relics, the endangered artefacts of a past which seems to have little connection with the present.[38] The manual work of manufacturing is one of these relics which is being preserved. The task of conveying some sense of work in the past is an important one, but the danger is that it becomes the eclectic collection of bits and pieces which the artefacts of industrial heritage sites often are. An even greater danger is that it produces some kind of romanticised image of the past where skilled men of great dignity work with huge machines making wonderful objects. The written evidence points to a world of harshness, exploitation, brutality and danger only occasionally peppered with fun and camaraderie. This too is just as likely to be a distortion of the reality. There is also a danger in seeing the past as a foreign country and the world of past work as quite different from the world of present work. The evidence suggests that long hours, low pay, exploitation of the young and of women, and sub-contracting are every bit as much features of contemporary capitalism. Understanding the past and present experiences of work remains important. No one means can achieve it. A coming together of as many ways as possible of seeing the past is necessary. The historic imagination and the artistic imagination need to be combined. The past of work as of anything else is a social construct and can best be comprehended by combining the skills of historian and collector with the insights of the poet, the novelist and the artist.

NOTES

1. For these and many other examples of 'heritage baiting' see Raphael Samuel, *Theatres of Memory*, Vol 1, 'Past and Present' (London: Verso, 1994), pp 259–73.

2. To be fair the NTS, which had Culross as its first acquisition, has perhaps been less inclined in this direction than its English counterpart.

3. Raphael Samuel, *Theatres of Memory* (Verso, London, 1998), pp 270–1.

4. J Burnett, D Vincent, D Mayall, *The Autobiography of the Working Class*, Vol 1 (Harvester, Brighton, 1984), p xvi.

5. C A Whatley (ed), *The Diary of John Sturrock, Dundee Millwright* (Tuckwell Press, East Linton in association with University of Dundee, 1997).

6. 'Life of a Handloom Weaver', *The Commonwealth*, 25 April 1857. This is one of a series of prize-winning autobiographies of Scottish working men published in this Glasgow newspaper between October 1856 and April 1857.

7. 'Life of a Journeyman Baker', *The Commonwealth*, 13 December 1856.

8. 'Narrative of a Miner', *ibid*, 25 October 1856.

9. D Kirkwood, *My Life of Revolt* (London, 1935), p 50.

10. Bob Stewart, *Breaking the Fetters* (1967), p 22.

11. 'Life of a Letterpress Printer', 7 February 1857. *The Commonwealth*.

12. W G Riddell, *Adventures of an Obscure Victorian* (Greenock 1965, first published London 1932) has various examples.

13. James Dawson Burn, *Autobiography of a Beggar Boy* (first edition, London: Tweedie, 1855: Europa, London, 1978 edition, D Vincent ed), p 125.

14. Riddell, *Adventures*, p 15.

15. Edwin Muir, *An Autobiography* (London, 1980), p 91.

16. 'Dundee Factory Boy', *Chapters in the Life of a Dundee Factory Boy*, James Myles (ed) (Dundee, 1855), p 45.

17. John Paton, *Proletarian Pilgrimage* (London, 1935), p 139.

18. Muir, *Autobiography*, p 133.

19. *The Life of Mansie Wauch, Tailor in Dalkeith, written by Himself* (Edinburgh 1828), p 43.

20. Manny Shinwell, *Lead with the Left: My First Ninety-Six Years* (Cassell, 1981), p 27.

21. 'Life of a Cotton Spinner', *The Commonwealth*, 27 December 1856.

22. 'Life of a Blacksmith', *ibid*, 17 January 1857.

23. Kirkwood, *My Life of Revolt*, p 77.

24. *The Life of James McCurrey* (1876).

25. Muir, *Autobiography*, p 15.

26. Stewart, *Breaking the Fetters*, pp 23–4.

27. J F C Harrison, *The Early Victorians, 1832–1851* (Weidenfeld & Nicolson, London, 1971), p 35.

28. 'Narrative of a Miner', *The Commonwealth*, 25 October 1856.

29. Robert Smillie, *My Life for Labour* (London, 1924).

30. John Hodge, *Workman's Cottage to Windsor Castle* (London, 1931), pp 84–5.

31. Jean Rennie, 'Every Other Sunday' (1955), quoted in John Burnett, *Useful Toil. Autobiographies of Working People from the 1820s to the 1920s* (Allen Lane, London, 1975), p 235; Jane Stephenson (ed), *'Five Bob a Week'. Stirling Women's Work 1900–1950* (Stirling, 1988), p 28.

32. *Ibid*, p 25.

33. Jane D Stephenson and Callum C Brown, 'The View from the Workplace: Women's Memories of Work in Stirling *circa* 1910 – *circa* 1950', in E Gordon and E Breitenbach, *The World is Ill-Divided* (Edinburgh University Press, Edinburgh, 1990), pp 9–27.

34. Stephenson, *'Five Bob a Week'*, p 30.

35. George Gray, *Recollections of Huntly as it was Seventy Years Ago* (Banff, 1892), p 27.

36. *Ibid*, p 27.

37. Muir, *Autobiography*, p 131.

38. The point is Samuel's in *Theatres of Memory*, pp 220–1.

6

JANET McBAIN

Romancing the Industry:
Business and the Cinema in Scotland

THE place of film within Scottish historical studies has been hard fought. The Scottish Film Archive was founded in 1976, in an era when little was known of Scotland's filmed past, neglected and misunderstood as an historical record in its own right. Asked at the time why he never used film in his teaching of history, the distinguished academic who replied, 'Sir, I educate my students – I do not entertain them' would now, thankfully, be in the minority. Historians are increasingly turning to moving images as one of a number of sources of evidence of modern Scottish social, cultural and industrial life.

The Scottish Film and Television Archive was established at the same time as trailblazing historians Michael Moss and John Hume were actively collecting records and writing about the long-established industries in the west of Scotland that were during that decade going into decline with alarming speed. In the early 1970s, the Upper Clyde Shipbuilders' records were brought in to Glasgow University Archives, requiring archivists to spend long dusty days manhandling volumes, blueprints and technical drawings from Andrew Barclay's locomotive works in Kilmarnock, to Mirrlees Watson's sugar machinery works in Glasgow and Beardmore's Parkhead Works. Among the material that came to light was the film *A Romance of Engineering*, made to promote Beardmore's at the 1938 Empire Exhibition. The use of film at the 1938 Empire Exhibition was the culmination of a developing relationship between cinema as the vehicle through which to reach the marketplace and industrial concerns who had a product or an image to sell, thathad its roots at the very beginning of cinema itself. British film producers were making advertising films by the turn of the century but films promoting one single product, what we would today describe as a commercial, are nevertheless rare in the early period of cinema.

The more familiar kind of screen product was a kind of company profile along the lines of 'a visit to so-and-so's works' or the production line 'from raw material to finished goods'. The earliest surviving examples in Scotland are *The Making of a Great Daily Newspaper* (1911) made for D C Thomson to celebrate fifty years of *The Courier* as a daily paper and *From Wool to Wearer* (1913), made for Peter Scott & Co, hosiery manufacturers of Hawick. Sub-titled *The Romance of Pesco Underwear*, the latter carried inter-titles in both French and English being intended for screening at the Ghent International Exhibition in Belgium and then the following year at the Royal Highland Show held in Hawick. (See Figure 1).

It may have been the lack of an established nation-wide circuit of permanent cinemas that held up the development of promotional films. They were relatively simple to have made, there being a burgeoning section of cine-photographers setting up in business, but the distribution of special interest films and the sporadic geographical spread of permanent cinema screens did not make for easy or systematic access to the public audience. In fact D C Thomson eschewed the existing distribution set-up and having commissioned the above film

Figure 1. A still image of a street seller taken from the film, *The Making of a Great Daily Newspaper* (1911), D C Thomson & Co.

from the Gaumont Company, they bought projector apparatus, and employed a man from Dundee to travel its hinterland showing the film in village halls, cinemas and anywhere where the equipment could be installed – to great public interest. The film was a well-made, thorough presentation of all aspects of newspaper production, including a shot of 'DC' himself arriving at the Editorial entrance in his motor car, and wonderful shots of urchin street-sellers rushing out with the latest edition under their arms. *The Courier* reported:

> *The Courier* film proved the attraction of the cinematograph [sic] entertainment given in the Masonic Hall, Ladybank, last night under the auspices of the local branch of the Amalgamated Railway Servants Society. The profits were given to the widows and orphans fund. The hall was packed, many people being present from Kettle, Pitcairlie and the surrounding district. When the *Production of a Great Daily Newspaper* was announced there were cries of 'good old Courier'. From start to finish the large audience closely followed the unfolding of the newspaper story, every now and again a warm appreciation being exhibited. The other films shown by Mr P Feathers, Dundee, were of an amusing character, and the entire entertainment was voted a great success and one of the best ever given in the burgh.[1]

The twenties and thirties saw increased production in film promoting products and industrial concerns. The simple factual account of production line processes continued, but more ambitious ways were being found to market the product. Using a light narrative, placing characters into situations where they purchased products or services, or presenting scenes that would intrigue audiences with limited horizons. In 1928 MaCallum Orme, steamship operators commissioned the Glasgow film company Topical Productions to film a trip on the SS *Hebrides* on her regular sailing out through the ports on the west coast and the Hebrides to St Kilda. Intended for west of Scotland urban cinema goers there is a sense of a great adventure into remote and curious places. The tone of the inter-titles highlights cultural differences between the city dweller and the rural Scot (see Figure 2). The fact that the film alludes to the harsh struggle of the island community so soon to be evacuated heightens the poignancy, but has left us with some unique images of a lost way of life.

In 1931 Isaac Benzies' department store commissioned *Out For Value* to promote the delights of a day's outing to the store, seen through the eyes of the Mackenzie family and their friend, Mrs Grant, who shop, take tea, have their hair done and even partake of a bath – all facilities on offer under one roof.

Figure 2. The team of Topical Productions on location in St Kilda showing a group of island children their cine apparatus, when visiting to make the film *St Kilda, Britain's Loneliest Isle* (*circa* 1928).

Figure 3. An extract from the film *Seeing is Believing* (1931), made for George Guthrie, Butcher, illustrating a crucial stage in the process of making 'quality' sausages.

Figure 4. A scene from *Wealth of a Nation* (1938), by Scottish Film Productions for Films of Scotland, illustrating the pride in Scottish industry which characterised the film.

Throughout the thirties a steady stream of promotional film was produced for industry, providing for a number of Scottish film production units the bread and butter of their order books. Well into the era of the talkies, silent advertising films continued. Jay's Film Service produced silent advertising films in the early to mid-thirties for Aurora Lamps, Brunton's Wire Rope Manufacturers, Castlebank Laundries and Guthrie's, Butchers. One can only conclude that although shown in cinemas the films had other non-commercial outlets where sound technology was yet to be introduced. Indeed Guthrie's used their series of four short advertising films promoting the quality of their product, including *Seeing is Believing* (on the latest techniques in sausage making) to great effect by means of an ingenious back projection system in the shop window (see Figure 3). Folk memory records that the police were forced to request Guthrie's to limit the number of times they showed the films as the crowds of fascinated passers-by were spilling over into Maryhill Road and obstructing the tramcars.

Government came belatedly to recognise the enormous propaganda opportunities presented by film. Here was a captive public audience in the habit of visiting the cinema two or three times weekly, often 'en famille'. Apart from overt propaganda films shown in cinemas during the First World War Scottish Government departments had not actively

engaged with cinema in the way that industry had. In anticipation of 1938, when Glasgow was to host the Empire Exhibition, a six month extravaganza celebrating the achievements of Empire, the Scottish Office set up a Committee to arrange for the production of films about Scottish life to show in the special Empire Cinema to be established within the exhibition arena.[2] The Films of Scotland Committee produced seven documentary films on Scotland, including titles on fishing and agriculture and *Wealth of a Nation*, directed by a Scot, Donald Alexander, who had emerged from the Grierson-inspired documentary movement in the south.

Wealth of a Nation gave a government view of Scottish industrial achievement and took a lofty overview of the industrial traditions of the past, the effects of the depression of the thirties, the role of the people and state in determining the future economic policy (see Figure 4).[3] These and other films commissioned directly and funded by Scottish industrial concerns, seized the unique opportunity of reaching not only a United Kingdom market but vast numbers of overseas visitors who were to attend the six-month exhibition. David Colville's steel making company proudly trumpeted in *World of Steel* its contribution in making the girders that formed Tait's tower, to be seen on the hill at the centre of the arena. Beardmore's aforementioned

A Romance of Engineering and Scottish Oils' *Paraffin Young* extolled the achievement of Scots industrial entrepreneurs and inventors. Crouch and Hogg, who had created the colourful fountains and cascades lining the exhibition avenues, recorded their engineering achievements in *Water Displays At the Empire Exhibition.*

Alongside these heavyweights municipal authorities such as Falkirk and Stirling screened films highlighting business success and community values and educational institutions such as George Heriot's School encouraged parents to enrol their offspring by illustrating the excellent academic and supporting facilities on offer.

During the Second World War many industrial porduction lines were turned over to war-related purposes and the overt promotional film largely gave way to training or propoganda films. In *Tribute to Wartime Production* the King and Queen are seen visiting Templeton's carpet factory converted for the manufacture of army blankets. H Morris & Co, Furniture Manufacturers, commissioned film of their wartime production of rifle stocks. *Wood Goes to War* opened with the screen credit: 'A lasting

record of the part this Glasgow firm played in the Second World War.' Shot during 1942 and 1943, the film was not released until hostilities had ceased.

The post-war period saw developments in the use of film by industry as a training medium and for practical use within their own organisations. Roger Whitney, in his paper to the Business Archives Council in 1987, attributes this to the development of the specialist film at a time of an increasingly professional approach to business and industrial management and cites *Introducing Work Study* (1955) as the most heavily booked title in the Central Film Library's catalogue in 1957.

Within Scotland, certainly, the Scottish Co-operative Wholesale Society (SCWS) led the field with a suite of product information and publicity films and a series of staff training films aimed at all levels of the retail sector of the business, ranging from *Counter Courtesy* (1947), on how to be a model sales assistant, to *Know Your Business*, for the branch manager. [4]

The use of the magazine film became a familiar feature of fifties industry. The National Coal Board's regular monthly *Mining Review* was

Figure 5. The Thames & Clyde Film Co. on location at Martin Black's wire rope works, Coatbridge, *circa* 1946.

introduced in 1947 with newsy items about latest technological developments, chatty stories about social and welfare clubs around the country and designed to tell the miners the important economic and social role that they were playing in British society. Outwith the nationalised industries the heavy industries tended to dominate the use of the magazine film with titles such as the *Ingot Pictorial* (1948–58) and *Unilever Magazine* (1951–58). In Scotland Babcock and Wilcox's review *Home and Away* was screened in local cinemas in Renfrew, the company town, and at staff social clubs and community venues around the plant. Mixing technical and 'out-of-hours' stories these magazine films evoke the atmosphere of 'family' and industrial paternalism of the single employer within a discrete community. In issue ten of *Home and Away* (1956) can be found a story of the Babcock special – a locomotive to take Babcock employees and their families to Blackpool and Morecambe for the Fair fortnight summer holiday.

The traditional links with the cinema screen began to decline in this period as cinema itself went through a recession and endured the inexorable rise of television. Films purely made as interest or shorts for cinema audiences were now re-cast in the form of short snappy TV commercials for a new audience. The SCWS took to the new medium proudly, promoting its breakfast oats, for example, with a model family happily singing and dancing around the breakfast table.

Meanwhile cinema was not entirely excluded. The establishment of Films of Scotland in 1954 created an agency with a broad remit to make films 'about Scotland' for theatrical distribution in cinemas both at home and overseas and non-theatrical circulation through education film libraries, the British Council and film societies. Over its thirty-year existence, through partnerships with local authorities, national agencies and industrial concerns, some one hundred and sixty documentary films were produced chronicling the diverse fabric of Scottish society. Of these about fifty were produced in direct collaboration with the commercial industry sector, ranging from iron and steel production (Colvilles sponsored three titles), petro-

Figure 6. Men at work on the hull of a ship at Clydeside, a glimpse of a fading industry featured in *Seawards the Great Ships* (1960), by Templar Films for Films of Scotland and Clyde Shipbuilders Association.

leum, textiles, banking, whisky, power, car manufacture, construction engineering and of course shipbuilding, exemplified by *Seawards the Great Ships* (1960) (see Figure 6). This tribute to Clyde shipbuilding, not to any one particular company, broke the mould for the hitherto familiar industrial 'prestige' film with the guiding hand of the veteran producer John Grierson and the fresh approach of young American Hilary Harris. The film won a Hollywood Oscar in 1961, was released commercially into cinemas with Alec Guinness's tour de force *Tunes of Glory* and was dubbed into some fifteen foreign language versions. It was one of the most popular British information films ever shown in the USSR. By the time of the demise of Films of Scotland in 1982 the production of publicity and promotional material for industry was switching over to the new technology of videotape, with production facilities becoming increasingly affordable and accessible to small businesses. The link with cinema was largely broken.

So far, in considering Scottish industry's engagement with film, we have investigated the official, public face of industry presented on the screen. An alternative source of film evidence also exists in the collections of amateur film held in the Scottish Film and Television Archive, made by individuals from within the industrial community whose hobby was cinematography. From the examples in the Archive it would appear to be a pastime most frequently associated with senior figures in family-owned firms – those with a disposable income to put towards the purchase of 9.5mm or 16mm cameras and projectors and the costs of film stock. Examples of such are George Scott (of Peter Scott & Co, hosiery manufacturers), Jack MacFarlane (of MacFarlane Lang biscuits) and Jack Mavor (of Mavor & Coulson). In considering the value of this amateur footage concerning industrial life, it is prudent to reflect on the relative exclusiveness of film-making as a hobby in the inter-war years. One exponent recalled that his first roll of 16mm colour film purchased in September 1936 to film the *Queen Mary* leaving the Clyde cost him half of what the ordinary working man would expect to earn in a week.

It is perhaps not surprising, then, that the amateur films made in this period were made largely by the firms' owner and manager class and reflect their experience of working life rather than that of the ordinary labourer on the shop floor. After the war, with the introduction of slightly cheaper 8mm equipment and film and the increased prosperity of the worker, the relative cost of cine equipment fell in relation to earnings and there followed a wider penetration of camera ownership across the social strata and a subsequently broader view of everyday life, culminating in today's virtually prerequisite videocam coverage of lifestyle such as family holidays, weddings, offsprings' progress and social gatherings.

The earliest example in the Archive of the industrialist-as-cinematographer is private footage shot by Kenneth Dundas of Melville, Dundas and Whitson, builders of the King George V Bridge across the Clyde from 1924 to 1927.

One of the largest and, in the author's opinion, more interesting, collections of this nature was made by Norman Stein, director of John G Stein & Co Ltd, brickmakers of Bonnybridge and member of the family dynasty founded by his father in 1887. The 16mm films he made between 1932 and 1946 reflect family life at Millfield, the Steins' house near Polmont, school sports days at Glenalmond, family holidays at home and cruising in the Mediterranean and social occasions. There is footage shot inside the company's Manuel brick works showing both technical processes and informal shots of the employees. The interface between employer and employee is alluded to in the scenes of the annual Staff Garden Party at Millfield where brickworkers are entertained to tea on the lawn and enjoy the freedom of the grounds, and to civic events in Castlecary and Allandale, a village built to provide homes for the workforce, such as the opening of the Bowling Green (by Mrs Annie Stein) and Coronation Day celebrations in 1937.

The potential for this kind of material as a source for historians and for teaching has yet to be fully explored. With far-sighted proponents such as John Hume, however, the raw material that is the original film is being collected and preserved for the future use of historians. The collecting is being done by the Scottish Film and Television Archive with the help of the broad archival community of Scotland. However, in terms of industry's corporate output it is at best haphazard and reliant upon the goodwill and co-operation of the companies who have collections of obsolete promotional films. Many more are now commissioning 'prestige' productions in the new era of the corporate video and are presenting themselves to the world through television. Video is by its nature short-lived and re-usable and the chances of libraries of video productions surviving in the hands of commercial concerns beyond their immediate currency is unlikely. That we can point to a growing set of moving image evidence of our industrial past in the first half of this century is encouraging, but to be sure of collecting now for the future some support is required. Proposals are being crafted in the late 1990s for an extension of legal deposit to include non-print published works, which will embrace moving image materials. If the historians of the future are to be able to study through the medium of the moving image the industrial history of the last decade of this century and beyond, state support through such as a system of legal deposit could make all the difference.

ACKNOWLEDGEMENTS

Invaluable source material for the above on the history of industrial film came from Roger Whitney, 'Film in Business History', a paper presented to Business Archives Council, 1987, and published in the *Proceedings* of the Business Archives Council.

As a young archivist, introduced to the sharp end of archival collection by Michael Moss, newly launched on a professional career, and certainly new to film as an archival medium, I was welcomed into the fold of practising historians and archivist's by John Hume, with his refreshing, open-minded and at that time unusual assumption that film was an historical record in its own right. I was fired by the encouragement and enthusiasm for industrial history that John communicated to his students. I remember the paeans of delight that one of his postgraduates met on hearing of a discovery of film of tile making in Ayrshire in 1951. It was, although it did not really sink in until later, an inspiration, a morale boost to a young archivist who felt that a medium dealing exclusively with twentieth-century records could not really be a proper archive!

NOTES

1. From *The Courier*, Saturday, 25 March 1911.
2. For further information see *To Speak its Pride, the work of the Films of Scotland Committee 1938–1982*, Jo Sherington (Scottish Film Council, Glasgow, 1996).
3. A critique of the film *Wealth of a Nation* by Richard Butt can be found in *With an Eye to the Future*, Scottish Film Monograph (Scottish Screen, Glasgow, 1997).
4. See *The British Co-operative Movement Film Catalogue*, compiled and edited by Alan Burton (Flicks Books, 1997).

7

MATTHEW HUME

Scottish Industrial History, as Represented by Summerlee

Introduction

The heritage boom of the 1970s and 1980s led to the establishment of several 'site museums', interpreting social and industrial history on a larger, yet more intimate scale than was normal in 'traditional' museums. One of these was Summerlee, on a derelict site in Coatbridge. John R Hume was among those involved in creating the vision that this project hoped to achieve.

When the proposals were unveiled in 1984, it was seen as a potential 'Beamish of the north', drawing on the success of the similar English developments of the previous 15 years. It was to encompass the history of the area, which had only become heavily populated after the Scottish ironmaking revolution of the 1830s. The centerpieces of the site were to be the remains of the Summerlee Ironworks, representing this revolution, a large exhibition hall to house machines of national significance, and a local history gallery, to display the collection of the former Airdrie Museum. The final development plan differed from this initial proposal, and remained fluid until the Trust was taken over by Monklands District Council in 1995. This flexibility was one of the main benefits of being independent (although supported by the Council), and allowed the development of some ambitious projects which would now be unlikely to find support.

Many of the problems and successes of Summerlee are shared with other institutions, but the way forward for the next decade will require ingenuity, foresight and determination, against a background of increasing financial constraints.

Historical Background

Scotland has been well served since the mid-nineteenth century by a large number of museums, ranging from the small town museum to the great municipal and national institutions in the main cities. These museums have preserved, and to some extent interpreted, Scotland's history in applied and fine art, in curiosities and in objects relating to the more interesting of the obsolescent crafts.

Industry also was portrayed, largely in objects and models gathered as educational tools to improve knowledge and assist in the process of producing intelligent artisans. The Royal Scottish Museum, founded in the early 1860s, had one of the finest contemporary collections of items from late Victorian Scottish industry, many of which have, alas, vanished along the way. Even the smaller museums, such as that at Airdrie, had examples on display of local coal and iron ore, steam engines, and more exotic economically important minerals from across the globe.

This wealth of material suffered from the reaction against the 'improving' use of museums from the First World War onwards. Among the intelligentsia, industry in Scotland was in retreat, and hence was no longer a fit subject for treatment. The newer industries, such as electrical goods and manufacturing failed to retain a specific Scottishness, and the relics of the older heavy industries were not yet of antiquarian interest. Furthermore, the movement, born between the wars, which laid emphasis on traditions in vernacular architecture and rural crafts, could not, by its nature, find any relevance in the buildings and living conditions of the industrial nineteenth century, nor in industries which were still alive, albeit in their death throes.

So it was that by the 1960s, although the mass destruction of the built industrial heritage had already begun, there were few who saw the importance of recording, and where possible, preserving the surviving relics. This seems to have been the case especially in the museum world; of the pioneers of industrial archeology in Scotland, only a few including Wood and Walden came from museums; the rest were academics, archivists or men who had worked in the disappearing industries. It is solely thanks to this small but devoted band of acolytes that, when the significance of industrial history began to be recognized, there was anything to display and interpret.

The first large-scale industrial processes in Scotland were extractive and chemical, the chemicals industry being closely followed by iron smelting as the West of Scotland in particular became a manufacturing base. Unfortunately, the evidence of such industries tends to disappear quickly (high scrap value, acreage of land), and also has seldom fired the imagination of preservationists and enthusiasts. This lack of appeal, coupled with the desire of local authorities to obliterate sites which are not only perceived to be eyesores, but also monuments to failure, meant that by the end of the 1970s there was little surviving in the Coatbridge area to show for the vital place it had held in the iron revolution.

The Birth of Summerlee

A proposal by John R Hume in 1978 to preserve the Victoria Rolling Mill in situ as a museum site came to naught; it was still just too early for a District Council to make such a leap of faith.[1] The machinery was preserved, but was moved to Edinburgh by the National Museums. The proposal may, however, have sown the seed, for in the 1980s Monklands District Council began to follow the fashion in large-scale site museums, which had been pioneered

over a decade earlier in the North of England. The urban regeneration of Coatbridge had already begun, with the landscaping of sections of the infilled Monklands Canal. There was clearly a growing feeling in the area that its history was in danger of being forgotten, and the proposed 'Heritage Park' would have the dual advantages of providing a focus for interpretation, and of encouraging extra-district visitors to an unpromising destination.

The site selected was 50 acres of derelict land almost in the centre of the town. Lying on a branch of the Monklands Canal, it had been the Summerlee Ironworks until 1937, when most of the site was cleared. Although the former workshops had remained in use for colliery maintenance, latterly under the National Coal Board, the main building on the site was the craneworks of Lambert & Co Ltd, a Glasgow firm building hydraulic mobile cranes under the name 'Hydrocon'.

By 1980 the Hydrocon works, a steel portal-frame structure of 1951 with a prominent office block, was in its turn derelict and vandalized. The site, which belonged to the Council, was unattractive to industry due to restricted access, and the terrain limited its use for housing. A report was therefore commissioned from a firm of consultants to comment on the feasibility of its use for a heritage attraction.[2] The report was presented in 1984; it showed the possibilities of dual use, with the western area sold for private housing, and the rest turned into an industrial museum, albeit with a preponderance of green landscaping. Central to the plan was the re-use of the main factory building as an exhibition hall to house machinery which was available from other institutions, notably Glasgow Museums and the Royal Scottish Museum. Other features were to include a reconstructed coal mine, a passenger-carrying railway, the rented offices of 1836, and the excavation of the Summerlee ironworks' remains, with reconstructed blast furnaces.

While on reading the report, it must have seemed ambitious, perhaps unreasonably so, the Council nonetheless had enough confidence to begin the process by appointing a general manager and a small staff. At the time, the Government's Manpower Services Commission scheme, which provided work for the long-term unemployed, was crucial to the initial stages. A changing body of 300 men was employed for some three years; their work included landscaping, and crucially, excavating the ironworks remains under supervision of archaeologists.[3]

The main hall was re-clad; the former ironworks offices were taken down and re-erected, and other work carried out with considerable capital funding from the Council and the European Regional Development Fund. Naturally, the plans changed as time went on. It is arguable that the flexibility and autonomy of independent trust status were vital to the early success of Summerlee. As an example, the mineral railways of the proposal became instead an electric tramway; less overtly industrial, but no less relevant and possibly even more of a visitor attraction (see Figure 1).

In museum terms, the most significant development was the concentration on one site of most of the important machine tools and process equipment in Scottish museums. The Strathclyde Regional Council's collection arrived en masse. Many of the machines collected by the Scottish Society for the Preservation of Historical Machinery (SSPHM), and stored at the RSM, came to be displayed for the first time; and some very significant items came from Glasgow museums, rescued from neglect, if not worse. These were supplemented by machinery

Figure 1. The Summerlee Electric Tramway, with Brussels car No. 9062; the steam crane is from the Dalzell Steelworks in Motherwell.

Figure 2. Steam-powered plate bending rolls in the Coatbridge boilerworks of Thomas Hudson Ltd. (Photograph by John R Hume, 1974)

and other artefacts acquired by the Trust either as donations or by purchase. For the first time a high profile museum was eager to take large, indeed very large items, and several items and groups were saved which would otherwise have been lost.

As examples of unique and important acquisitions, mention can be made of spade and shovel making machinery from the Chieftain Forge near Bathgate; the contents of a brass finishers' workshop (Gardners of Greenock), and machinery from Hudson's Boilermakers, Coatbridge. The last group includes, vertical plate bending rolls, dish turning lathes and a set of steam-powered bending rolls, all unique in Scotland and possibly in Britain as a whole (see Figure 2).

Among the items on loan from other museums, perhaps the most notable is the atmospheric beam winding engine from Farme Colliery in Rutherglen. Preserved by Glasgow Museums in 1920, it arrived

as an incomplete kit of parts and has been reconstructed by Summerlee staff over several years, from drawings fortunately made by apprentices of Sir William Arrol & Co.

From its inception Summerlee was set aside from other independent museums by its ability to undertake mechanical restoration in-house. Arguably the retention of traditional engineering skills is as important, if not more important than, preserving mere static exhibits. Unfortunately, a proposal for an apprentice-training scheme was not followed through, but despite retirement of key staff and redundancies, one highly experienced engineer remains in the Conservation Engineering Workshop. This is becoming one of the last such general engineering workshops in the West of Scotland, and it is vital not only as a centre of excellence for conservation and restoration, but as a surviving skills base for the next millenium.

In 1995 Summerlee's independent status was ended when it was subsumed by Monklands District Council. This was done largely to safeguard the revenue funding in anticipation of changes stemming from Local Government reorganization in the following year. While the immediate future was thus safeguarded, and it no longer faces the same struggle for survival that afflicts the other independent industrial museums, Council budgetary restrictions have inevitably meant a curtailment of developments and new projects. This is by no means altogether a bad thing. The rapid pace of expansion led to a tendency to leave projects unfinished, and collection management, while adequate, now requires integration with the systems used by other component authorities of the new North Lanarkshire.

A relative latecomer as an industrial heritage attraction, Summerlee nonetheless had to learn many important lessons anew. Although no new large-scale museums of this scale are likely to be established, these lesson are worth repeating for the smaller institutions. Perhaps the most important is location. As long as visitor numbers are regarded as the prime indicator of success, any attraction must be clear as to the visitor constituency at which it is to be aimed. Summerlee was planned both as a local museum and as a tourist magnet; it was fortunate that the size and nature of the site allowed special events to be held, attracting tens of thousands of visitors annually (see Figure 3). This, together with repeat local visitors and school parties, meant that an upper limit of 144,000 visits was achieved in 1994. It is clear, however, that if the West of Scotland catchment area had not been accessible, with motorway and railway stations nearby, the number of extra-district visitors would have been far smaller. Dunaskin, Newtongrange, and to some extent, Irvine, have suffered from a relative lack of large

Figure 3. Visitors and exhibits at one of the successful special events at Summerlee, 1990.

local population bases. Not only does this restrict visitor numbers, but it makes investment from Councils and others less likely, though by no means unattainable. Summerlee was undoubtedly born under a lucky star, with a funding commitment from local authority, and local communities which felt it to be their own.

Despite these advantages, it would have been easy to go from a promising beginning to slow death. The success of Summerlee has largely stemmed from its accessibility. The word is used here in all its meanings. Free entry has always encouraged repeat visits; geographical location has made it a popular destination; but most of all it has managed to appeal to a broad cross-section of the larger community. This is less due to initial planning than to hard work, and, crucially, 'vision and humanity'. Comparisons could be drawn with the Motherwell Heritage Centre. This was carefully designed as an entity; it has all the fashionable trappings of audiovisual presentations and computer interactives; but the building is not particularly welcoming. Publicity is helping, but Summerlee was self-publicizing from the start; and it became a familiar name very quickly.

The accessibility of museums has been debated at length for many years, and it is more vital perhaps for industrial museums than for others. In a sense this is odd, for industrial and social history is familiar to most, and especially to those who have traditionally felt excluded from museums. However, if interpretation of these subjects is still attempted in a text-based format, as is still often the case in museums, this will inevitably tend to alienate a large and vital section of the public. There is, of course, a place for didactic displays, but their limitations must always be borne in mind. This stricture applies with equal or greater force to computer interactives; the amount of information conveyed by on-screen text is limited, and the quality of associated images is generally poor. Flawed though its execution may be, the concept explored at Summerlee of working machinery in appropriate environments conveys understanding of the effects of the Scottish industrial revolution to a wide public which often includes the direct descendents of those who originally worked with these machines.

The most striking aspect of most heavy industry is its assault on the senses: noise, heat, smell, and above all the sheer scale of the machinery and processes, are all difficult to convey in a museum setting. Even set re-creations are not always effective, while to display machines as silent monoliths, however striking they may be as sculpture, destroys much of their meaning. The display of industrial objects in an appropriate setting is no easy task; the decision has to be taken as to whether the setting is to be representational or a re-creation.

The coal mine at Summerlee is a set re-creation containing very few genuine artefacts. Nonetheless, many visitors, including former miners, have expressed disbelief that it is not a real mine. The curatorial team visited the last drift mine in Lanarkshire and drew on this experience in their attempts to convey the realities of work underground. Although the rock and coal faces were cast in glass-reinforced concrete, all other materials used were real; the stone used in the longwall 'packs' came from the drift mine at Forth. At times the curators went to extraordinary lengths to steep themselves in the hardships of a miners life (see Figure 4). Imagination, attention to detail and a certain passion, together with a clear understanding of the processes and working practices involved, must all therefore be brought to bear on design and interpretation.

It is all too easy to see a collection as complete, especially when items have been acquired at a rate which perhaps precludes proper collection management and conservation. As a collection grows, it is often necessary to weed out, and actively to acquire items to fill gaps rather than wait until wanted items become available. Nonetheless, as newer industries rise and fall, it is vital to represent them in industrial museums. John Hume wrote, in 'A New Head of Steam', '... much has been achieved in the field of industrial preservation, but we must be careful to avoid complacency.'[4] Almost a decade later, these words should be remembered, and perhaps written on every industrial curator's wall. Apart from the necessity of improving and consolidating the existing collections, we must always be alert to opportunities arising. As an example, the closure of

Figure 4. The author in the longwall face in the Summerlee coal mine reconstruction.

the Ravenscraig integrated iron and steel works at Craigneuk near Motherwell provided an opportunity for the collection of a wide range of clothing and small artefacts, but a combination of lack of political will and shortage of resources precluded the acquisition of any large artefacts such as a blast furnace bell. Thus there is no monumental object surviving to represent this huge works, or to commemorate the end of the iron smelting tradition in Scotland after more than 200 years.

We must also guard against erosion of the existing preserved material. Alone perhaps among museum disciplines, industrial collections are vulnerable to thoughtless and ignorant disposal. On grounds of decay, irrelevance, size and lack of visual appeal, objects can easily be consigned to scrap, especially if documentation is poor. For this reason, the synoptic centre, as suggested by John Hume,[5] if it ever came to fruition, would number among its important functions the ability to advise on disposals, and perhaps assist in transfers between

museums (still often seen as undesirable by more parochial local authorities).

In order to produce interpretation and displays which will attract, educate and entertain the public, museum professionals must combine awareness of interpretative techniques and human psychology with deep knowledge of their subjects. In an industrial historical context, however, it is equally important to have a broad overview of social and economic influences, and to understand interdependencies. For example, to interpret the iron smelting industry it is necessary to take into account geology, chemistry and the chemical industry, the cast and malleable iron trades, steel production, and Scottish imports and exports. Obviously few can have detailed knowledge of all these subjects, but it is important to aim at a generalist approach. For a museum professional in our field, nothing from Church history to the computer revolution is an irrelevance. These arguments, of course, can and should be applied to all fields of museum work. A generalist approach implies flexibility and constant intellectual challenge, and these can only benefit museums as a whole.

We have left the growth period when heritage attractions could and did spring up like mushrooms, and we are entering a time of retrenchment when we may well see a decline in numbers of institutions and increasing competition for limited funding. It will be all the more necessary to keep the twin objectives of preservation and interpretation in sight when it is easy to become bogged down in administration and subordinate to political decisions. But, as long as we have men and women with the vision and the courage to influence decision makers at the highest level, it will be possible to continue the work begun by John Hume and his contemporaries. 'It behoves us all not to betray their vision, and to carry the torch into the next millenium, always remembering not to devalue the intellectual dimension in what we are all trying to do.'[6]

NOTES

1. J R Hume, 1998, pers comm.
2. Feasibility Study, Land Use Consultants Ltd, Glasgow 1984.
3. Summerlee excavation reports (unpub), John Lewis *et al*, 1986–88.
4. J R Hume, 'A New Head of Steam', in *Introducing Scotland's Industrial Past* (Scottish Museums Council, Edinburgh, 1992), pp 9–12.
5. *Ibid.*
6. *Ibid.*

8

JAMES E ARNOLD

New Lanark: Rescue, Preservation and Development

Foundations

A wooded gorge described in the Old Statistical Account for Lanarkshire as 'almost a mere morass ... and of difficult access'[1] seems today an unlikely location for the largest cotton mill in Scotland (see Figures 1 and 2). Yet the site of New Lanark was chosen with deliberate care to take advantage of the cotton-spinning patents secured by the English inventor, Richard Arkwright. These allowed yarn to be spun in water-powered mills on a previously unprecedented scale. Arkwright visited Scotland in

Figure 1. View of New Lanark in about 1817, before the destruction by fire of Mill Number Three in 1819 (by John Winning, courtesy of John R Hume).

1783 to inspect the Falls of Clyde, a well-known tourist attraction, with the intention of considering the establishment of a new factory. In Glasgow he met David Dale, a leading West of Scotland linen yarn merchant and agent of the Royal Bank of Scotland. This initial partnership was short-lived and Dale undertook the development on his own, based on the power of Dundaff Linn, the smallest of the Falls. He feued the land from the local owners, Lord Braxfield and the Incorporation of Shoemakers in Lanark. With the quashing of Arkwright's patents in 1785, any involvement by the English inventor ceased. The first mill at New Lanark went into production in 1786, and was followed by another, until four mills had been built. Crompton's spinning mule replaced Arkwright's water frame, because it was capable of manufacturing finer yarn.

As the mill buildings were completed and filled with machinery, it became necessary to provide housing for workers. The gorge of the River Clyde offered only a very restricted site (see Figure 2), so houses were built in blocks of three or four storeys in height, in contrast to the lower buildings

Figure 2. Aerial view of New Lanark, 1975 (Crown Copyright: RCAHMS)

favoured at other Scottish cotton mills. By the late 1790s, the working population approached 2000, and the manager of the works, William Kelly, had been experimenting with methods to make the mules self-acting.[2]

David Dale was well known as a humane employer, and as an unusually just and kindly man. As a magistrate, he won the golden opinions of his fellow citizens as he tempered justice with mercy. He treated his employees well, and employed destitute children, keeping them well clad, housed and fed. At New Lanark, the school he established had, in 1796, 18 teachers for 510 pupils, giving almost a modern pupil-teacher ratio. There were eight classes, and children progressed by achievement rather than by age. The scale and sophistication of this provision was altogether exceptional for the period. As the most successful cotton spinner in Scotland, he provided an important example of the application of a religiously inspired social conscience. He was also responsible for the main part of the physical fabric of the village of New Lanark which you can see today. The general layout of the site, and the ambitious scale of the project, follows his design. The materials used in the buildings, local sandstone for the random rubble walls, and slate for the roofs, met his construction requirements.[3]

Robert Owen and after

Caroline Dale became the object of Robert Owen's affections when he visited her father on cotton business. In 1799 he married his bride, formed a partnership to take over New Lanark, and, on New Year's Day 1800, took up occupation in the centre of the village. He tightened up the administration of the mills, introducing new standards of book-keeping, stock control, and factory discipline. By around 1809 he had begun to introduce significant new physical elements to the village. He had brought Mill Number Four into full production, instead of using it to house children and mechanics. These were relocated to an apprentice house at Nursery Buildings, and a new Mechanics Workshop. Almost in parallel, his social views had begun to develop more fully, and the success of the business allowed him to act on his revolutionary opinions. He had become convinced that by treating his workpeople as responsible for their actions, and by encouraging them to realise their mutual dependence, productivity in the mills would increase, and a community spirit would develop. He also realised that an educated workforce was more likely to realise his objectives, both in the context of the village and on a universal scale. In 1809 he started to build his 'New Institution for the Formation of Character', but he found that he was unable to carry his partners with him. After two changes in the partnership, he secured a grouping that allowed him to complete the Institute in 1816 and to add a School for Children in the following year.

Owen took delight in receiving visitors, and the combined tour of the village and the Falls of Clyde became one of the great features of a tour of Scotland. Contact with distinguished visitors, and a high level of public consciousness, helped to propel Owen on to the wider stage. His vision of a society without crime, poverty, or misery had a broad and immediate appeal in the depressed years following the end of the Napoleonic Wars. He wrote and travelled widely to promote his views. In 1824, after a series of quarrels with his partners about his educational methods, he began to disengage from New Lanark. He left to develop a community at New Harmony, Indiana, USA, on the co-operative lines which he had described in his 'Report to the County of Lanark' in 1820.[4] For the rest of his life he continued to develop his ideas of co-operation and how to establish a more rationally based society. He travelled extensively and became an internationally known and much respected figure.[5]

Robert Owen, wise and good,
Better known than understood;
Too often putting wisdom's tools
In the very hands of fools.
Many hear you theorize,
And with wider mouth than eyes,
Swallow all you have to say,
As 'twere food for them to-day;
Dreaming not your mental eye
Is lighting dim futurity.
   (*Poor Man's Guardian*, 29 September 1834)[6]

New Lanark was purchased from the surviving partners in 1828 by the Walker brothers. They continued to spin cotton and to operate Owen's Institute and School. The School was superseded by the State system in 1875, and the Walkers sold the mills in 1881 to a partnership which introduced net-making and canvas weaving. From them it passed into the hands of the Gourock Ropework Company, the world's largest rope and net-making firm, who ran the mills, making cotton canvas and nets, until 1968 (see Figure 3, which shows New Lanark as it was in 1961). Essentially this represented nearly 200 years of successful enterprise and economic activity based on the capacity and ingenuity of management and workforce. While the presence of Owen in the early days did represent an added dimension, the core achievement was very considerable in its own right.[7]

By 1968, the historic importance of the village was beginning to become internationally recognised. In countless textbooks throughout the world, Robert Owen's visionary name was coupled with that of historic New Lanark.[8]

Decline and Decay

When, in 1963, the Gourock Ropework Company decided it could no longer maintain the housing in the village, a Housing Association was formed to modernise the interiors, while retaining the buildings' original appearance. Before the second phase of this rehabilitation had been completed, the mills had closed. The mill complex, including Owen's Institute and School, was sold in 1970 to a scrap metal company. With administrative responsibility split, wholesale demolition seemed almost inevitable, until, in a last-ditch attempt to find a future for the village, New Lanark Conservation Trust was formed as a trigger for a programme of revivification

Figure 3. School, lade, mills and boiler-house chimney, New Lanark, 1961. (Crown Copyright: RCAHMS)

on a scale unprecedented in Scotland, and with few parallels elsewhere.

Essentially the historic village remained intact, substantially as it had been built by its great founders, Dale and Owen. Both would be able to find their way around the modern New Lanark with no difficulty, so little has been the change. Both would recognise the magical visual impact of the site and the overwhelming sense of it as a unique place. Economic competition had always been a significant factor in the operation of the factory, but for the village's twentieth-century owners, the Gourock Ropework Company, it had become overwhelming. They were subject to take-over and amalgamation in a way which has now become commonplace. Also, there were genuinely more difficulties involved in production from an eighteenth-century cotton mill than would have been the case with a flat, concrete-floored, modern factory shell with proper access doors and services. Cheap national fuel policies had meant that the water-power advantage of being located on the Falls of Clyde had been gradually eroded. [9]

Visually this decline could be identified by the deteriorating condition of the buildings, especially the housing rows. The 'Gourock' had desperately tried to divest itself of the main village housing offering it to the local housing authority. It was no longer appropriate that a factory should also own the houses of its workers, and 'the Gourock' could not afford the major restoration works required to bring the dwelling units up to post Parker-Morris standards. In 1963 the charitable housing association, New Lanark Association Ltd, was formed to take over this responsibility. [10] It is still in existence, and at the time of writing it continues to operate the village housing.

This same problem was evident elsewhere within the mill complex, despite the company's best efforts. The 1931 Boving water turbine, at the heart of the power-generating system, was patched together to keep it going. Like most of New Lanark, it needed a thorough overhaul to make it efficient and bring it up to date. After nearly 200 years this was unavoidably true of much of the village. Closure in 1968 represented a local disaster, and an already difficult situation was made even worse by the loss of 300 jobs and the sale of the mill site to the scrap metal company. The efforts of the housing association were rendered ineffective, and prospects were bleak. Another major Scottish industrial heritage site appeared to be in imminent danger of being reduced to rubble.

New Lanark Conservation Trust (NLCT)

A small group of individuals and organisations combined to support the 1974 formation of New Lanark Conservation Trust: central and local government, the Scottish Civic Trust, and the University of Strathclyde, represented by John Hume of the Department of Economic History. He, and Harry Smith, the Chairman of the 1972 Working Party on the future for New Lanark, and Provost of the Royal Burgh of Lanark, were probably the key individuals at this stage. [11] Although there were organisations involved, it should not be forgotten that the individuals were of crucial significance. The Trust continues to be supported under planning legislation, on an annual partnership basis, by the successor bodies to the original statutory founders, South Lanarkshire Council and Historic Scotland. The problems of the absence of any committed capital budget, and of revenue funding approved on an annual basis, have remained as a major financial and restrictive issues throughout the period of operation of the Trust.

'Revivification' of the village was the policy adopted by the Trust. This is a very positive approach, which seeks to introduce new life and appropriate development within the existing architectural framework and historic traditions. Statutory protection was provided when all the buildings were listed Category 'A' under the Town and Country Planning (Scotland) Act 1972, and a Conservation Area established and declared 'outstanding' under the same act and the Town and Country Amenities Act 1974. Additional protection was realised in 1996 when the boundaries of the Conservation Area were extended to include the Falls of Clyde and the landscape setting of the historic village. This was partially caused by various planning applications for modern housing and development near to

Figure 4. Mantilla Row, New Lanark, 1976. (Crown Copyright: RCAHMS)

New Lanark, which, if approved, would have been seriously detrimental to the historic site. This extension represents a major additional safeguard.

The restoration of New Lanark was a seriously daunting task for the tiny and new New Lanark Conservation Trust and its newly-appointed, naïve and young Village Manager. Housing was the first priority. It had been agreed that the new Trust would provide assistance to the housing association. Financial re-structuring was achieved and the Association re-established on the relatively sound footing which it enjoys to this day. A similarly successful application of a wide range of appropriate mechanisms has effectively restored the historic housing of New Lanark. A total of 65 new homes have been created within the original fabric of the tenement rows. In 1998, only Double Row awaits rehabilitation. This will create perhaps ten additional house units. Only one housing block, Mantilla Row (see Figure 4), comprising three house units, has had to be demolished because of structural instability. It remains the ambition of the New Lanark Association and Trust to complete the village, including these two housing projects, and a multitude of ever

more complex applications are in place to try to achieve this increasingly elusive objective.

In the industrial area of the village the major single step forward started in 1979. Clydesdale District Council, the local planning authority, issued a Repairs Notice in response to the non-repair of buildings of historic and architectural importance. In 1983, after a visit of inspection by George Younger, the Secretary of State for Scotland, all the buildings owned by the scrap metal company were compulsorily acquired, to be passed over to New Lanark Conservation Trust to allow works of preservation and restoration to commence. Such a procedure has been used very rarely, and in this case it required the Secretary of State to act against the advice of his officials. Once again the support of an individual proved crucial for the development of the project.

A major programme of restoration and development has since been established in the industrial area. Virtually all the most significant buildings have been restored and adapted to new uses. The Institute forms the reception for a major visitor facility which leads into the Mill Number Three and incorporates working mill machinery and the 'Annie McLeod Experience', a dark-ride system designed to tell the Robert Owen story and to attract visitors.[12] In 1994 the water power system was re-established and the electricity generated supplies the site, with the surplus being exported into the national grid system. In 1998 Mill Number One and the Waterhouses were opened as a four-star, 38-bedroom hotel (see Figure 5), with eight self-catering units attached. The Mechanics' Workshop and Dyeworks have been restored and are let to tenants, including the Scottish Wildlife Trust, who manage the adjacent Falls of Clyde Wildlife Reserve. There are still outstanding projects: the completion of the School interior as an audio-visual interpretative facility; Mill Number Two interior; structural and retaining walls; and projects to improve access in the area around the village. However, the prospect is much improved since 1968.[13]

World Heritage Status

Characteristically the rescue and preservation of New Lanark has never been an easy project. The World Heritage story illustrates this well. In the end it is likely that the village will achieve this status, but apparently not without a struggle. At the shortest possible notice, in 1986, the Trust was invited by Historic Scotland to participate in the preparation of the submission for the village to UNESCO. The preparation work was undertaken by John Hume for Historic Scotland and by me, as Village Manager. At that moment I became an addition to John Hume's very extensive list of collaborative authors, though this was for something of an official publication. We had a very short time in which to prepare the document, which had to conform to a Historic Scotland format, and which was ready and signed by the appropriate Scottish Office Minister of State on 30 December 1986. Preparation costs were shared by New Lanark Conservation Trust and Historic Scotland, and inevitably there were cost overruns. These amounted to several thousand pounds, and were borne by the Trust. Thus did we become probably the only site in the world to have paid for its own World Heritage submission. Not only this, but we became involved in a wider

political issue involving a general appraisal of world industrial heritage. Our proposal was deferred while studies could proceed, and this remains the position today, more than a decade later.

It requires fortitude and some resolution not to be deterred by this position of general difficulty, partly because it seems to be inherent in the structure of an independent trust. New Lanark Conservation Trust has annual revenue funding supported by partnership government agencies, and no capital budget for restoration projects. Therefore, it needs to maintain support from its funding agencies, and also seek additional, project-based support for each individual proposal. It is not likely that such a formula would ever be easy to operate. It is difficult to think of a revenue funding agency with which there has not been some difficulty over a period in excess of 20 years. Local government has changed its structure three times, and no other agency is quite the same as it was. Inevitably the operation of the Trust has been the subject of virtually constant review, as each new funding body emerges or disappears. In these circumstances the solidity of core intellectual and emotional support is vital, particularly because the immediate uncertainty is usually real, and pressing.[14]

The Magnificent Seven and the Big Picture

A site of the size of New Lanark, with at least some permanent staff on some sort of temporary basis, could hardly ever escape some of the wider obligations to industrial heritage. Involvement in this area of activity brought together the group of industrial sites which formed AIIMHS, the Association of Independent Industrial Museums and Heritage Sites. The first meeting was held in March 1984 with representatives of most of the major sites, and John Hume attended to give us support. With his help the major independent Scottish sites came together: New Lanark (I have been temporary chairman for twelve years); the Scottish Maritime Museum at Irvine; Doon Valley Heritage at Dalmellington; Wanlockhead Lead Mining Museum; The Scottish Mining Museum at Newtongrange; Bo'ness Heritage Trust; and occasionally Summerlee at Coatbridge was able to be a member, depending on its local authority status. Originally there was a total of seven sites, with Dundee Industrial Heritage being involved later, and occasionally they must have been magnificent in somebody's eyes – hence the title.

This contact structure was important for the member sites because it made them more aware that their problems and institutional arrangements were common across Scotland. It has become a way of sharing information and techniques for dealing with common issues. Perhaps most important of all, it has allowed a group of institutions to come together to make common representations to central government and related agencies. Therefore, the organised voice of industrial heritage practitioners could be made heard and their views at least taken into account. Probably the clearest recent example of this development has been the 1996 publication of a government policy statement on industrial heritage. Of the twelve Steering Group members for this report and ministerial statement, three were from AIIHMS.[15]

A similar position exists in respect of support for the voluntary societies. These provide an important bedrock for the appreciation of industrial heritage in Scotland. Characteristically voluntary support in Scotland has been less obvious than in neighbouring England. The position was made as strong as possible in 1984 when John Hume helped to pilot the amalgamation of the Scottish Society for the Preservation of Historic Machinery (SSPHM – the famous 'scrap-iron club') and the Scottish Society for Industrial Archaeology. The new body, the Scottish Industrial Heritage Society (SIHS), brings all the interested parties together in one group with fewer administrative requirements and fewer overheads. These examples illustrate how important it is for site-based activities to take into account the outer world, even if the outer awareness usually has to be confined to Scotland. It is very easy to be contained by the immediate, often overwhelming, problems associated with running a major site.

However, it would be inappropriate to leave this point without making some mention of the difficult position in which most of the major Scottish 'national' industrial heritage sites have been

placed. Central government has contrived broadly to ignore a sequence of reports (Williams/Bute/Miles) which have commented on various aspects of an unsatisfactory situation. While there has been significant change at the establishment centre, there has been virtually no alteration at the periphery. In 1986, in the report 'Museums in Scotland', Professor Hamish Miles quoted a small part of my submission:

> We can provide a unique location for an industrial museum of international standing and interest, concentrating on areas in which a special contribution can be made. Alternatively it can develop as a fairly lightweight visitor centre, with minimal collection, and concentrating on public entertainment and amusements. Given the lack of real support from the museum bodies there is very little effective choice.[16]

The current revenue funding crisis which is being experienced, in one form or another, by most of the sites, is caused by an underlying condition that was diagnosed more than a decade ago. Even the effort made by New Lanark to concentrate on 'entertainment and amusements', will only provide a temporary palliative. We must make every effort to achieve a more satisfactory funding base. Perhaps the establishment of a Scottish Parliament will mean that it will be less easy for a national government to evade its responsibility for these industrial heritage sites of 'national significance'. The 1986 Miles Report started its industrial chapter

> No other part of Scotland's heritage is abandoned and ignored to the same extent as industry; no other part of Scotland's heritage is as relevant to its population as industry.[17]

To some degree this generalisation addresses the central issue involved with the rescue and preservation of New Lanark, which was how to achieve physical restoration within the constraints of the prevailing economic position of central government, and the unavoidable requirement to operate commercially once physical restoration had been achieved because of limitation on publicly funded revenue support. In a real sense the issue of 'preservation' did not really exist. At that time, as now, there were virtually no funds available for strictly preservationist projects. Financial support was hardly ever available for any project simply to preserve the historic monument of New Lanark. Therefore, restoration through economic development was the unavoidable alternative. This remains conceptually difficult even for the present Trustees, who can be seen yearning for resources which are not available to them. Preservation, based on the inherent value of the object, with support from public funds, is a comfortable option which has not been available to us. It is this absence of any real policy choice that has substantially shaped the current form of physical and economic development in the village.[18]

There is absolutely no doubt that we would have done things differently if the position had been more favourable. As it is, virtually all the village buildings have to provide an economic return which will sustain their future. This has meant that the original millworkers' houses have had to be extensively modernised within the historic shell. There are some external changes, but these have been minimised. Internally, however, the modern homes bear only an outline structural relationship to the original dwellings. This can be seen when it is considered that the nine main housing blocks originally contained over 2000 inhabitants. Now the 45 domestic tenancies and 20 owner-occupier units provide accommodation for around 180 people. On full completion there will be around 200 inhabitants in the village. The main remnant of preserved originality is in one Museum Stair in one of the tenement blocks.

This is similarly true in the industrial area of the village. The development has focused on significant tourist activities being located in the buildings. New Lanark mill buildings tend to be very large, in excess of 36,000 square feet, and this requires major revenue flows to be derived from tourist activity. There is no question of free entry, rather the issue is the elasticity of demand in relation to the tourist product and price. This has meant that our mill buildings are converted as a visitor centre, café, large retail shop, and hotel. Our Mechanics' Workshop

is developed as 12,000 square feet of lettable space. Our tenants are: a high-tech audio-visual creative and training company; a furniture and rug retail showroom; a leather-worker's shop; and a darkroom for the local camera club. It is not a replication of the site where over 200 skilled men worked to keep the cotton factory in operation. It is not a joiner's shop on the top floor, a light engineering shop on the middle floor and a heavy engineering and casting shop on the ground floor. Mill Number One, one of the most historic buildings in Scotland, has been converted to an hotel. It is not difficult to recommend that on this basis Edinburgh and Stirling Castles should follow the same development pattern. Holyrood Palace would make a particularly interesting hotel; but it is going to be more difficult to find appropriate economic functions for some of our other monuments, and they could have to be abandoned.

These types of issue are representative of those which will challenge any strictly preservation-based project, and it was the imperative to develop a more pragmatic approach which encouraged the Trust to proceed on the basis that it was unavoidably committed to looking after its own financial future, insofar as that was possible. Even now this seems less than simple or just. It produced many hours of debate for Trustees and other advisory agencies. It tended to focus on specific project proposals, rather than on general principles. In the end, difficult judgements were always required to proceed with the best alternative of the series of worst options.

New Lanark is often used as a symbol of success. It has become a major rural tourist attraction with over 400,000 visitors per annum, and of these a peak of 150,000 p.a. have paid to enter the visitor centre and undergo the 'Annie McLeod Experience', and participate in the other interpretative facilities. Major awards have been won, including a Civic Trust Award (1971 and 1979), a Europa Nostra Silver Medal (1986), the British tourism 'Oscar' – the BTA Come to Britain Trophy (1986), various Scottish Tourism Awards, and an Historic Scotland Award for the restoration of Mill Number One (1996). This is a selection from more than 20 major awards.[19]

The main fabric of the historic village is restored, apart from one or two major remaining projects. There are many people who have contributed to this achievement. On the occasion of the publication of this collection of articles, the retirement of John Hume from his post as Chief Inspector of Historic Buildings for Historic Scotland, it is appropriate to acknowledge his contribution to this specific project at New Lanark. He has acted with characteristic determination and consistency. New Lanark acknowledges the debt which it owes to John, which it can never fully repay, but I hope that he finds encouragement in our determination to capture the currently breaking wave of enthusiasm for the future as represented by the words of Robert Owen. (Who else could it be?)

'What ideas individuals may attach to the term 'Millennium' I know not; but I know that society may be formed so as to exist without crime, without poverty, with health greatly improved, with little, if any misery, and with intelligence and happiness increased a hundredfold; and no obstacle whatsoever intervenes at this moment except ignorance to prevent such a state of society from becoming universal.' [20]

ACKNOWLEDGEMENT

This article relies heavily on the 1986 submission made to UNESCO for New Lanark's inscription on the World Heritage List. The main author of the submission document was John Hume, and I am pleased formally to acknowledge his assistance.[21]

NOTES

1. *The Statistical Account for Scotland*, Vol XV, 1795, p 34.
2. For additional background see *The Industrial Archaeology of New Lanark* by John R Hume, in *Robert Owen, Prince of Cotton Spinners* (David & Charles, Newton Abbot, 1971).
3. See D J McLaren, *David Dale of New Lanark* (Caring Books, 1999).
4. See D Hardy and L Davidson, *Utopian Thought and Communal Experience* (Middlesex Polytechnic, London, 1989), as well as very extensive publication range from Historic New Harmony, Indiana, USA.
5. See *Selected Works of Robert Owen*, 4 vols, G Claeys (ed) (Pickering & Chatto, London, 1993).
6. See E Royle, *Robert Owen and the Commencement of the Millennium* (Manchester University Press, 1998).
7. See *The Story of New Lanark* (NLCT, New Lanark 1993).
8. See *Select Bibliography* (NLCT, New Lanark, 1998).
9. See G Blake, *The Gourock* (Glasgow, 1963). Also, the extensive manuscript records held by University of Glasgow's Business Archive.
10. *Rules* of New Lanark Association Ltd 1963, Model H. 7 1962 (Charitable).
11. *A Future for New Lanark* (Lanark County Council, 1973).
12. *Heritage: The New Lanark Story*, ed J M Fladmark (Donhead Publishing, Shaftesbury, 1993).
13. For economic background information see, CR Planning – *Economic Impact of New Lanark*, 1993, available from Lanarkshire Development Agency.
14. I Donnachie and G Hewitt, *Historic New Lanark* (Edinburgh University Press, 1993).
15. *Industrial Heritage and Tourism in Scotland: A Review* (The Scottish Office, Edinburgh, 1996).
16. *Museums in Scotland*, Report by the Museums & Galleries Commission (HMSO, Edinburgh, 1986).
17. *Ibid* p 74.
18. See L Davidson and D Hardy, *Thinking of Heritage* (Middlesex University, 1991).
19. *Awards List 1971–99*, available from NLCT.
20. Robert Owen, Address to the Inhabitants of New Lanark, New Year's Day 1816.
21. *New Lanark*, submitted by the Secretary of State for Scotland to UNESCO, 1986.

9

IAN GOW

'The Most Learned Drawing Room in Europe?': Newhailes and the Classical Scottish Library

THE National Trust for Scotland's acquisition of Newhailes is the most important rescue bid in Scotland to be supported and made possible by the Heritage Lottery Fund and Historic Scotland during John Hume's tenureship as Chief Inspector of Historic Buildings for Scotland. The key to understanding Newhailes lies in its remarkable Library and this paper attempts to set it in the contemporary Scottish context.

The Library of the typical eighteenth-century Scottish country house has three characteristics: it is almost always located high up in the house to an extent where it can be described as skied; it is often unusually architectural and grand while, finally, it was often the most comfortable and welcoming room in the house. These last two characteristics are perhaps difficult to reconcile and were to give rise to a degree of creative tension as the century progressed.

This characteristic skying may be the outcome of the prevailing verticality of our national architecture where any kind of new specialisation in room use had, of necessity, to fall out high-up in man-made tree-houses like Craigievar.

But the development of the Library presupposes the achievement of a critical mass of books and, at least architecturally, this seems to have occurred in the late seventeenth century. The Library, however, appears to be secondary to the development of the fireproof, stone-vaulted and floored Muniment Room protected by its iron door and window shutters. The importance of land demanded the provision of secure depositories to protect the

all-important charters. The best known of these, in a newly built house of 1698, is perhaps that designed by Sir William Bruce at Hopetoun. These Muniment Rooms, in new houses, were often situated in close proximity to the Laird's private accommodation and thus, in contrast to the skied library, often fell-out on the ground floor, where his apartment was often placed to allow the landowner to interview retainers in its outer rooms who would not normally be permitted in the body of the house. The grandest expression of the fireproof Muniment Room, at national level, was to be Robert Adam's Register House of 1774, one of the most important buildings of the Scottish Enlightenment.

The development of the Library must have been equally practical in Scotland because few landowners could live solely off their rents and the law, then as now, was to be the most important profession and an established route to political office in a country which lacked a resident Court after 1603, a Parliament after 1707 and had developed an egalitarian Established church. A country with few natural resources was inclined to value learning highly and the country house Library could be viewed as an educational investment for the heirs of a dynasty. A sequestered situation high up in the House was conducive to study, and also kept the precious books away from damp vaults and basements.

Small collections of books cannot have made very pressing architectural demands. The handsome bracketed library shelves at Ferniehurst Castle may have been a response to a larger than average collection and are among the earliest to survive in

Scotland. In 1887 they attracted the attention of MacGibbon and Ross who illustrated this proto-Scottish classical Library in their *Castellated and Domestic Architecture of Scotland* (see Figure 1).[1] Ross's sketch shows rather tricksey shaped fretted brackets, embellished with carving, supporting shelves around the perimeter of a circular tower room, under a timber ceiling which relates to plasterwork from the second quarter of the seventeenth century. The Library at Craigston Castle, with its timeless shelves fitted-in amid the restrictions of tower house living, is perhaps representative of the pragmatic norm before architects intervened.

Nothing prepares us, however, for the suave urbanity of William Adam's design of *circa* 1726 for the skied Library at Arniston, and he was himself sufficiently proud of it to have the section engraved for his projected *Vitruvius Scoticus*. His design must have been constrained by the dimensions of the Dundas' existing tower house but the position of the Library was given a new axial coherence in the published plan by siting it immediately above, and over, the central two storied coved entrance hall.

Although the attic position might have limited the height of the Library, Adam was to give it a sense of spaciousness and importance by breaking its cove up into the roofspace. An architectural presence was imparted with the dignity of an Order. His choice of the Ionic order may have been reflected its historic association with learning and

Figure 1. 'Fernieherst Castle, Ceiling of Library', the proto-classical library illustrated in MacGibbon and Ross, *Castellated and Domestic Architecture of Scotland*, Vol II.

LIBRARY FERNIEHURST

DETAIL OF BRACKET

scholarship but, while Sir William Bruce's earlier Scottish interior system had depended on paired pilasters framing the central chimneypiece, Adam carried his Ionic pilasters, which have no pedestals, all around the room under a correctly pulvinated frieze, which, most skilfully, dodges the uneven window spacing imposed by the Library's falling-out behind the external frontispiece under the pediment. The internal Library bays were linked by attic arcades, framing and cherishing classicising busts. Perhaps the most luxurious refinement of all was the glazed doors that protected the contents of every case. In execution this overall architectural control was to be relaxed a little by asymmetrically skittish naturalistic stucco-work – presumably by Enzer, who executed that in the Hall immediately below. Although now sobered under later graining, Pat Wigston, who has researched the Adam decoration of Arniston, has discovered that it was initially painted white with gilded ornaments heightened by painted festoons down each pilaster.

Adam's Arniston Library was to provide a model that was frequently imitated in Scotland. In his own smaller house designs like Haddo and House of Dun where the coved Great Dining Room centred on the garden front was planned as the largest interior volume and rose higher than its adjacent rooms, it was logical to squeeze the Library in above this, at a mezzanine level, stealing additional space and height from the roof after the Arniston model. But the format was to be taken up and copied by others like Sir James Clerk in his new house at Penicuik and the unknown architect of Auchinleck. Few of these libraries were to vie with the showy interior architecture and decoration displayed at Arniston. A particularly charming rustic, and possibly contemporary, version, within a tower house, survives at Traquair (see Figure 2). It may have been

Figure 2. The principal library within the earlier tower house at Traquair House, Peebles. (Crown Copyright: RCAHMS)

designed by John Douglas but it is not clear if James West, the Edinburgh house-painter, was repairing its original decorative painting in 1823 or introducing a fanciful departure of his own.

In spite of the undoubted splendour of the Arniston Library, it was to lack one refinement that was certainly included in the specification for both Haddo and Dun because it has no Library Closet. In both of the latter houses, small closets opened directly off the Libraries, and both, significantly, were equipped with fireplaces. It is easy to see how these snug warm closets would have been a very practical addition to the usefulness of a library sequestered in a remote part of the house.

But we must not necessarily assume that these libraries were solely the resort of the serious minded. In 1781, the Reverend John Waugh, recently appointed tutor to the Erskine boys, wrote a long letter to his sister describing his life at the House of Dun which was quoted at length by Violet Jacob in her *Lairds of Dun*, 1931.[2]

> There is a large room or Hall contiguous to my apartment where the Library is, In it is likewise a grove of myrtles and aromatic shrubs, a telescope and maps, pictures with cabinet of shellwork and a Hobby horse and battledore for the Ladies. The billiard table is out of repair, which is no disappointment for I should be apt, as has formerly been the case to spend too much of my time at this bewitching game. Here I frequently sit and read or in the evening play on the fiddle ...

The privacy of the Library Closet therefore may also have supplied a refuge from the distractions of the varied and surprising uses to which the adjoining larger room was being subjected. As well as being a repository for books, the library seems to have attracted the characteristics of a popular everyday living room imbued with a spirit of informality in contrast to the showy materials and best behaviour demanded by the state apartment on the *piano nobile* below.

But all was not well in the Library at Dun because John Waugh was to complain that the father of his pupils 'does not read, not for want of opportunity but from want of inclination', and it is possible that the tutor was lodging in the Library Closet and ordinarily using the Library as a sitting room apart from the gentry in the equivocal social position of later Victorian governesses. However atypical conditions may have been at Dun, the development of the classical Scottish country house library probably embraces the paradox of a room designed apparently to be removed from the central bustle of the household and then being gradually annexed as the life and soul of family life.

Although most Scottish libraries of this period share these characteristics, their skied form is by no means unique to Scotland. Chicheley House in Buckinghamshire is celebrated for its curvaceous Baroque facade of *circa* 1719 and, high up on the attic floor, an apparently conventional panelled room, graced by Corinthian pilasters, contains a surprise when it is revealed that its apparently normal-looking panels are hinged to reveal adjustable bookshelves, riding in wooden slots.

Clearly there was no tradition of tower house verticality in Buckinghamshire which makes one wonder if these skied libraries could be a misreading of something with a specific Italianate context in published engravings. A likely candidate are the *Guardaroba,* or fitted wardrobe rooms with their own loggias high up on the roofline of Roman Palazzi to attract the air, and misinterpreted – their patrons possessing no purple vestments to be preserved from moth – as libraries, and thoughtlessly mimicked to a more practical British purpose. Their true function and purpose was revealed by Patricia Waddy in her *Seventeenth-Century Roman Palaces*.[3]

Having established the norm, the extraordinary qualities of Sir David Dalrymple's Library at Newhailes can be more fully appreciated. At the time of writing, however, many aspects of the building history of Newhailes remain obscure. In 1709, Sir David had purchased the house, which had been designed and built from scratch as a pioneering neo-Palladian villa in the proximity of Edinburgh, by the celebrated architect, James Smith, for his own use. Smith had himself purchased the estate, then called Whitehill, in 1689 (see Figure 3). Smith's tenure at Newhailes, however, is not as clear-cut in

Figure 3. The entrance front of Newhailes House, Inveresk. (Crown Copyright: RCAHMS, 1994)

the surviving documents as one could wish. As the home of one of Scotland's leading architects, and one who also occupies a key position in the history of English Palladianism through influence upon Colen Campbell, one might expect to encounter the architecturally extraordinary at Newhailes. Campbell's architectural drawings, now deposited in the British Architectural Library, were discovered in Yorkshire in 1966. They included not only designs for many buildings firmly documented as being designed by him but also many theoretical designs displaying a penchant for precise bi-lateral symmetry. The Campbell drawings include a recognisable study of Newhailes.

Even today visitors to Newhailes express their astonishment when they pass from Smith's lowly seventeenth-century rooms at the core of Newhailes, to the vast oak lined library on the *piano nobile* that rises through two stories to a coved attic and is flooded by light from its five immensely tall, arched sash windows. The effect must have been the more remarkable for Sir David's contemporaries because

they were more familiar with smaller skied libraries. The Newhailes Library is practically equal in volume to Smith's entire existing house (see Figure 4). Although Sir David's new Library could not but be conditioned by the constraints imposed by this existing house, its importance depends on its relatively early dating in the development of the classical Scottish library. Dr W B McQueen's survey of the Newhailes Papers in the National Library of Scotland, undertaken on behalf of the National Trust for Scotland, has established that the Library was constructed between *circa* 1718–22, and it thus predates Arniston, which must have been begun in a spirit of rivalry.[4]

Given the diminutive scale of Smith's little proto-Palladian villa, a traditional skied library would have been a non-starter at Newhailes if we presume the achievement of an impressively critical mass of books as the occasion for its construction. But the existing house still dictates the dimensions of the adopted design in that the *enfilades* along each front of Smith's house were continued as entrance axes to

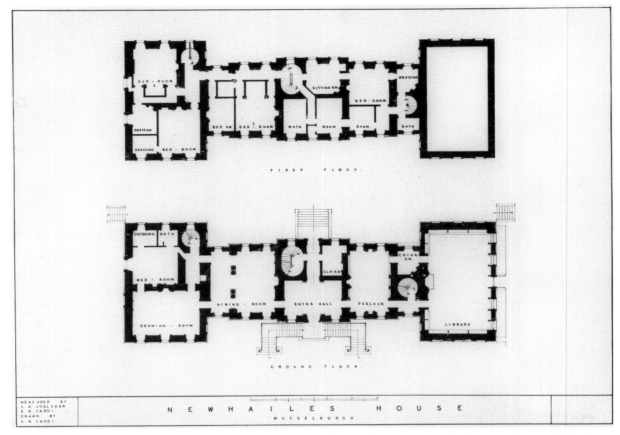

Figure 4. Floor plans for the ground and first floors at Newhailes, showing the proportionately large area designated for the Library. (Crown Copyright: RCAHMS)

what could only be a new wing, or pavilion, but one turned through ninety degrees to the existing matrix (see Figure 5). The height of the floor-level and the wallhead was continued from the existing house. Sadly, the name of Sir David's architect is not recorded but Smith, and his partner Alexander McGill, must remain plausible candidates. Because details like the chamfered window surrounds, and the base moulding, were copied from the *corps de logis* there is nothing immediately idiosyncratic about its exterior architecture to identify a designer and Smith's quoins gave way to simpler stone fillets framing the expanses of external stucco – some of which, on the Entrance front, retains its smoothly lined-out imitation ashlar. Although the end walls of the Library pavilion were left unpunctured to provide maximum book space at each end of the room,

the provision of dummy windows on the exterior of this block perhaps presupposes that the Library pavilion was always to be replicated to provide the balancing Great Apartment block from the outset – although the latter was not certainly built before the later 1720s.

There was no attempt to utilise the basement below the Library as living space and it was partitioned up into vaulted cellars – presumably to keep the precious books dry. The entrance lobby to the individual cellars is not placed axially but has a valency towards the present Garden front and appears to be weighted towards the present spinal corridor shown on the ground floor of the Smith 'design' for Newhailes in the British Architectural Library. Access to the cellars thus also dodges the footings of the central Library hearth and flue above.

Figure 5. The Library Pavilion at Newhailes. The use of blind windows provided articulation to the external elevation while ensuring that no space was lost to the book shelves inside. (Crown Copyright: RCAHMS)

If the cellars were never intended for living space, to fit them as practical storage cellars their floor was excavated four steps below the ground level of Smith's existing house. The vault in this cellar Lobby runs parallel to this axial corridor and is an impressive space that recalls the dimly lit crypto-porticus passages of Roman ruins with their powerfully elemental great basket arched doorways, with broad stone surrounds, leading to the four paired cellars of different sizes opening to either side. The cellars are lit by shafts cut down from elegant port-hole windows below the Library windows showing a sense of design and a feeling for order. The final third of the Lobby is cut off to form the present wine-cellar. The vaults retain traces in the mortar of their original timber shuttering.

It was presumably logical to place the flue in the great Library room above and between the two *enfilade* doors, leaving the entire length of wall opposite for the 'real' tall windows which illuminate this deep room. It is on this side facade alone that the Library pavilion takes on an architectural distinction with its five arched windows – a new introduction to Newhailes's architectural repertoire – under deeply projecting attic panels, reflecting the cove that lies behind them. The keystones of the arch-headed windows are carved with shells – the first appearance of a feature that was later to become the *leitmotiv* of Newhailes's celebrated rococo interiors. The central window was treated as a door, and the stopping of its base-moulding appears to have been planned – although the step may have been lowered. This door-window led onto a raised terrace and seems to have been associated with an axial cabinet garden beyond, created from a shaped clearing in the policy woods. A tiny sundial was neatly slipped in over the central window.

This new Library pavilion, however, is buffered by an extra bay between it and the original house whose function seems to have been to provide the necessary Library Closet. This was perhaps a particular necessity in view of the vastness of the new room and has a practical and warming corner fireplace whose flue abuts the main Library flue next door. Between this and the new Lobby leading into the Library, was placed a circular service stair whose function was probably as much to provide access above as to connect with the service zone below. These circular service stairs – an old-fashioned usage in Scotland at this time – in this and the Great Apartment Pavilion recalls their extensive and idiosyncratic contemporary use by Campbell, in designs like Wanstead, who may have seen them as an Italianate Palladianism. Because both *enfilades* led into the Library, they do not necessarily shed any light on the re-orientation of the house that has certainly occurred since the design in the Smith/Campbell collection now in the British Architectural Library was drawn up. If the Library Closet was meant to be semi-private in character, there is the likelihood that this switch was related to this same building campaign.

The Library Lobby is lined with bolection panelling, which presumably reflected the finishing of Smith's original interiors, but may have been re-set – it has certainly affected by dry rot eradication. The closets on the floors above have all lost their original detail although that immediately above the Library Closet retains its dove-grey basket-arched chimney surround with original marble lining precisely matching that in the Closet below. This might suggest that it too relates to the function of the Library, perhaps being reserved for a clerk. At the upper reach of the circular stair the floor level in the attic over the Library has been raised in timber and the current attics over the Library appear to be nineteenth century in their finishings.

One of the Dining Room overdoor paintings depicting the Newhailes Estate, which are in themselves innovative for Scotland through their recording an actual, rather than an idealised classicised landscape, depicts the Library pavilion window face-on, like an isolated pavilion in the countryside (see Figure 6). These paintings are attributed by James Holloway to Isaac Vogelsang, the Dutch painter of landscapes and cattle who also worked in Ireland. The individuality of this facade appears to have been deliberately designed to be distinct from the pair of long facades, as though planned to be appreciated in isolation as a facade in its own right. This characteristic is accentuated by the surrounding terraces which mean that it is not very easy to circulate around the house from the present entrance front.

The oak-lined interior of the Library, at least in comparison to its later embellishment, appears to have been conceived as sober and unornamented space that would be conducive to a working Library under its not particularly architectural concave, and thus rather French, oak cornice. Although there are documentary references to as yet unidentified changes to the cases, the system of tiered slots, which allow the heights of the elegantly moulded oak shelves to be adjusted, must be original to the room because, in deference to an earlier mode of thinking that was anxious to utilise every inch of earlier tiny libraries, even the normally 'dead' spaces in the corners of the room were designed for book storage. This was made possible by the ingenious split corner shelves. It is hardly surprising that this inconvenient system – where up to half-a-dozen books were incarcerated – was later abandoned and the corners boxed over.

So austere is the design of the interior of Newhailes Library, that in the absence of any designer's name being revealed by the family papers, there is nothing about it that sufficiently distinctive visually to allow one to hazard the name of any designer. But this austerity was to be shortlived and one suspects that, rather as at the House of Dun, a Library intended for serious scholarship and legalistic swatting, was found to have more hedonistic benefits. In 1743, Sir David's son, Sir James Dalrymple, called in Thomas Clayton to add the stucco flourish to the upper zone of the chimney-breast and it seems logical to assume that the insertion of the

Figure 6. One of the Dining Room overdoor paintings at Newhailes depicting the Newhailes Estate, in an idealised classicised landscape with the Library Pavilion as an isolated pavilion in the countryside (attributed by James Holloway to Isaac Vogelsang). (Crown Copyright: RCAHMS)

sadly undocumented, but luxuriously decorative, broad red, green and yellow polychrome marble chimneypiece, with its purest white statuary ornaments, was the occasion for this improvement. It certainly dictated the width of the new stucco chimneybreast which incorporates Medina's portrait of Sir David Dalrymple (see Figure 7).

Although the acanthus and palmette stucco ornaments of the concave cornice and the fleshy rinceau over the chimney-shelf are typical of Clayton's work elsewhere, the design of the over-mantel is rather more elegantly Palladian than anything that appears in his own oeuvre. But we can guess exactly where Clayton's inspiration for one element, the stretched lion-pelt, came from, because it is clearly inspired by the Kentian pelt on Cheere's Dining Room chimneypiece of 1739. Unlike its original, however, it cuts across its architectural framework through being crowned with a panache of ostrich feathers.

It cannot have been easy to relate the stucco upper section with the, presumably existing, oak-panelled lower zone of the chimney-breast, and it seems at least possible that the sanding of the chimney-breast, now gilded, was an attempt to unify a tricky interior design problem – the sanding on the flanks below the chimney-shelf is certainly laid over timber lining which could be the original panelled chimney breast. The still glittering, if now, like so much else at Newhailes, enchantingly mellow, gilding might be assumed to be secondary but for the survival of an earlier over-door painting in its sanded and gilded frame. The original overdoors were displaced at some as yet undocumented date in the early nineteenth century by the arrival of new over-door paintings by Thomson of Duddingston, a friend of the family. The brilliant pools of gilding certainly lift the sombre penumbral gloom of the oak and the expanses of leather bound books to great decorative effect. The original frame to the

Figure 7. The Library at Newhailes *circa* 1930 before the removal of the books. (Hew Dalrymple Collection, Crown Copyright: RCAHMS)

survivor of the earlier, displaced painting, which is also attributed to Isaac Vogelsang by James Holloway, is much plainer, with its simpler egg and dart carving, than the elaborately knulled surround of the present pair of over-door landscapes by Thomson of Duddingston.

The long tripartite panels between the new chimneypiece and the entrance doors, may well recall the vestige of an earlier Brucian Order, characteristic of Scottish classical rooms, but the upper rail appears to relate directly to the frieze of the over-mantel and it feels more like work of the earlier 1740s than the 1720s. The voids, behind these tall panels, with their dovetail ties into the adjacent woodwork, suggest that the bookcases may originally have extended on either side of the entrance doors, and the voids remained accessible by slip cupboards which can only have been planned to retain the use of these voids as book storage zones – although now put to alternative use for later services.

The colourful marbles, over-door paintings, decorative stucco and lavish gilding thus radically altered the character of the room and this was continued through to the Library Closet. In 1739 the carver William Strachan was paid for 'carving sixty-four corner pieces for the panels in the Library Closet'. Their present oak graining has tended to disguise the fact that these corner pieces, like the gold edges framing each of the main panels with attic panels above, are removable fillets holding in the loose panels as Timothy Clifford was the first to realise. On a trial removal of these fillets by Stewart Colquhoun, of the National Trust for Scotland, it is clear that each panel was once covered with tightly stretched silk, and there is thus every reason to think, in combination with the shaped corner pieces and the eccentric carved detail round the corner chimneypiece and the strange geometric carving around the window reveal, that the Closet was given an exotic chinoiserie treatment to create

Figure 8. The Library Closet, Newhailes, adapted *circa* 1822 as a china closet. (Crown Copyright: RCAHMS)

a rococo masterpiece whose present sobriety is highly misleading. Although the present arrangement of the room as a china closet is thought to date from *circa* 1822, this was merely an extension of its original character and was perhaps necessary when the silk had tarnished – it was certainly cut from each panel with a sharp blade before they were re-papered to form a darkly contrasting green background to set off the porcelain (see Figure 8).

A peculiarity of the Closet is the fitting of the inner door between it and the Library, which is not only end-pivotted, rather than hinged, by the fixed edge, but this edge has been rounded off to fit closely and turn within a matching groove. This fixed edge happens to be nearest the corner fireplace and is presumably intended, from the care with which this detail has been considered, to act as a draught-excluder in the cosy closet.

The appearance of the Library after 1743 was thus much closer to the grandeur of William Adam's Arniston Library. Curiously, William Adam's *Vitruvius Scoticus* supplies an unexpected link between the apparently different approaches exemplified in the skied Library of Arniston and the outsize *piano nobile* solution adopted at Newhailes (see Figure 9). As James Simpson realised in his commentary on the Plates in his 1980 reprint of Adam's unwieldy book, the as yet unidentified designers of both Rosehall (later rechristened Douglas Support) and Newbyth are likely to have been the same architect. At Rosehall, the skied attic Library pavilion proudly floats atop a roofline high above an Ionic frontispiece, whereas at Newbyth, which might have had a similar attic, the Library occupies an entire pavilion contiguous to the *piano nobile* and is a very large rectangular space, surrounded by wall presses, and lit by tall arched-headed sashes. William Adam was himself to adapt to this polarity in his patrons' choice between two poles in Library taste through his provision of similar large pavilion libraries at both Hopetoun and Duff – both so megalomaniac in scale that it is hardly surprising that they were not executed.

But the state apartment at Newhailes, fitted into the balancing wing, also shows signs of contemporary changes in the perception of the appropriate character that was deemed suitable for other public rooms in the Scottish country house. While the new Dining Room, fitted out during the 1730s, is characteristically Scottish in being the largest and showiest architecturally in the new suite, the adjoining Drawing Room shows a development from the older form of Withdrawing Room in its extravagant expanse of Chinese wallpaper creating an oriental panorama effect around the entire room, consciously distinguishing the room from the others in the suite. This is also indicated in the choice of purest white statuary marble, raised to a new sculptural pitch in the figurative sculpture of its Persian caryatids. These features combine to make the Drawing Room chimneypiece the most ambitious in the suite. These changes reflect a feminisation of the Drawing Room that was to be reflected in a related association of the Dining Room with an increasingly masculine character. We can also now surmise that this Drawing Room – although there are no Inventories before 1873 – was completed with the sumptuous set of two sofas, sixteen chairs and four stools made to display the tapestry depicting shells on cabriole-legged mahogany frames. Tragically, this suite had to be sold in 1928.

The great size of the Newhailes Library and its secondary decorative qualities imparted in 1743, were to be crucial for the survival intact of the Newhailes State Apartment. This precious survival is important for Scottish architectural history because in so many other houses, like Haddo, Hopetoun, and House of Dun, the State Apartment was to be altered drastically during the early nineteenth century. The rise of the Drawing Room was to be at the expense of the larger and more decorative Great Dining Room which was often converted to supply the outer Drawing Room. The adjacent Drawing Room and Bedroom, were then thrown together to create a new inner Dining Room, served by the back stairs beyond the Dressing Room and Closet, which were often gutted to provide dinner service.

At Newhailes, however, the existing and very large Library was simply waiting to be readily converted to a Drawing Room, when the vogue developed for larger reception rooms, by the simple expedient of transferring the tapestry suite across the

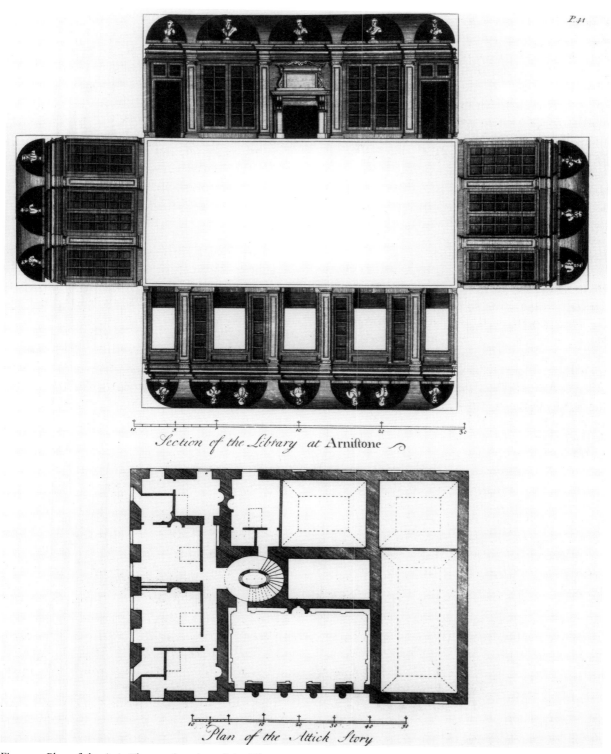

Section of the Library at Arnistone

Plan of the Attick Story

Figure 9. Plan of the Attic Floor and section of the Library at Arniston, Midlothian, by William Adam, from *Vitruvius Scoticus*, Plate 41. (Crown Copyright: RCAHMS)

House. The tapestry suite is readily spotted in the mid-Victorian watercolours of the Library. In the 1873 Inventory, the Library has been rechristened 'Drawing Room' but this may reflect a change of room use that had occurred long before. The two cut glass lustres, which may date from the middle of the eighteenth century, may reflect this change although their ceiling roses seem to date from Gillespie Graham's documented alterations to the roof of the Library block in 1815. A further watercolour of 1857, when the Drawing Room had been demoted to 'Schoolroom', may show the mid-eighteenth-century wool-embroidered Library sofa and chairs, that were swapped for the Drawing Room's tapestry chairs.

If it thus far from certain, when the full Drawing Room-isation of the Newhailes Library occurred, the hybrid room, was to have its apotheosis during the lifetime of Sir David Dalrymple, Lord Hailes (1726–1792) who succeeded in 1751, and was the grandson of the Sir David Dalrymple who built the Library. Lord Hailes was a distinguished author in his own right and knew many of the leading literary figures of his day to an extent where the Library at Newhailes was allegedly dubbed 'the most learned drawing room in Europe' by Dr Johnson – although the source of this quotation remains unsubstantiated.[5] These pungent historical and romantic associations were vividly evoked by Sir Lawrence Weaver in his 1917 *Country Life* article:

> The chief interest of the building centres in the library, for it was there that this Sir David, who as judge bore the title Lord Hailes, did the literary work that has made his name honourable in the annals of British scholarship. There, also are preserved singularly interesting manuscripts, letters from Johnson, Boswell, Burke, Horace Walpole and other well known men of the day. We find Burke writing to Lord Hailes that the erudition of Scottish lawyers makes him a little ashamed of the English Bar. Walpole is caught confessing in a letter of 1772, that his own learning is superficial, a verdict which posterity is inclined to accept. It is however, to the Boswell letters that we turn with most satisfaction.[6]

The convenient *piano nobile* version of the Scottish Library as pioneered by Newhailes, creating a comfortable family living room, was to have a brilliant future. One of the most celebrated later exemplars is Robert Adam's Library at Mellerstain of *circa* 1771 which opens, *en enfilade*, on the *piano nobile* from the central Great Dining Room in the opposite axial direction from the State Apartment and a Gallery takes the place at the top of the house of the traditional skied Library. But Adam was also to create one of the most thrilling and final variations of the skied Library in 1785 at Dalquharran atop a circular tower rising high above the roofline of this Castle Style house (see Figure 10). The bookcases, windows are curtains were brilliantly integrated into a cyclical design that captures much of the brio of his father's design for Arniston with a careful attention for practicality in that the hinged pilasters of the presses provide storage for rolled maps – a detail that also applied in his ground floor Library at nearby Culzean.

The most vivid description of the popularity of the Library as a general family rendezvous is provided through a series of bulletin progress reports – as with so many areas of Scottish life – by Elizabeth Grant of Rothiemurchus in her *Memoirs of a Highland Lady*.[7] During 1813, her father completed a number of further improvements at their home, The Doune:

> The next stirring event was another alteration – a final one it proved – of the principal staircase, the painting and papering of the new part of the house, and the fitting up of the drawing-room as a library. We had lived so long with doors and shutters of plain deal, cane backed chairs and sofas, common Scotch carpeting, etc, that the chilly air of our half-furnished apartments never struck us as requiring improvement. My mother had long wished for more comfort around her, and the books having accumulated quite beyond the study shelves my father determined on removing them; he gave himself great credit for his choice in his bookcases; they were made of fir from his forest, picked pieces of course, highly varnished and relieved by black mouldings. The

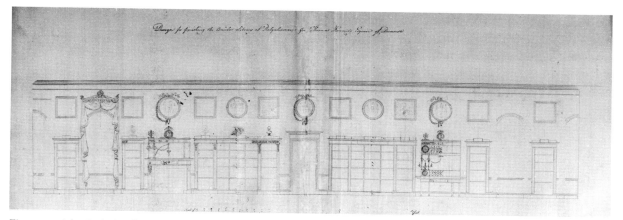

Figure 10. Adam's design for a skied Library of 1785 at Dalquharran Castle, Ayrshire, at the head of a circular tower. (Soane Museum: Crown Copyright: RCAHMS)

room was large and lofty, and really looked well when finished, but it was a work of time.

Similar libraries, were to become a standard component of early nineteenth-century Scottish country house, as codified by William Burn, where the Drawing Room was relieved by an adjacent Library, to which it was connected by double doors, with the detached Dining Room forming the third component of the public rooms. During the last quarter of the nineteenth century a new Library was created on the *piano nobile* at Arniston and Adam's resplendent original cases were given over to a museum-like display of old china. By chance if at Newhailes the National Trust for Scotland is responsible for the most important and earliest Scottish classical Country House Library, it also has the last, at Haddo, in its care too. The Haddo Library is a spectacular pastiche in the Adam Revival manner of *circa* 1880 by Wright and Mansfield of London, which just happens to occupy an entire pavilion, at *piano nobile* level, in William Adam's house. Its two Wedgwood chimneypieces support over-mantel portraits of the first Marquess and Marchioness of Aberdeen, and were copied from one in the collection of Lord Tweedmouth, the Marchioness's father. It was perhaps through his interest in collecting Wedgwood jasperware that Lord Tweedmouth became a leading pioneer of the Adam Revival. The care that Wright and Mansfield bestowed on the huge runs of cedar Library cases

was more usually limited to cabinet-furniture in the eighteenth century and each shelf is lined with morocco in this most *de luxe* of variants on the Adam family's designs for libraries.

The final alterations to the Newhailes Library were to be carried out by Lord Hailes's daughter and heiress, Christian Dalrymple (1765–1838), who transformed it into something more akin to a family shrine. It was presumably she who replaced the earlier over-doors with moody Romantic landscapes by the local artist, The Reverend John Thomson of Duddingston, a family friend, one of which depicts Hailes Castles, the Dalrymples' ancient seat. These were given new gilded oak frames whose peculiar knulled ornament is so close to the doorcases below, as to make one think that the entire doorcases and over-doors above, are really grand dynastic picture frames. The frieze of the doorcases are vaguely Kentian with their cushions of acanthus leaves, but the solecism of these cushions straying over the lugged frames, again make one think that they preserve the ghost of earlier lugged doorframes – a similar detail occurs in the Hall doorcases. The splendid new grate must also date from Christian Dalrymple's improvements but is equally undocumented. By now the Library was surely seen as a fully-fledged Drawing Room where instead of serious scholarly study, a dance might as readily have been held.

In 1839 the shrine-like character was completed when William Burn was instructed to estimate for 'projecting the centre and ends of the library, and making them to contain the large volumes, putting new doors and divisions on under presses all round to be made to open freely, and provided with good locks, also to fit up additional cases on each side of fire place, the whole to be finished in a corresponding manner and in keeping with the style of present bookcases'. These new elegantly curvaceous cases must have supplied a major deficiency of the Newhailes, as a mere villa, in that it did not have a Muniment Room.

Between the windows, these cases pack the final surprise of the Newhailes Library, in that each cupboard contains a resplendent, and readily removable, parquetry oak cabinet with a fall front, that rests in a bureau-like position supported by folding metal brackets. Presumably, when propped up on trestles or a convenient table, these were portable offices. Each cabinet has storage drawers in various configurations and a substantial lock with an ingeniously concealed catch for opening them disguised as one of the hinge plate studs. As a type they recall the Spanish *varugueno*. Similar pieces exist with provenances from other Scottish houses but the Newhailes cabinets have the distinction of being the only known set. It is difficult not to think that they are an original component of the Library, displaced, with their bureau flaps, now at a useless ankle height, when Burn's cupboards were added to extend their manuscript storage capacity. They are eloquent of Newhailes capacity to astonish.

The twentieth century was to see the richness of the Newhailes Library grievously diminished. In 1928 the two suites of tapestry furniture were sold and after the death of Sir Mark Dalrymple in 1971, the Library books were accepted in lieu of death duties and transferred for safekeeping to the National Library of Scotland. The challenge that now faces the National Trust for Scotland, and is the express wish of the Heritage Lottery Fund terms under which Newhailes was saved for the nation, is to match, at Newhailes, the controlled environment that the books enjoy in the National Library of Scotland to permit their return to the house. In 1998 two of the tapestry chairs, sold from the Library in 1928, appeared on the New York art market. Sadly the National Trust for Scotland were the underbidders but, if they failed to return these two chairs to Newhailes this time round, they are now aware of the whereabouts of all four chairs from this set, and eagerly await the rediscovery of the 'shell suite'.

Acknowledgements

This article has its origins in a lecture given to the Edinburgh Book Festival at the invitation of Elizabeth Strong. I am grateful to many friends and colleagues, both old and new, for their advice including Duncan Bull, Dr Iain Gordon Brown, Timothy Clifford, Richard Craig, John Cornforth, Althea Dundas-Bekker, Lady Antonia Dalrymple, Richard Emerson, Mark Hopton, Betty Leviner, John Maclean, Dr Bill MacQueen, Professor Sir James Dunbar-Nasmith, Simon Redburn, Veronica Steele, Charles Strang, Jackie Stewart, Jane Thomas, and Ruth Wimberley.

NOTES

1. David MacGibbon and Thomas Ross, *Castellated and Domestic Architecture of Scotland*, Vol II (David Douglas, Edinburgh, 1887: James Thin, 1980), Fig 617, p 159, 'Ferniehurst Castle, Ceiling of Library'.
2. Violet Jacob, *Lairds of Dun* (London, 1931). The original document is in the Ailsa papers in the National Archives of Scotland.
3. Patricia Waddy, *Seventeenth-Century Roman Palaces: use and the art of the plan* (MIT Press, Cambridge, Architectural History Foundation, New York, 1990).
4. Dr W B McQueen's survey of the Newhailes Papers in the National Library of Scotland: see 'The Newhailes Collection', National Library of Scotland, HP2.98.4889, National Trust for Scotland, Edinburgh, 1997.
5. Lady Antonia Dalrymple's verbal version of this tale, in calling the Library a Dining Room – its later manifestation – tends to confirm its bogusness.
6. Sir Lawrence Weaver, 'Newhailes', *Country Life*, Vol XLII, 8 September 1917, p 228.
7. Elizabeth Grant of Rothiemurchus, *Memoirs of a Highland Lady* (Canongate, Edinburgh, 1988: first published, J Murray, London, 1898).

DAVID WALKER

Designing the Royal College, Glasgow

ALTHOUGH rarely mentioned in architectural studies of the period, the Royal Technical College of Glasgow was one of the greatest building projects undertaken anywhere in the United Kingdom during Edwardian times, far bigger than Aston Webb's almost exactly contemporary Royal College of Science in South Kensington of 1900–06. At 346 feet its main frontage was almost one hundred feet longer than that of the nearby City Chambers and its height, at one hundred feet, was some twenty greater. Yet the College attracted relatively little attention even when it was built, and the few modern architectural writers who have made reference to it have had difficulty in perceiving its merits. Thirty-five years ago the writer was incautious enough to characterise it as 'red and ugly with hardly a detail which might be said to be at all correct':[1] Elizabeth Williamson, writing in the Glasgow volume of *The Buildings of Scotland* twenty-five years later, was only marginally less unkind, though certainly more perceptive in commenting on its affinities with contemporary warehouse and commercial building design.[2] But as Christopher Hussey once tersely but courteously answered when taxed with an opinion written four decades earlier, 'one's ideas change over the years.'[3] The Royal College has always tended to be too narrowly measured against the modern of Mackintosh and Salmon & Gillespie on the one hand and the Pascal-inspired Beaux Arts classicism and neo-Baroque of Burnet, Campbell and Paterson on the other. But Beaux Arts in several respects it is: the less directly historicist aspects of Beaux Arts design were simply less well understood in the 1960s and 1970s than they are now.

As an institution the Glasgow and West of Scotland Technical College (as the Royal College was titled prior to 1912) had a complicated evolution and a very scattered collection of buildings. It was a product of the Educational Endowments (Scotland) Act of 1882, the commissioners appointed under that Act having re-united two pre-existing institutions and incorporated two others in 1886–87. The oldest and largest of these was Anderson's College, originally Anderson's Institution, founded in John Street in 1796 and in 1828 transferred to the former Grammar School in George Street (1787), a handsome Adamish building by John Craig. This was remodelled for the purpose by Robert Scott and James Watt, who added an Ionic portico and a fine domed museum.[4] In that same year (1828) the Institution assumed the title of Anderson's University, but difficulties in obtaining a charter and securing a working relationship with the University of Glasgow caused it to relinquish that status in 1877. It then became Anderson's College. By that date the original institution had been enlarged by the building of the Young Department of Technical Chemistry at the corner of George and John Streets in 1870 and by the acquisition of the Georgian buildings between them – the gift of William Ewing – which became the Model School. Next in seniority was the College of Science and Arts, originally the Mechanics' Institution, which had separated from Anderson's College in 1823 and since 1860 had been housed in James Salmon's monumental building on Bath Street. The more recent foundations incorporated into the College were the nearby Allan Glen's Institution (a day school of 1853 with a large technical block of 1889, transferred to the

School Board of Glasgow in 1912) and Atkinson's Institution (1861) which had no building of its own.

A representative body of Governors was appointed to manage the College and raise funds. The difficulties they faced were considerable. The main activities of the College were concentrated in the Anderson and Young buildings on George Street and on Montrose Street, where Anderson's College had occupied the former City Public School and Pupil-Teachers' Institute as annexes. But many of the College's activities were still in Bath Street, supplemented by a number of rented premises elsewhere in the city centre.[5]

The first step towards equipping the College with more suitable premises was the building of Anderson's College of Medicine to designs by James Sellars in 1886–88. For the convenience of the students this was sited on Dumbarton Road adjacent to the city's main teaching hospital, the Western Infirmary. Sellars died during its construction and its completion passed to his pupil John Keppie, then in partnership with John Honeyman, rather than to Sellars' partner Campbell Douglas.[6]

But within five years of the amalgamation it became evident that the other departments of the College also required a major rationalisation of the teaching accommodation. The Governors, probably with John Chesser's recasting and enlargement of Edinburgh's Heriot Watt Institute buildings in mind, recommended a reconstruction of their George Street buildings in 1891. But it was quickly realised that in the longer term the College would require an architectural identity worthy of its scale and academic standing, and the initial decision to rebuild completely anew on the George Street site was taken early in the following year.

The Governors appointed a Special Committee on New Buildings to consult with the professors and prepare a statement of the accommodation required by each class on the basis of the numbers then current, plus sufficient accommodation for an increase equal to that of the previous three years. Together with museum and library, this was found to amount to 127,300 square feet. Perhaps because John Honeyman was a Governor of the College, Honeyman & Keppie were not re-commissioned.

In June, R A Bryden, whose services had previously been restricted to adaptations to the existing buildings and valuations, was instructed to prepare designs for a new college on the site of Anderson's and the adjoining buildings on George Street for a fee of fifty guineas. The Committee was authorised to apply to the Trustees of the late Misses Steven of Bellahouston for a sum sufficient to finance its construction.

Robert Alexander Bryden (1841–1906)[7] had been a pupil of Clarke & Bell, into which firm George Bell II (1854–1915) hurriedly took him into partnership, evidently in the belief that the commission was for real. If they did so believe, then they were mistaken. Although Bryden had an extensive practice, and had been elected a Fellow of The Royal Institute of British Architects as early as 1878, he was an architect of limited ability. His scheme is unlikely to have appealed to the representative of the architectural profession on the board of governors, John Honeyman – even although Honeyman had nominated him for election to The Royal Institute – or to the head of the school of architecture within the College, Charles Gourlay (1865–1926), a pupil of Duncan MacNaughtan and James Chalmers; Gourlay had been appointed in 1890 and was to be given the title of professor in 1895.[8] In general arrangement Bryden's scheme formed a symmetrical 'E' (see Figure 1). It was to have occupied the whole of the site between St Paul's Church and the Young Building on John Street to the west, and Montrose Street on the east. Its end blocks were to have been quadrangles of classrooms with central glass-roofed atria. No examination hall was then planned, the only large space being the museum to the rear of the central staircase. Bryden's four-storey elevation to George Street was a conventional centre-and-ends composition in which the gables did not express the width of the wings behind them. Stylistically it followed the Netherlandish free Renaissance then in vogue south of the border. A tall and broad stepped and scrolled Dutch gable marked the centre of composition and corbelled turrets with stilted domes turned the corners.[9] Echoes of its style are to be found at his Ocean Chambers of 1899 at 188–194

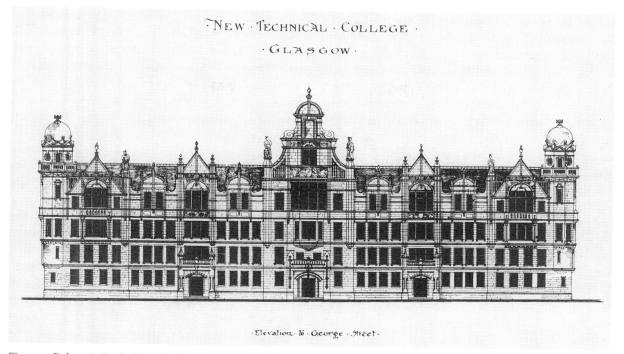

Figure 1. Robert A Bryden's Netherlandish free Renaissance design for the College, a design requested by the Governors in 1892, before the formal competition. (Strathclyde University Archives)

West George Street. The concept of a fully integrated institution had not yet taken root, the George Street elevation having three entrances of almost equal importance.

No significant discussion of Bryden's design is recorded in the minutes of the Special Committee on New Buildings, its appointment having been allowed to lapse. The Governors' belief that the Bellahouston Trustees would provide the whole of the sum required had proved unfounded. But early in 1894 the Finance Committee was instructed to obtain a report on the price of the site to the east of the Andersonian buildings at the corner of Montrose Street, and on the motion of its convenor, the Governors re-appointed a Special Committee convened by the civil engineer and boiler maker William Robertson Copland (1838–1907), who was also a Town Councillor. Their remit was initially to consider other possible sites, and, if they saw fit, to complete the negotiations for the Montrose Street corner. The Committee met on 5 and 12 September and discussed several sites, none of them

identified in its minutes. It was divided in its opinion, eventually narrowing its recommendations to the Anderson site and one not-then-specified new site which were then submitted to the Governors for a decision. None was actually reached, but the Governors recognised the key issues as being, firstly, a site central enough for their evening students and, secondly, the uncertainty of being able to raise a sum sufficient to purchase a completely new site as well as to construct a building. On 16 November it was agreed to make known to the public that the scheme required at least £100,000, £25,000 being needed immediately to take advantage of an offer from the Bellahouston Trustees to contribute the same amount. The concept of matching funding is by no means new.

The decision to re-launch the appeal was taken five days later. The Lord Provost, Sir Samuel Chisholm, agreed to convene a public meeting in December to consider the scheme, the case for a new building being put forward by J G A Baird, MP. It resulted in the formation of a committee to raise new subscriptions with a target of £120,000 in addition to the £30,000 already raised. A supporting paper was circulated in its support calling for a college building 'on a scale commensurate with its importance and the dignity of the City of Glasgow'. The paper had two illustrations, pointedly contrasting the Anderson buildings with Spalding & Cross's design for The Manchester Technical Schools, then under construction at a cost of £250,000.[10] On this occasion industrialists, merchants, shipowners, professionals and public alike rose to the challenge, £180,000 being raised within two years.

At that date there was still no decision on location. The Special Committee's alternative site was subsequently disclosed as being a large one owned by the City in North Street. In 1896 the City was requested to reserve it for the College, which it agreed to do for two years. But while this site had the advantage of being flat, it was much less central and was not pursued further.

Given the sums required for the actual building, and the difficulty and cost of assembling a more central site than that in North Street, there can never have been much real doubt about the final location despite the limitations and practical disadvantages of that of Anderson's College. The sections of Montrose Street not yet owned by the College were acquired in April 1900, and on 5 October that year the Governors appointed a third Special Committee to select an architect. This was again convened by Copland, who was now also chairman of the Governors. It held three meetings. Although the scale of the building would have justified open competition, it was decided to restrict invitations to eight practices drawn from a narrow circle within Glasgow, all long-established firms with the necessary staff resources already in place. The conditions conformed to none of the Royal Institute of British Architects' rules and assumed a considerable degree of public spirit on the part of the participants. The invitees were each to receive £50 for their expenses and the Governors were to adjudicate themselves, with only Gourlay and a measurer as assessors. The winner was to receive no premium but would be paid the customary 5% commission with an advance of £500 if the work did not proceed before 31 December 1902.

John James Burnet could not be prevailed upon to compete on those terms and let it be known that an invitation would be declined prior to its formal issue. Invitations were thus sent to only seven: of these the eventual winner, David Barclay, was an obvious choice. He had had more experience of building educational institutions than any other Scottish architect. John Honeyman (1831–1914) was another obvious candidate, since he had been a Governor and had, with his partner John Keppie (1862–1945), completed Anderson's College of Medicine as described earlier. Even more relevantly they had submitted a much admired design for the Manchester Technical Schools competition.[11] William Forrest Salmon (1843–1911) also had links with the College: his firm had been architects to the Mechanics' Institute and to the original Trustees of Allan Glen's, designing its technical department just prior to its incorporation into the College in 1886. James Miller (1860–1947) had the support of the railway engineers and Thomas Lennox Watson (1850?–1920) that of the naval architects and shipbuilders through his brother George, while John Thomson (1859–1933) and Robert Douglas Sandilands (1854?–1913) had established a reputation for the successful organisation of very large hospital projects. The conspicuous absentee was the College's own architect, Bryden. It musthave been with considerable chagrin that he found that Clarke & Bell had been invited, his partnership with George Bell II having been dissolved again some two years earlier on completion of their Christian Institute on Bothwell Street.

On 15 November the Governors delegated the task of adjudication to an augmented Chairman's Committee. The brief finally issued to the competitors was short, not much more than a detailed schedule of the accommodation needed by each department, the libraries and the administrative offices, with a requirement for fireproof construction. The floor area to be provided had now risen to 154,510 square feet. Designs were to be drawn to a scale of one-sixteenth of an inch to a foot, coloured only to indicate materials, and accompanied by a description: perspectives were not asked for. The problems the competitors faced were, however,

Figure 2. The revised perspective proposal which David Barclay presented to the Governors in November 1901, worked up from sketch proposals within five days. (Strathclyde University Archives)

not at all easy to resolve. The steep and irregular configuration of the site, very shallow at the west end because of the presence of St Paul's Church on John Street, meant that a balanced disposition of the plan could not be achieved. The presence of a railway tunnel in the hillside, the crown of which was above George Street level, together with the retention of the properties not in the College's ownership on Rottenrow at the north end of the site, imposed severe restraints on excavation. A continuous ground floor level through to the back of the site was thus not possible. The steepness of John Street and particularly Montrose Street made access for large-scale engine and machine components particularly difficult. Classrooms, libraries and examination hall had to be, as far as possible, so disposed as to be insulated from the sounds of engines, turbines, dynamos, machinery and noisy trades generally. All of these requirements had to be met within a cost-limit of £120,000 'if it is possible to do so', with the options of retaining the Young

Building or omitting the north block in whole or in part to stay within that figure. The latter was a variable option because the City School and the Pupil-Teachers' Institute on Montrose Street both offered the possibility of retaining existing classroom accommodation. The Governors were thus indicating the possibility of up to four different solutions.

The content of the brief was summarised in *The Building News* of 18 January 1901, almost the only reference to the competition in the national architectural press. The Governors were stated as having acknowledged that 'it was not an ideal site, but it was near the Municipal Buildings' and that the brief was more in the nature of suggestions than actual conditions. It was not an auspicious start and Miller withdrew before the closing date of 17 April, pleading pressure of other business. This reduced the number of competitors to only six; none of these provided more than one scheme, only the possibility of sections being left unbuilt. Predictably the

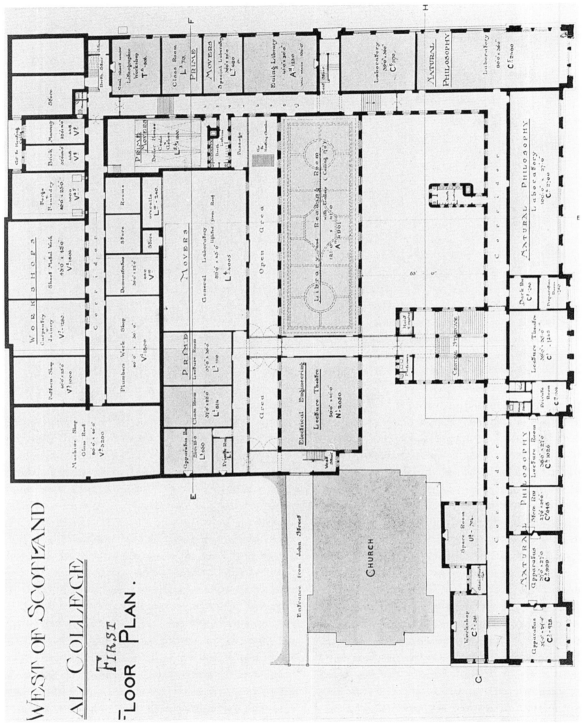

Figure 3. The first-floor plan from Clarke & Bell's first ambitious scheme. The plans were accompanied by grand elevations. (Strathclyde University Archives)

competitors were in serious doubt as to how the brief was to be interpreted.

Barclay, whose winning scheme will be discussed later in the context of the building as executed, was the only one to read the Governors' minds correctly, concluding that they would opt for constructing the whole development in a single campaign if they possibly could (see Figure 2). He and his measurer somehow kept the total cost of his design down to £124,733, calculating that the additional £5,000 would probably be found. Nevertheless Barclay fixed the width of the frontages of his corner pavilions at that of the Young Building so that the western could be deferred if the Governors deemed this absolutely necessary.

None of the other competitors offered anything so straightforward for the sum available. Clarke & Bell – by that date George Bell II and his chief draughtsman, the Alexander Thomson scholar James Hoey Craigie (?–1930) [12] – assumed from the appeal leaflet that something as ambitious as The Manchester Technical Schools was sought to complement the nearby City Chambers and Parish Council Offices, and offered domed grandeur at a cost of £138,398 (plus £1,600 if an alternative, more elaborate elevation were to be preferred), with the option of bringing the cost down to £123,000 by omitting the north block. Like Barclay they assumed that the Young Building would be demolished, but made no provision for interim retention. On plan their scheme comprised four blocks in the form of a reversed 'E' with arms of unequal length (see Figure 3). The front block on George Street comprised mainly class'r4ooms; the middle range, which was to be parallel with it, contained the library at ground level, the electrical engineering theatre (which doubled as the public lecture theatre) at first floor level and the societies' room and examination hall on the second floor; the northern range consisted of laboratories and classrooms, raised up over the prime movers' laboratory and noisy trades workshops; and, linking the three together, the east range on Montrose Street housed the engineering museum, the Ewing Library and assorted laboratories, classrooms and workshops. The circulation had the merit of being simple and clear with south, north and east

corridors round the courts these ranges formed, the circuit being completed by a three-decker glazed bridge corridor running north from the main staircase. This was designed to form the central spine of the building if it were ever to achieve a complete rectangle between John Street and Montrose Street. The main advantage of the scheme was that it concentrated the public spaces of library, hall, public societies' room and principal lecture theatre in the heart of the building, close to the main stair but insulated from the sound of George Street traffic and the noisiest trades, the latter being located at the very back of the site. The elevations were characteristic of Craigie's predilection for a rather dry neo-Baroque with neo-Greek orders as exemplified in the top floors he added to Alexander Thomson's Grosvenor Building on Gordon Street. He offered two alternatives. Design A, marginally the better of the two, had channelled rustication at ground and first floor levels, and a giant order of Roman Doric pilasters breaking into Ionic columns at the tetrastyle pedimented centrepiece (see Figure 4). Above rose a baroque dome with a scrolled broken-pediment aedicule, answered by smaller domes and aedicules at the corner pavilions. A curious feature of the design, and one which would have proved unsatisfactory in execution, was the different treatment of the central of the three double-bays which linked the middle and end pavilions. Design B, which brought the giant order down to the first and second floors with a dwarf order at third floor and an eaves gallery at fourth floor, was more successful in that respect, but much less so at the somewhat frenzied composition of the arcaded screen and tall aediculed and domed towerlets which fronted a much enlarged dome and cupola (see Figure 5). Clarke & Bell described these elevations as being 'in a simple style of Italian architecture ... we have endeavoured to obtain dignity of effect in a simple and economical way, and not by the use of elaborate ornament or other expensive work, in which, we trust, the Governors may think we have succeeded.' Much less effort was made with the Montrose Street elevation, which simply petered out in an irregular and perfunctory arrangement of windows and pilasters.

No drawn record of the scheme prepared by

Figure 4. Clarke & Bell's more economical design for the College. (Strathclyde University Archives)

Figure 5. Clarke & Bell's more expensive design for the College, in what they described as 'a simple style of Italian architecture'. (Strathclyde University Archives)

Watson,[13] an ex-assistant of Alfred Waterhouse, and his new partner, Henry Mitchell, survives. Their description indicates a solution which had points in common with Clarke & Bell's, although the middle range, comprising the examination hall, the engineering museum and the model room, was more satisfactorily re-orientated north and south, dividing the area of the building into two courts, the western two-sided because of St Paul's Church and the eastern a quadrangle 136 by 102 feet. Hall and museum formed a semi-public area in conjunction with the double-height natural philosophy classroom, at the centre of the George Street elevation, all these being congregated off the main stair. The scheme thus offered the possibility of a symmetrically disposed plan if the site of St Paul's Church could be acquired. The façades are not described but a Glasgow baroque similar to their exactly contemporary Ashfield House on Sauchiehall Street can be assumed. As options for phasing they offered to omit the greater part of the George Street frontage, bringing the initial cost down to £82,850, or the Montrose Street frontage of the eastern quadrangle, bringing the figure down to the specified £120,000. Neither option would have been satisfactory if the Governors had been unable to raise funds for further

building. Nevertheless, within what was then believed to be a volume of 4.56 million cubic feet, it seems to have offered considerable clarity of planning, for the future as well as for the present. But it also had a cost: the excavation required to achieve this unified plan put the price of some parts of the building as high as one shilling per cubic foot, with an overall average of 7.834 pence, resulting in a total estimated cost of £148,850.

Of Thomson & Sandilands' design we have only a perspective, belatedly exhibited at the Royal Glasgow Institute in 1905 (see Figure 6). It hardly did justice to the design, but read with the description it tells us a great deal about the scheme.[14] Clearly Sandilands, as might be expected of a product of the *atèlier* of Julien Guadet, saw the College as the Glasgow counterpart of Henri-Paul Nénot's Nouvelle Sorbonne in Paris, albeit without the chapel and the sumptuous interiors. As always with Sandilands, the plan seems to have been very efficiently organised, meeting all the requirements within 4.46 million cubic feet, half-a-million less than in Barclay's scheme. Like Watson & Mitchell he foresaw, even if the Committee at that stage did not, that St Paul's Church would have to be bought out sooner rather than later, both schemes being

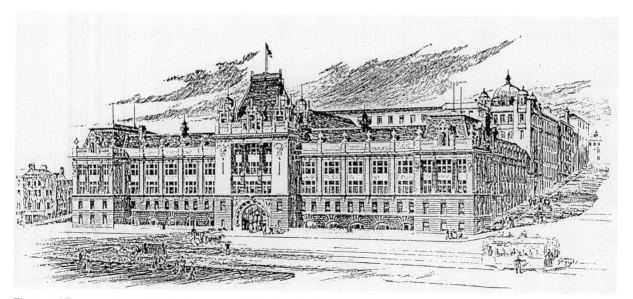

Figure 6. Thompson & Sandilands' design as exhibited at the Glasgow Institute of Fine Arts and published in *Academy Architecture*, 1905, volume 1, in their Beaux Arts baroque manner, as seen at the nearby Parish Council Offices (1900).

conceived as a first 75% phase of a symmetrically planned double quadrangle with a central hall orientated north and south. To achieve a consistent plan from first floor level upwards Sandilands planned to excavate the area within the site right down to the arch-ring of the railway-tunnel and beyond. This created southern and northern ground floor levels, the northern area beyond the tunnel being occupied by the prime movers' laboratories, lit from rooflights at the bottom of the courtyards of the northern block of classrooms. The front section of the ground floor was, however, no semi-basement as it is in Barclay's executed design, housing the College's administrative offices. A cleverly planned entrance stair-hall provided as good access to these as to the examination hall and public offices at first floor level. Beneath was a true basement which housed workshops, foundry, forge and boiler room, together with a large bicycle room reached by a ramp in the front area.

The upper levels of the building were designed to limit the height of the George Street frontage to four storeys and attic. To compensate, the rear quadrangle was to have risen five storeys above the Montrose Street pavement with two basement storeys beneath, the three-storey difference in the eaves-line between the front and rear portions of the building being skilfully masked by a tower. This had a dome flanked by orielled towerlets with cupolae, the whole being a miniaturised version of the top of Sandilands' Parish Council offices (1900). Sandilands' George Street elevation was architecturally extremely ambitious. A giant five-storey and attic central pavilion crowned by a huge French roof was answered by oblong corner pavilions, their front elevations reminiscent of those of his Govan Town Hall but on an altogether larger scale. The intervening sections were to have been of five bays with wide three-light windows set in a giant order of anta pilasters answering those of the corner pavilions. The details were 'modern French' with a double-height arched portal reminiscent of that of Burnet's Fine Art Institute and a Greek Ionic giant order. At the central pavilion this was at a higher level than at the corner pavilions, a solecism unexpected in an *élève* of Guadet's and one which would probably

have been resolved in execution had Sandilands been successful. Flanking the central pavilion roof were to have been domed towerlets, their swan-neck Edwardian baroque pediment details rather at odds with the restrained *Troisième Republique* classicism of the remainder. Inevitably such architectural grandeur and the excavation necessary to secure efficient planning did not come cheap. Sandilands' average cost per cubic foot was much the highest at 8.06 pence, resulting in an overall cost of £149,971. This was almost £30,000 above the cost-limit and there was no option for reduction by retaining existing buildings.

The two remaining designs took a much more pessimistic view of the prospects for the College's future expansion, and assumed that the College would be built incrementally over a longer timescale. Of Honeyman & Keppie's design we have no proven record but the description [15] is interesting in two respects. Firstly, it is headed, in Keppie's handwriting,

John Honeyman RSA
John Keppie IA
CR MacKintosh [*sic*]

although Mackintosh did not become a partner until the end of the year, suggesting he had some input into the design; and secondly it tells us a fair amount about the planning, though not the elevations. Their scheme was based on the retention of the Young Building:

> The fact of the great depth of the site from the back of St Paul's Church to Montrose Street and the permanent nature of the 'Young' Laboratory Buildings has induced us to make the general divide of the plan in the centre of the portion representing this main depth. In the centre of this portion is the main entrance to the building.

The plan consisted of a rectangle enclosing three courts, two approximately square on the south and a single long rectangular one on the north, somewhat awkwardly described as 'front sides and back buildings with a connecting block through the space thus formed and another connecting portion from the front to the middle block.' From the description we further learn that the end blocks of the main elevation were to be treated as corner towers. There must therefore be a distinct probability that the now lost tracing illustrated by Howarth as a preliminary study for Glasgow School of Art – which we know today that it cannot be, given Newbery's competition specification for the studio windows – represents Mackintosh's scheme for the George Street elevation. The 1/16 scale, the corner towers, central entrance, number of storeys and length of frontage appear to correspond.[16]

Honeyman Keppie & Mackintosh's strategy was to keep excavation and demolition to the minimum consistent with the sensible planning of the site, and to pile the accommodation high at the back, very much as in Thomson & Sandilands' submission. But, even retaining the Young Building, the cubic area was still over 4.5 million square feet, resulting in a total cost of £144,500. The only savings offered were the fourth and fifth floors of the rear blocks, reducing the estimate to about £128,000.

Of James Salmon & Son's scheme we know much more as a perspective and alternative elevation

were published in *The British Architect* on 11 October 1901[17] (see Figure 7). Although William Forrest Salmon was still the senior partner, and may have had some hand in the planning of their submission, all design work had been delegated to his son James (1873–1924) and his partner John Gaff Gillespie (1870–1926). The accompanying description[18] is particularly informative and tells us much about the philosophy behind the design. Their conclusions on the probable phasing of the building of the College, and in turn on the planning of the site, were similar to Honeyman Keppie & Mackintosh's, but they were more ambitious and offered far more options. In responding to the possibility of retaining not merely the Young Building but the Model School, and still having a George Street frontage which read as a complete architectural unit, they considered that

the best position for the main entrance is in George Street, at the centre of the large rectangular piece of land, rather than at the centre of the whole extent of the ground ... This

Figure 7. The competition design for the College by John Gaff Gillespie and James Salmon, from *The British Architect,* 11 October 1901. Perspective by Gillespie and inset alternative by Salmon Junior.

arrangement, besides expressing honestly the formation of the College ground and giving opportunity for greater architectural variety of grouping and treatment, is in truth the most central and convenient.

In addition to the possibility of completing the George Street frontage in two phases they offered almost infinitely variable possibilities in relation to the Central School and Pupil-Teacher Institute on Montrose Street, although 'no temporary arrangement should be allowed to impair the final perfection of the plan as a whole'. With an eye on the success of the appeal, enthusiasm got the better of them in suggesting the inclusion of a gymnasium and additional lifts, hydraulic and electric, for the instruction of the students, resulting in an area of 5.76 million cubic feet as against Barclay and Craigie's 4.96, and a correspondingly high cost of £178,000 with two suggestions for reduction to bring the cost down to £120,000. Of the alternative elevations, that prepared by Gillespie was fresh and original, 'the application of classic motif to modern requirements more especially in regard to lighting … All the windows are flush with the ceilings at the top, which not only gives maximum direct lighting but illuminates the ceiling without shadow and secures the addition of reflected light therefrom'. The asymmetrical element on the Young Building site was crowned by a steel-framed dome adapted from the Capella dei Principi at San Lorenzo in Florence, 'the least costly way of obtaining a striking feature which will give the College a character distinct from all the other buildings in the area.' They had a point: it would have been a prominent corner feature whereas Clarke & Bell's dome would have been little seen, set back behind the main elevation a hundred feet from street level. Gillespie's dome was to have contained the suggested gymnasium. Salmon and Gillespie proposed red tile roofs, again with the object of giving the College a striking identity different from that of its neighbours. Despite the steepness of the slope their Montrose Street elevation was to have been symmetrical, and to have had the same arch and bay window central motif as that to George Street.

Salmon's alternative elevation was still in the Art Nouveau of his St Vincent Chambers and Anderston Saving Banks (1899) and by 1901 may have appeared just slightly out-of-date. Nevertheless the bays between the centre and end pavilions were more modern in concept than Gillespie's and offered significantly larger glazed areas. Salmon's was also marginally cheaper.

The Chairman's Committee thus found itself confronted by a confused outcome to the competition which illustrated the options but in which like could not be compared with like. The cubic area of the designs varied from Thomson & Sandilands' 4.46 million to Salmon's 5.76 and the cost per cubic foot from Barclay's 6.34 pence to Thomson & Sandilands' 8.06. To help the Committee come to some conclusion each design was recalculated at the highest and lowest figure per cubic foot, which made Thomson & Sandilands' the cheapest (£112,135 and £149,791) and Salmon & Gillespie's much the most expensive (£144,816 and £193,440). Each scheme was then costed as a standard 5 million cubic feet at its architects' own quoted rate per cubic foot which resulted in Barclay being the lowest at £125,062 and Thomson & Sandilands' the highest at £167,916. None of this was at all informative as Thomson & Sandilands and Watson & Mitchell's savings of nearly half-a-million cubic feet in the planning of their buildings had been achieved by excavating the site to ground floor level resulting in the higher unit costs which the other competitors had thought it safer to avoid. All that it did was confirm that Barclay's design appeared to provide the best value in terms of accommodation for money, and that it was the only one to offer the possibility of completing the whole project within £5,000 of the stipulated cost-limit.

Predictably these calculations did not satisfy the Committee, which then instructed its newly appointed measurer, Henry Herbertson & Co, to produce a more meaningful set of figures. Every scheme was completely re-measured, and all but one of the competitors were found to have underestimated both cubic volume and cost. Barclay's cubic volume rose from 4.961 million square feet to 5.264, Clarke & Bell's from 4.968 to 5.117, Honeyman &

Keppie's from 4.535 to 5.184, Thomson & Sandilands' from 4.46 to 4.889 and Watson & Mitchell's from 4.56 to 5.25, which probably eliminated them from the competition as their floor area was the second lowest at 171,095 square feet. Only Salmon's cubic volume fell, from 5.76 to 5.6. Barclay's now became the second most expensive design at £154,667 and lost its overall cost advantage, largely due to its generous circulation area (69,728 square feet), but it offered the second largest useable floor area at 174,533 square feet.

Apart from these corrections Herbertson's figures were not much more helpful than the first set as they had been priced at a standard cost per cubic foot without any allowance for excavation or underpinning of adjoining properties. The Committee was clearly perplexed and on 29 April it delegated the task to Gourlay and the Board of Studies. Honeyman & Keppie, Salmon & Son, Thomson & Sandilands and Watson & Mitchell were all quickly eliminated 'because of obvious unsuitability arising from insuperable difficulties of access, imperfect lighting of corridors and rooms, expensive excavation, or other structural defects'. That left only Barclay and Clarke & Bell in the race, and their plans were thereafter reported on by each of the College's departments. Only the prime movers found serious fault with Barclay's scheme. Clarke & Bell's attracted little support, the Departments of Mechanics and Applied Mathematics and of Machine Design, together with the librarians, alone being content with it. Some of the reports from the other departments were so damning as to preclude any possibility of selection. The Board reported on 13 May and the Governors duly appointed Barclay on 17 June. No announcement was sent to the architectural journals. It may have been thought best to avoid critical comment on the conduct of the competition. Effectively the competition had been decided by a vote of the academic staff for their own departmental interests without overmuch thought being given to the planning of the building as a whole, or as to how it might develop in the future, and it may have been thought best to avoid critical comment.

At the time of his win David Barclay (1846–1917)

was fifty-five and had a highly successful career behind him.[19] He had won by long experience in competitions, and in school buildings in particular. The origins of the scheme, and still more of the executed building, lay in his classical designs of the 1870s, 1880s and 1890s. Although he still practised under the name of H & D Barclay, his eighteen-years-older brother Hugh (1828–92) had been dead for nine years and he had not yet taken Colin Sinclair – who was to continue the practice into the mid-1950s – into partnership. Hugh had founded the practice with another former pupil of William Spence's, Alexander Watt, as Barclay & Watt in the mid-1850s. They established a reputation almost at once with the remarkable triple-arched cast-iron façade at 60–66 Jamaica Street in 1856–57, and with the refined and original classicism of the Roman Doric Ewing Place Church on Waterloo Street and the Corinthian Corn Exchange reconstruction on Hope Street in 1858. On 1 January 1861 David joined them as an apprentice. Legend has it that James Sellars, who was three years older, was also apprenticed to Hugh on that same day. Although Sellars had died some four years before Sinclair joined the firm, Sinclair knew of the close friendship between Sellars and the Barclays which continued long after Sellars had left. Probably Barclay simply did not have enough work to keep him on at that time since Watt also left to recommence practice on his own. But by 1871 Hugh's business had picked up sufficiently for David to become a partner, their first joint work being the very sophisticated Italian Romanesque Duke Street United Presbyterian Church, long since vanished. The Convalescent Home at Kilmun followed in 1873. By the very early 1870s both Sellars and the younger Barclay had been drawn into Alexander Thomson's circle, and in 1875 the Barclay firm made its name for a second time with the Albany Academy in Ashley Street. It established their reputation for educational buildings and set the pattern for a long series of rather Germanic Italianate-profiled board schools with sophisticated neo-Greek details of the Thomson-Sellars school, some of them French-influenced. Nearly all of these schools had simple well thought-out rectangular plans and broad-eaved hip roofs, Schinkelesque banded rustication, pilastrades, architrave frames spanning several bays, unfluted Ionic columns and herms, these being the Barclays' favourite motifs. Considerable numbers of these schools were built from the later 1870s onwards: Melville Street (1878), Pollokshields (two blocks, 1879 and 1882), Abbotsford Place, (two blocks again, 1879 and 1893), Springfield (1881), Harmony Row and Rutland Crescent (1883), and Hillhead High (1884) in Glasgow; and Jean Street (1883) and Clune Park (1886) in Port Glasgow. All of these were board schools. The grandest was the privately funded new building for Glasgow Academy at Kelvinbridge (1878).[20] Of these schools Rutland Crescent differed somewhat from the others, being virtually indistinguishable from the work of Sellars. It lent credence to Sinclair's somewhat unspecific recollection of a working relationship between the Barclays and Sellars when the practice became overcommitted,[21] which it most certainly was in 1883. Echoes of Sellars's buildings of the 1880s, particularly Wylie & Lochhead's factory on Kent Road, are to be seen in some of the details of the Royal College as built.

In 1879 Charles Barry, Junior, President of the Royal Institute of British Architects, had awarded the Barclays the commission for the new Municipal Buildings at Greenock. They were at this time by far the most ambitious project of the kind undertaken in Scotland, with a central public hall and an internal carriage drive closely modelled on English precedents, and they escalated in architectural pretension during construction when the Municipal Buildings in Glasgow threatened to put them in the shade. In deference perhaps to the assessor's known preferences, their façades were more Renaissance than Greek, with domed corner towers, pedimented attic pavilions, and a 250 feet tower crowned by a Corinthian peristyle, all liberally enriched with granite-shafted columns and caryatid figures.[22] Greenock took the firm into the premier league and enabled it to ride out the professional disaster of David's arrest on a charge of culpable homicide – of which he was acquitted – as a result of the collapse of a playshed at Pollokshields in 1882. The brothers won the competition for the unbuilt municipal buildings opposite the Clark Town Hall in Paisley in 1883[23] and secured the commission for the giant Sellarsesque Greek Ionic temple of St George's-in-the-Fields in 1885, clearly designed as a challenge to Thomas Lennox Watson's Roman Corinthian Wellington UP Church of 1882.[24]

In the later 1880s, in parallel with Sellars, the Barclays abandoned pure neo-Greek in favour of more Renaissance-influenced treatments, although characterised by a Grecian sharpness of detail. Their schools now took on straightforward Italian palazzo forms, first seen at Annette Street in Govanhill in 1886, but best exemplified at Lorne Street, Govan (1892), where the Ionic aedicules, fluted dwarf attic pilasters and diamond panels of the final design for the Royal College first appeared. These buildings were still very chaste in design; but with Hugh's last illness and death on Christmas Day 1892 the shackles were off, and uninhibited competition with the Northern European early Renaissance forms of the likes of James Thomson and his sons became the norm: indeed David Barclay seems to have set the pace for it in his competition win for J & P Coats' Central Thread Agency Buildings on Bothwell Street in 1891,[25] a long façade of thickly crowded aedicules, gables, turrets and chimneys which completely outdid the pioneer Glasgow examples of the genre, Thomas Lennox Watson's Citizen Building of 1889 on St Vincent Street Place and Alfred Waterhouse's Prudential Building of 1890 on West Regent Street. Much more impressive as architecture than the Central Thread Agency was the giant Cumming & Smith warehouse of 1892[26] on Sauchiehall Street with its towering façade of deep giant arched recesses, extruded bay windows and dwarf-colonnaded eaves gallery, the arched recesses being enlarged and enriched red sandstone variants of those of his brother's cast-iron façade in Jamaica Street of thirty-five years earlier. It reintroduced the giant scale, bold projections and arcaded forms which were to feature in the final design for the Royal College.

The design with which Barclay initially won the College competition had little of the robust quality of the Cumming & Smith warehouse or of the still bigger but more austere American-inspired Hunter-Barr warehouse on Queen Street which had followed

Figure 8. The design with which Barclay initially won the College competition. (Strathclyde University Archives)

it in 1899[27] (see Figure 8). The savings Barclay and his measurer had had to make were everywhere apparent. Except for some sculpture the College was to have been simplest board school architecture without any formal axial qualities in the plan, these having been dispensed with to make best use of the unequal depth of the site. Barclay's solution to this problem seems to have been inspired by contemporary hospital design. In the angle of the 'L'-plan blocks to George Street and Montrose Street he proposed a rectangular court, as large as St Paul's Church would allow. Within the court at basement level were the toplit boiler house and prime movers' laboratory, i.e., all the heaviest equipment. The north range of the court, parallel with George Street, comprised classrooms, laboratories and, at its upper levels, the museum and model room. Along the north side of this range were corridors, linking with those on the east and west in an 'H'-plan arrangement; and from these north corridors ran two blocks, parallel with that on Montrose Street, in a Nightingale ward type arrangement. The western comprised classrooms, the eastern the examination hall, and the Montrose Street block the double-height Natural Philosophy classroom, the societies' room and further classrooms. The

other principal apartments, the board room, staff rooms and library, were located in the George Street block.

The scheme had its merits as it offered the possibility of extending the ward-block type arrangement to a fourth range fronting John Street, by-passing St Paul's Church if that proved impossible to acquire. Its weaknesses, both the results of ruthless cost-cutting, were the lack of a central stair or any axis through the building from the George Street entrance, the main stair being relatively small and located west of centre at the junction of the south and west corridors. The public entrance was to be not on George Street but on Montrose Street. The eastern ground floor corridor was thus to be the public foyer and linked across the north-east court to the examination hall, making the position of the latter more logical than it might appear to be now.

Although the channelled rustication at the centre and end pavilions provided the George Street elevation with a reasonably strong if rather shallow architectural framework, the triple windowed bays between them were as economical as they could be, divided off by pairs of downpipes rather than by pilasters and minimally accented by second floor aedicules. Only at the middle was economy at all

Figure 9. The College building to John Street and George Street, as built to David Barclay's design, a classic of the semi-industrial genre of much French Beaux Arts architecture. (Strathclyde University Archives)

Figure 10. The College's centrepiece in George Street, photographed soon after completion, with the architects' signature at the foot. (Strathclyde University Archives)

relaxed with a large arched entrance, columned upper floors, rusticated aedicules, an armorial panel, and a sculptured segmental pediment at the parapet. The most adventurous section of the design was the south end of the Montrose Street frontage where the public entrance was rather grandly sculptured and flanked by two asymmetrical Italianate towers. These framed the arch over the windows of the public lecture theatre, the cills of which were stepped with the rake of the floor. Beyond it the Montrose Street elevation was as unadorned as the bleakest poor law hospital.

Although its sheer scale gave the design a monumental warehouse-like dignity, Barclay and the Governors did not allow it to be published in the architectural journals, perhaps because even then it was realised that it could not be the final design. It received only private circulation within the College and its major funders. Probably Barclay had intended from the very beginning to upgrade both plans and elevations once the competition was won, but in the event the decision was taken for him. The Governors lost no time in sending their newly-appointed architect, together with the College Secretary, Herbert F Stockdale, on a tour of the eighteen principal Technical Schools in England to help establish how the points raised by the Board of Studies might best be resolved. Barclay submitted revised sketch designs on his return, which attracted further comment. The Board's crucial recommendation had been an increase in height at the library floor to make the library comparable with that in the Clarke & Bell scheme. This necessitated a complete redesign of the elevations which could now be tackled with more spirit thanks to the success of the appeal. The Montrose Street elevation was now consistently treated with that on George Street. Further sketch designs were produced for the Building Committee on 13 November at which Barclay was instructed to produce 'a large perspective drawing' and such other large scale drawings as time permitted for the Governors' meeting on 18 November (a Monday, i.e., three working days). If there are some imperfections in the final design they may be attributed to that period. What the Governors approved was what was built. Looking today at that

big sepia perspective,[28] and at the washed-in elevation which appears to have been part of the exercise, the wonder is that they could have been drawn out and tinted within that timescale. The Sabbath may well have been broken.

Whether Barclay extended his English tour to Paris, whether he had searched through the French books in his office library or begun buying Julien Guadet's *Eléments et Théorie*, the first part of which was issued in 1901, we do not know. But what is fairly apparent is that the revised elevations of The Royal College with their classical buttresses and large arched openings owe their inspiration, directly or indirectly, to Guadet's Nouvel Hôtel des Postes on the Rue du Louvre of 1880–84.[29] The discs in the spandrels of the library floor's arched windows are also French and so are the dwarf Ionic pilaster orders of the dramatically heightened central and corner pavilions, now of much bolder projection. These dwarf orders had featured at Duban's buildings at the Ecole des Beaux Arts in the 1830s and in numerous derivatives. The simplified Greek Ionic capitals at the aedicules are also Beaux Arts in origin and the boldly scrolled shouldered treatment of the ground floor windows with their inner recessed lintels is probably French too, although of a somewhat older-fashioned kind. Indeed the only recognisably British Edwardian features about the design are the exaggerated keyblocks of the attic windows, the baroque angle turrets which frame the balustraded parapets of the corner pavilions, the deeper relief of the pilasters and the enormous projection of the cornices. All these details were less refined than a Frenchman would have made them but it has to be borne in mind that they were designed for the dark red sandstone and for the lower light levels of the none-too-clean atmosphere of Glasgow at that date. The design has its faults: the relationship of the buttresses to the corner pavilions is not as subtle as it is at the Hôtel des Postes, the rustication of the corner pavilions does not answer that of the central one, and the arched ground floor windows of the former are too small in scale for those of the openings above – a fault less apparent in the drawings than in the executed building – but otherwise it was a classic of the semi-industrial genre of much French

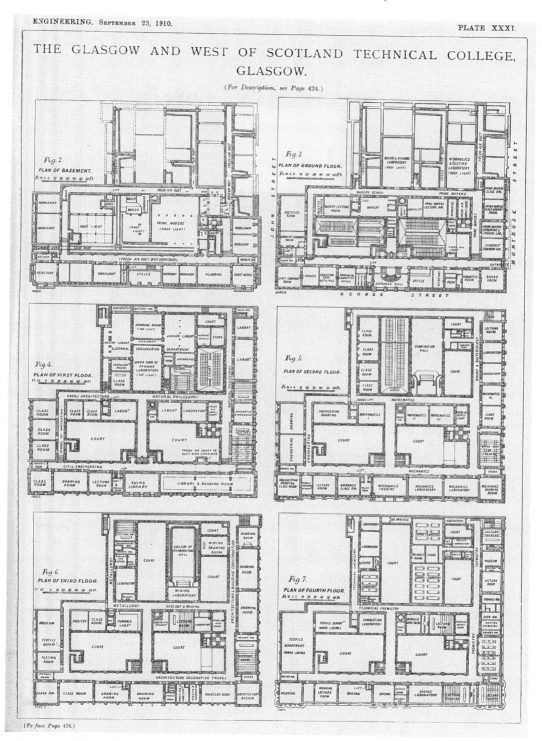

Figure 11. Floor plans of the College by David Barclay showing the complexity of planning, with lines of communication arranged centrally to allow the classrooms and offices to benefit from the maximum of light. Taken from an article written to celebrate the completion of the College in *Engineering*, 23 September 1910. (The Trustees of the National Library of Scotland)

Figure 12. The spacious interior of the Library as designed by David Barclay, now destroyed. (Strathclyde University Archives)

Beaux Arts architecture of the 1880s and 1890s, with a scale and visible structural strength peculiarly appropriate to what was indeed as much an industrial building as an educational one (see Figures 9 & 10).

The redesign was not confined to the exterior. Economy was forgotten and the stairs and corridors replanned centrally as they should have been from the outset (see Figure 11). Moreover, the increase in the ceiling heights of the library floor resulted in a general aggrandisement of the scale of the whole interior which has a remarkably spacious, larger than life-size quality (see Figure 12): the same clean-cut semi–industrial character is in evidence throughout. In the final scheme the entrance hall was trebled in size. Within the hall bowed stairs rose up to ground floor level between semicircular bastions: these had giant scrolls to the balustrades enclosing the upper flights, all very Beaux Arts (see Figure 13). At their head a screen of Ionic-columned openings led into a wide corridor. A further screen opened into a very grand central stair rising the full height of the building and owing something to Burnet's at the Clyde Trust Building in its use of columns. From this stair spinal link corridors now divided the court, providing the axis the original scheme lacked, even if the position of the hall remained something of an anomaly once the Montrose Street entrance had lost its original significance. At first floor, the library now became an even more handsome apartment than Clarke & Bell's would have been, galleried on the north side and divided into three compartments by Serlian

Figure 13. The dramatic, Beaux Arts-inspired entrance hall at the College. (Strathclyde University Archives)

arches. Clean white tile walls and dados with under-stated but distinctive chequer borders characterised the whole interior. And although plenum vent-ilation and heating system had been planned from the start, an air-washing plant was introduced in the south-eastern court consisting of an inverted pyramid of glass louvres 31 feet by 18 with a sprinkler system, the water and filters of which had to be changed every three days.[30]

Before proceeding to specification and contract stage Barclay circulated printed notes on building materials to the Building Committee in January 1902.[31] They provide a great deal of interesting in-formation on the business of construction at that time. White sandstone would clearly have been preferred – and would have made the Beaux Arts character of the design more obvious – but carriage from Northumberland ruled it out (75% more ex-pensive). Dumfriesshire stone was therefore favoured over Ballochmyle and Arran, which Barclay thought too porous. White glazed brick was preferred both to cream or salt glazed brick and to terra cotta since it would keep its colour better in the Glasgow climate and have some reflective value, even though, as Bar-clay pointed out, the courts were as wide as streets. Rubble stonework was ruled out because of the cost of window dressings. For the classrooms and corri-dors he suggested brick linings, glazed only at the dado, as he had seen in the newer colleges in Eng-land; this avoided the maintenance associated with timber dados. Only the administrative rooms, hall, museum and libraries should be plastered. These recommendations were largely accepted. The natural philosophy lecture theatre, that used for public lec-tures, was unique in adopting a less austere wainscoted treatment.

On the steelwork Barclay sought instructions as to whether contractors should be confined to Scot-tish or English rolled steel since German or Belgian would be cheaper, although of less value for strength. For the floors he advised Portland cement, broken brick and ash concrete rather than the hollow tile floors he had used at Hunter Barr's because subsequent fixings could result in the bot-tom of the tile falling out: tenders were to be taken from the several patent systems then on offer.

For flooring he gave the Committee the options of granolithic, wood block or marble tessera, the two latter being the dearer. Maple was recom-mended as the hardest wearing wood for those floors which were to be timber. Carolina wood or Ameri-can canary wood were proposed for linings because of the fine stain they took. Wired glass we think of as a fairly modern material, but Pilkington's wired glass was recommended for the roof-lights to avoid external netting and the risk of falling glass if broken. The whole document is a testimony to the thoroughness with which Barclay dealt with clients and undertook contracts.

Barclay's recommendations in respect of broken brick concrete and tessera floors were accepted by the Building Committee on 17 January. His propo-sal for white glazed brick in the internal courts was referred to the Governors who agreed to it four days later. The final plans and specification were then approved for contract on 3 July. Obtaining Dean of Guild consent was a more difficult matter as the increase in floor heights had taken the building to one hundred feet above pavement level, but after advertisement a waiver was granted. Copland took a direct hand in the award and management of the contracts along with Barclay, and, as they advised, as much of the work as practicable was contracted for on a separate trades basis to avoid mark-up on sub-contractors' work, which Barclay estimated at about 10%. The first contracts were for the Mon-trose Street and northern blocks, for which P & W Anderson secured the mason and steel work (£93,703, re-negotiated later to £103,747 because of excavation problems) and George Ferguson the wright work (£14,764, subsequently reduced to £14,528). They did not have an easy time as the College conducted tests on the materials to be used throughout. King Edward VII laid the foundation stone on 14 May 1903,[32] the walls were up and being roofed in by January 1904, and the design at last received wider circulation, being exhibited at the Royal Scottish Academy exhibition of 1905. What had been built was formally opened by the incom-ing Secretary of State, Captain John Sinclair, on 21 December of that year, the original invitee, the Marquess of Linlithgow, having left office in

Campbell Bannerman's reshuffle. The contract had in fact been completed ahead of schedule and the building occupied since September. The total cost of this first and largest section was £152,177.

In the meantime the success of the appeal had enabled the Governors to proceed to a decision which should have been taken much earlier – the purchase of St Paul's Church. It was a burgh church and the agreement of the City as well as that of the congregation had to be obtained. An attempt in July 1902 to relocate the congregation inexpensively to the redundant St John's Free Church opposite the College on George Street failed and it was only with an offer of £15,000 to build a new church in June 1903 that agreement was finally reached. This enabled Barclay to complete the western court to correspond with that on the east, but by that date it was much too late to plan the College as it should have been, with consequences still evident to anyone who tries to find the examination hall from the main entrance on George Street without guidance.

The purchase of the church, coupled with a decline in subscriptions as a result of the recession, left little in hand with which to undertake the next section, but a £25,000 grant from The Scotch (sic) Education Department enabled work to begin. Construction of this second section, the George Street block, was therefore carried out in two phases, partly to stay within the funds available and partly to keep the Young Building in occupation for as long as possible. It cost £43,282. The statue of James Watt by John Greenshields was removed from Bath Street and set up in the entrance hall in September 1906, but it was not until two years later that construction was completed.

The third and fourth sections on John Street had to wait on the congregation vacating St Paul's. These were instructed in quick succession early in 1909 at a cost of £22,182 and £33,187 respectively by negotiating extensions of the rates of the contractors without further advertisement. They were completed very rapidly, the final section being available for classes in September 1910. The event was celebrated by a series of long articles on the College buildings and equipment by Dr John Kerr, these

being published in *Engineering* from September 23 to December 2.

Work finally came to an end early in 1911 without further ceremony. The Building Committee thanked Barclay for his services, Professor Magnus Maclean, their consulting engineer on the electrical installation, and the College Master of Works, Robert Park, who had acted as their clerk of works. The convenor, Robert Goodwin, wrote with justifiable satisfaction after the last meeting in May that

> In presenting their final report the Committee do not propose to give any elaborate statistics regarding the buildings: the outstanding fact that they are adapted to the purposes of the college has long been obvious to all concerned in the work conducted within them and the experience of six years which have elapsed since the first section was completed suggests nothing of importance which could be changed with advantage if the work were to be begun again, although the buildings are the largest single structure devoted to education.

In his statement there was perhaps just a hint that had the decision to acquire St Paul's Church been reached earlier, the College might have been better planned. But, as Goodwin observed,

> The Committee have always kept closely in view the economical expenditure of funds committed to their charge, and the Governors are to be congratulated on the fact that, thanks mainly to the methods laid down by the late Sir William Copland during the first section, the total expenditure has exceeded the estimates by only about £1000 or one-fifth of one per cent. If allowance be made for the cost of the work due to the unexpected difficulties met with in excavating the site [additional underpinning of adjoining properties proved necessary], the expenditure has been substantially within the estimates … The cubic contents of the buildings amount to 7,292,382 cubic feet, and the cost exclusive of the site but inclusive of professional fees, has been under 9d per cubic foot.

Barclay's competition scheme had been 5,264,000 cubic feet. Sandilands's scheme, which would have resulted in a more unified plan with a central hall, had been ruled out, because it would have cost 8.06 pence per cubic foot. The Governors' failing, if failing it were, was that they had never planned ahead of what they could pay for. Nevertheless the executed building had achieved grandeur far beyond anything dreamed of in 1901. The final accounts showed that £272,329 had been spent on building work, more than twice the original cost-limit. A further £46,153 had been spent on lands and buildings not previously in the ownership of the College, and £34,746 on machinery and equipment. Grants and subscriptions amounted to £367,263, leaving a balance of £14,034 for painting and for machinery and apparatus still to be delivered. To mark the completion of the project George V was reminded of his father's part in it and petitioned to grant the title of the Royal Technical College, Glasgow. As it happened the King had just returned from India, where he had been impressed by the work of former students of the College in recent architectural and engineering projects. Lord Pentland, who had opened the building in 1905 as Captain John Sinclair and was still Secretary of State, conveyed to the Governors the Royal Assent on 9 February 1912.

Many, perhaps, will have reached the end of this tribute still rueful that the Special Committee and the Board of Studies did not retain the services of Honeyman & Keppie after the completion of The College of Medicine, and that no effort was made to resolve whatever difficulties there may have been in Honeyman Keppie & Mackintosh's competition scheme. That tantalising one-sixteenth scale tracing of Professor Howarth's might have been realised as a still greater international masterpiece than Glasgow School of Art, towering above George Street and Montrose Street. Indeed, if the brief had set clearer objectives the result of the competition might perhaps have been different. But even the best-regulated competitions were not won with a brilliant idea a century ago, as they sometimes are now, but with a scorecard of practical considerations in which artistic merit hardly figured, a simple verity

which other distinguished early twentieth century architects also discovered. Barclay's building may not have altered the course of architecture, but it is a serious building by a serious architect within a great European tradition, and a powerful architectural expression of what it is. Such faults as it has are not those of the architect but more of the circumstances in which it was built. Look at it again, as the writer has done, with a new respect.

Acknowledgements

This essay was essentially conceived as a tribute to John Hume's long association with the University of Strathclyde and his pioneering *rôle* in the study of industrial architecture and archaeology during his years there, to which the writer has been much indebted. The writer has also been conscious that the University's Royal College building is a subject on which his earlier writings required correction. The present volume has presented the ideal occasion on which to make amends.

The writer wishes to record the general help of Strathclyde University Archives towards that end. He is particularly grateful to the University Archivist, Dr Jim McGrath, who read the script, made some very necessary corrections and directed attention to sources of information which would otherwise have been missed; and to Samantha Searle who gave generously of her time in looking out the material, photocopying and arranging photography.

Sources

Most of the narrative in this essay has been based on the minutes of the Governors of the Glasgow and West of Scotland Technical College and their committees from 1891 to 1912. These were printed, but the relevant University of Strathclyde Archive numbers are E1/1/4 to E1/1/14. Individual references have not been given as the dates in the text provide a sufficient key. The best general accounts of the building as constructed are the *Notes upon the History and Objects of the College Issued on the Occasion of the Laying of the Memorial Stone of the New Buildings by His Majesty the King, 14 May 1903* (E7/1/4/1) and the series of articles by John G Kerr in *Engineering*, September 23 to December 2, 1910.

NOTES

1. *Glasgow Institute of Architects Year Book* (1965), p 91 (a pioneer account of central Glasgow which unwisely took received opinion and published information too much on trust).

2. E Williamson, A Riches, M Higgs, *The Buildings of Scotland: Glasgow* (Penguin, London, 1990), p 149; see also p 64.

3. See M H Port, *Imperial London* (Yale, New Haven & London, 1995), p 242. The South Kensington Royal College was demolished in 1973.

4. See T A Markus 'Domes of Enlightenment: Two Scottish University Museums' in *Art History*, Vol 8, No 2, 1985, and *The International Journal of Museum Management and Curatorship*, Vol 4, No 3.

5. For a general account of the period under discussion see J Butt, *John Anderson's Legacy: The University of Strathclyde and its Antecedents, 1796–1996* (Tuckwell, East Linton, 1996).

6. See John Keppie, 'The Late James Sellars' in *Scottish Art Review*, 1888, pp 191–3; and David M Walker, 'James Sellars Architect, Glasgow, 1843–1888' in *Scottish Art Review* (new series), Vol XI, Nos 1 and 2, 1967, pp 16–18 and pp 21–4.

7. For R A Bryden see *The Builder*, 21 April 1906, p 442 and *RIBA Journal*, Vol 13, 1906, p 340.

8. For Charles Gourlay see *Directory of British Architects 1834–1900* (Mansell Publishing, London, 1993), p 366; *The Builder*, 9 July 1926, p 42: *RIBA Journal*, Vol 33, 1926, p 542.

9. Strathclyde University Archives, E7/2/1.

10. Ibid E7/1/2/2.

11. *The British Architect*, 4 November 1892; reproduced in W Kaplan (ed), *Charles Rennie Mackintosh* (Glasgow Museums/Abbeville, Glasgow, New York, London, 1996), p 128.

12. Strathclyde University Archives, E7/1/1/3; plans E7/2/4. There is little published information on George Bell II beyond A H Gomme and D M Walker, *The Architecture of Glasgow* (2nd edition, Lund Humphries, London, 1987), p 290, and *The Directory of British Architects 1834–1900* (1993), p 72. For J H Craigie see *RIBA Journal*, Vol 37, 21 June 1930.

13. For T L Watson see *The Builder*, 22 and 29 October 1920 and *RIBA Journal*, Vol 28, 1921, pp 20, 78.

14. Strathclyde University Archives E7/1/1/3. For Thomson and Sandilands see D M Walker, 'Scotland and Paris' in J Frew and D Jones (eds), *Scotland and Europe: Architecture and Design 1850–1940* (St Andrews University Press, 1991), pp 33–5, and *The Builder*, 19 December 1913, p 687.

15. Strathclyde Univesity Archives E7/1/1/3. The literature on Mackintosh is too extensive to be listed here, but for Honeyman see D M Walker, 'The Honeymans' in *The British Architect*

16. *Charles Rennie Mackintosh Newsletters*, Nos 62, 63 and 64. A more detailed study has since been carried out by Alan Lamont but is not yet published.

17. T Howarth, *Charles Rennie Mackintosh and The Modern Movement* (Routledge, London, 1952, 2nd edition 1977), p 73.

18. For Salmon & Gillespie, see D M Walker, 'The Partnership of James Salmon and John Gaff Gillespie' in A Service (ed), *Edwardian Architecture and its Origins* (Architectural Press, London, 1975), pp 23–249. A full study of the practice by Raymond O'Donnell awaits publication.

19. Strathclyde University Archives, E7/1/1/3.

20. There is no good modern account of the Barclays. For both brothers see *The Building News*, 4 July 1890, pp 10 and 30 (portraits); for David, see *The Builder*, 27 July 1917; *RIBA Journal*, Vol 24, 1917, p 240. The group portrait of the Governors at Glasgow School of Art by Francis Newbery shows him as being of medium height, grey with a moustache, and bespectacled. His early friendship with Alexander Thomson is recorded in 'Greek Thomson: his life and opinions', *Architectural Review*, Vol 15, May 1904.

21. Good brief accounts of the surviving schools will be found in Williamson, Riches, Higgs, *The Buildings of Scotland: Glasgow* (1990). For Duke Street United Presbyterian Church, see J L Aikman, *History of United Presbyterian Congregations in Glasgow* (Thomas Annan, Glasgow, 1878 edition) with photographs of churches as well as the ministers.

22. Information from Barclay's partner Dr Colin Sinclair, *per* the late A G Lochhead.

23. *The British Architect*, November 1889: C Cunningham *Victorian and Edwardian Town Halls* (Routledge, Kegan & Paul, London, 1981), p 242.

24. *The Building News*, 19 October 1883.

25. *The British Architect*, 25 January 1889.

26. *Building Industries*, 15 June 1891, 16 March 1901.

27. Ibid, 16 December 1891.

28. Strathclyde University Archives, E7/2/3.

29. *Ibid*, P2/1/18.

30. For an (unsympathetic) modern account of this extremely well thought-out building, and an illustration, see Anthony Sutcliffe, *Paris: An Architectural History* (Yale, New Haven, London, 1993), pp 134–5. Guadet owed the concept of these classical buttresses to Léon Vaudoyer's *Aile Neuve* (1848) at the *Conservatoire des Arts et Métiers*, designed to answer the former refectory. See Barry Bergdoll, *Léon Vaudoyer: Historicism in the Age of Industry* (1994), p 168.

31. Illustrated in *Engineering*, 23 September 1910, p 425.

32. Strathclyde University Archives, E7/1/5.

33. Strathclyde University Archives, E7/1/4/1.

GUTHRIE HUTTON

Old Monuments for a New Millennium

THE Millennium Link, the project designed to bring the Forth and Clyde and Union Canals back to life, was given the go-ahead in April 1998. It was the culmination of years of hard work by dedicated people and signalled the restoration of two of Scotland's most important industrial monuments. The two canals span the canal building era; the Forth and Clyde coming early in Britain's years of 'canal mania', and the Union being one of the last major schemes.

There had been many plans for a sea-to-sea canal across central Scotland before the Yorkshire engineer John Smeaton put forward two schemes in 1764. One was to go from Stirling, across the Bog of Bollat and through Loch Lomond to the Clyde, but the debate centred on the other route, through the valleys of the Kelvin and Bonny Rivers. The canal that emerged from the lobbying was a compromise; a direct main line with branches into Glasgow and Bo'ness to assuage commercial interests in the two ports. Work began on 10th June 1768. Smeaton was assisted on the ground by a tough Scot, Robert MacKell.

The first, or sea, lock was on the River Carron beside the mouth of the Grange Burn. The little village that grew up around the lock became known as Grangemouth. It prospered at the expense of Bo'ness; the branch canal was begun, but never completed. From Grangemouth the canal climbed through Falkirk and Bonnybridge to Lock 20, near Banknock, the top lock on the eastern side. The summit pound was cut with some difficulty through unstable ground across Dullatur Bog, and on past Kilsyth. It reached Kirkintilloch in 1773 to complete the first operational section. With half the canal open, cutting continued westward. Stockingfield, near present day Maryhill, was reached in 1775, but by that time the Canal Company had run out of money and work ground to a halt.

Seizing the opportunity, Glasgow's merchants provided funds to cut the branch canal into Hamilton Hill. It was completed by 1777. The city had got what it wanted – a canal to the east coast and a river to the west. As it capitalised on this wonderful trading advantage, alarm bells rang in other parts of Scotland. Parliament was petitioned for money to complete the canal, but eight years were to pass before funds from forfeited Jacobite estates were made available. The delay had taken its toll. Smeaton had resigned and was now an old man; MacKell was dead. A new engineer, Robert Whitworth, was in charge when work restarted in 1785. The canal was completed to Bowling in 1790.

Also in 1790 the Glasgow Branch was extended from Hamilton Hill across Possil Road to Hundred Acre Hill where a new inland harbour called Port Dundas was created. Three years later, the Monkland Canal was joined into the basins bringing a new water supply and more trade. The canals gave Glasgow access to grain supplies from Europe and opened up inland coalfields, ensuring ample fuel. The upstart little city in the west was prospering, comfortable and growing.

Edinburgh wasn't pleased. It had a huge coalfield on its doorstep, but the Lothian coal-owners rigged the market, preferring highly priced exports to local sales. Resultant fuel shortages were made worse by dishonest carters selling short measure. The only way the capital could escape these restrictions was to cut a canal to the west; to open up the city to the same coalfields that were making Glasgow rich. Arguments over the choice of route became a growth industry through the 1790s. Some favoured a direct line from Leith to the Clyde while others pressed for a longer, lower route which linked the Monkland Canal to the east coast. The Napoleonic wars interrupted the debate.

The project was revived in 1813, but this time the arguments centred on a plan to cut what was in effect a branch canal to the Forth and Clyde. Leith was excluded. There was much wailing and gnashing of teeth as Edinburgh contemplated a proposal that would stop short of their port and hand a virtual monopoly of Scottish trade to the Forth and Clyde Canal Company, and its port of Grangemouth. The concerns were heightened because the scheme was designed by the Forth and Clyde's resident engineer, Hugh Baird. But it prevailed and work to cut the Edinburgh and Glasgow Union Canal started in 1818.

From the top of Lothian Road the route headed west through Slateford where a huge aqueduct was built across the Water of Leith. Another great aqueduct crossed the valley of the Almond River before the canal swept round a huge S-bend through Broxburn and Winchburgh (see Figure 1). After Linlithgow the third of the Union's magnificent aqueducts took the canal over the Avon Valley heading for Polmont and Falkirk. There William Forbes of Callendar House objected to the nasty industrial waterway passing close to his policies and forced the engineers to divert it through a six hundred and ninety yard, rock-cut tunnel – the first tunnel on a major transport undertaking in Scotland. A mile to the west, the canal descended a flight of eleven locks to join the Forth and Clyde at Camelon. It was completed in 1822.

While all this was going on the Forth and Clyde was prospering. It had become the focus for industrial and commercial development, and also for invention. William Symington conducted trials with steam-powered boats which culminated in his

Figure 1. Almond Aqueduct, near Ratho, on the Union Canal.

Figure 2. Port Hopetoun, the Edinburgh terminal basin of the Union Canal. (Crown Copyright: RCAHMS)

experimental tug, the Charlotte Dundas, pulling two laden barges from Lock 20 to Port Dundas in 1803. She completed the seventeen and half miles in just over nine hours. It was a triumph, but the Canal Company, fearful that the wash from the paddle wheel would damage the canal banks, stopped further trials. This was a sad end for the world's first practical steamboat.

The Vulcan fared better. She was Scotland's first iron-hulled boat and the progenitor of the country's great shipbuilding industry. She was built on the Monkland Canal at Faskine, near Calderbank, where the local iron-works specialised in casting flat plate. Her builder, Thomas Wilson, was mocked by people who believed that iron could never float, but

he had the last laugh; she was still afloat sixty years after her launch in 1818.

She was intended for use on the Forth and Clyde Canal as a passenger boat. Such boats had been operating on the canal from the early days, with regular sailings from Port Dundas to Camelon. They were clean, fast and comfortable compared to their bumpy, dirty, stagecoach rivals. The opening of the Union Canal made inter-city canal travel possible. Fast boats did the journey in under seven hours – better than the two days taken by stage-coaches – and slow boats operated at night. It was not as convenient as it sounds. Separate boats operated on the two canals and passengers had to change at Falkirk. The walk between the canals was shortened by extending the Union Canal to a new and unremarkable terminal called Port Maxwell.

The Union's Edinburgh terminal, Port Hopetoun, was altogether grander, with a large three storeyed warehouse jutting into the centre of the basin (see Figure 2). Passengers would be greeted by porters vying to carry their luggage, and the one to avoid was William Hare. He had worked as a navvy on the canal, as had the woman who later became his wife, dressed as a man. William Burke had also worked as a navvy on the canal in the Polmont area before moving to Edinburgh where he worked as a lengthsman. Scotland's most infamous serial murderers were therefore closely connected to the Union Canal.

A more wholesome claim to fame is the discovery of the solitary, or perpetual, wave by the marine architect and inventor John Scott Russell. In 1834 he observed that the bow wave of a boat continued moving after the boat had stopped, only dissipating on the bends of the canal. In his later ship design work, which included Brunel's Great Eastern, he tried to harness the wave's energy to assist propulsion. The electronics industry today is working to generate a similar, bell-shaped, perpetual wave called a soliton to send signals around the world by fibre-optic cables.

The development of public railways began soon after the Union opened, and in an attempt to stave off the looming threat, a rail-canal link was established in 1840. A trans-shipment basin was laid out at Causewayend near the Avon Aqueduct where trains travelling the Garnkirk and Glasgow, Ballochney, and Slamannan Railways could meet the canal boats. It was not a success. Boats sometimes missed the trains, stranding their passengers in the middle of nowhere, and stagecoach operators offered cheaper rail-coach deals undercutting the boats.

It made no real difference. In 1842 the Edinburgh and Glasgow Railway was opened and the Union Canal was in trouble; by the end of the decade it was finished. Having beaten the competition the railway could have left the canal to sink into decay and abandonment, but instead they bought it. Commercially it was an extraordinary decision, but it saved the Union for the future.

The Forth and Clyde, and the connected Monkland Canal, were in the right place at the right time to profit from the development of the iron industries of Coatbridge and Falkirk. To begin with the canals were the only means of moving the huge quantities of coal, iron ore and pig iron and the early railways acted as feeder lines to them. As railways developed, the volume of trade was still so great that the canals were kept busy.

The rise of railways meant that steam-powered boats were needed to compete. Early paddle tugs were not a great success although they came into their own in 1832 when cholera was rife in Kirkintilloch. The tugs towed other boats through the town without touching its infected banks. The first screw-propelled steam lighters appeared in the 1850s and very quickly became the workhorses of the canal. They were the first puffers – the *Vital Spark* was born at the Forth and Clyde Canal's little boatyards.

The lighters typically carried timber, coal, sand and chemicals. One of their principal trades was taking pig iron from ships in the Grangemouth docks to canalside iron-works. The docks were a valuable asset. Indeed, they were so valuable that in 1867, the Caledonian Railway was prepared to buy the entire Forth and Clyde and Monkland Canal system in order to acquire them, thus gaining a foothold on the east coast.

Railway owners often wrecked canals, but because the Forth and Clyde went through territory dominated by the rival North British Railway, the Caley used it to compete. So the canal survived and for a time thrived, although it gradually declined up to the outbreak of the First World War. The Admiralty closed the Forth Ports to commercial traffic for the duration of the war, throttling trade through Grangemouth. It never recovered. In the 1930s many of the old wooden bascule bridges were replaced by steel swing and lifting bridges to make road transport easier. The Second World War saw some increased activity for the little boatyards, building and repairing landing craft, but the inexorable decline continued through the 1950s.

The Monkland Canal, moribund since the 1930s, was officially abandoned in 1950. Its deserted weed-choked waters and derelict locks became a playground and death trap for children from the tenements and towns to the east of Glasgow. There were many tragedies. There were drownings too on the Forth and Clyde. The canals became the targets for press outrage. They were relics of a bygone industrial age – dirty, dilapidated, decaying and dangerous; they had to go.

The road transport lobby pushed for their demise too. The routes of the canals were seen as ideal for new roads. The M8 motorway, from Townhead to Easterhouse in Glasgow, was laid along the line of the Monkland Canal – every bend and every bridge on the road replicated the old canal. The narrow Forth and Clyde bridges, even those that had been rebuilt to ease traffic flow, were causing bottlenecks. Calls for them to be 'modernised' were, in effect, calls for the canal's closure. Other transport systems were caught up in the same mad rush to clear the streets for motor vehicles. Glasgow's last tram, the No 9 Dalmuir West to Auchenshuggle, which crossed the canal bridge at Dalmuir, was taken off in September 1962.

A few months later, on 1st January 1963, the canal was closed. The official reason was to save £160,000 for a lifting bridge at Castlecary on the new A80 dual-carriageway road from Glasgow to Stirling. It was a decision made easy by the prevailing attitudes. Some people opposed the closure but their voices were drowned by the negative clamour.

The Union Canal had survived for over a hundred years against the odds. Most of it was still there although the Edinburgh basins had been closed in 1922 and the Falkirk locks removed in 1933. With the other canals gone it became the target for the same pattern of opposition from a hostile press, and roads campaigners seeking 'improvements' to narrow bridges and aqueducts. Again canal supporters, crying in the wilderness, failed to prevent closure in 1965.

For a few mad years a flurry of road improvements took advantage of the canals' pariah status. The favoured installation was the drowned culvert. It blocked the canal with two four foot diameter pipes sunk in the channel, the space around them being filled in and the road driven across the top.

Partial blockages were created by Armco culverts which restricted the channel in a narrow tunnel-like pipe and flat, ugly, concrete bridge decks that maintained the channel width but restricted headroom. Over thirty crossings of the Forth and Clyde were fixed in this way and two large sections, at Blairdardie and Grangemouth, were filled in and piped. The section through Clydebank was made shallower to a depth of between two and three feet. The most damaging action was the lowering of the water level by an average of about two feet; separate pounds were set at different levels. It was meant to reduce maintenance costs, but it removed support from the banks and they collapsed. Some disused canalside buildings were allowed to fall into disrepair. They were mostly demolished and much of the canal's distinctive character disappeared with them.

The Union suffered from the attentions of 1960s and 1970s planners too. Six roads were culverted, one of them being the M8 east of Broxburn. It was a crass piece of work which not only blocked the channel, but severed the towpath too. In comparing the way canal, rail and road engineers solved the problem of crossing the Almond valley, the builders of the motorway came a very poor third. The planners of Wester Hailes, the large housing estate on the western edge of Edinburgh, didn't do too well either. They culverted about a mile of the canal to make way for their grand design.

The culverts were necessary to maintain the water flow. Canal water is not stagnant, it pours in constantly and any surplus is discharged by overflow weirs. The systems are extensive. Each canal has a catchment area sanctioned by parliament; for the Forth and Clyde it is up to ten miles on either side. Across the Kilsyth Hills, small burns are channelled into reservoirs which feed water down a lade to the canal at Craigmarloch. There are other feeders, like the Bothlin Burn at Lenzie and Possil Loch. When the Monkland Canal was extended to join the Forth and Clyde in the 1790s, it provided an aqueduct for water fed down the North Calder Water from the huge Hillend Reservoir at Caldercruix. Other reservoirs in eastern Lanarkshire were linked to the system too. The Union's principal feeder is a remarkable feat of engineering. The lade takes its

Figure 3. The *St John Crusader II*, the Seagull Trust's most recent vessel, near Ratho, on the Union Canal.

water from the River Almond at Mid Calder, about three miles from the canal. It crosses the river on a small cast-iron aqueduct and runs along the steep eastern side of the river valley through four small tunnels before entering the canal beside the Almond Aqueduct. A back-up supply was needed to top up the river if the canal deprived mills of water in dry weather. This was provided by a 'compensation reservoir', Cobbinshaw Loch, twelve miles away in the hills above West Calder.

The water was a problem and a saviour. The canals had been around for the best part of two hundred years and had become an essential part of land drainage. Buildings had been erected on old flood plains and to turn the water off at source would cause widespread flooding. The only option was to pipe the flow, as had been done with the Monkland Canal through Coatbridge and under the M8 in Glasgow. But the cost was high, and those who wanted to fill the canals in faced a daunting financial reality.

They also faced growing opposition. As the folly of what had been done became apparent, people reacted against it and in 1971 gathered in Edinburgh to form the Scottish Inland Waterways Association (SIWA). Although the canals were in a mess, they remained substantially intact and the Association's aim was to seek their restoration. Active campaigning began with public meetings, rallies and work parties. Attitudes began to change. A plan to drive a motorway along the canal from Port Dundas to Milngavie was shelved after pressure from people in Maryhill. It was the last major road scheme that might have provided funds to bury one of the canals in a pipe.

When the orgy of destruction had run out of steam, and those hostile to the canals had lost interest, British Waterways Board (as it was then called) was left with a legacy of decay and dereliction. It also had a band of enthusiasts snapping at its heels demanding improvements which it could

Figure 4. The new Hermiston Aqueduct, over the Edinburgh City By-pass.

not deliver. The Board was in a quandary. It could either fulfil its statutory role and preside over continuing decline, or it could give covert encouragement to people who were prepared to cover themselves in mud at the bottom of lock chambers, but whose enthusiasm offered some hope for the future. To its great credit the Board chose the latter, and an initially hostile relationship evolved into one of mutual interest.

As the volunteers and enthusiasts grew in confidence, boats started to appear. The first was a restaurant boat at Ratho followed by a small boat for disabled people also based at Ratho and run by a charitable organisation called the Seagull Trust (see Figure 3). The Trust has since expanded its Ratho cruising operations and developed others at Falkirk and Kirkintilloch (and at Inverness on the Caledonian Canal). A local canal society was established at Linlithgow and it started to operate a little trip-boat there.

SIWA's most significant achievement was to campaign successfully for an aqueduct across the new Edinburgh by-pass road at Hermiston (see Figure 4). It made little sense at the time because the canal only continued for a few hundred yards before disappearing into the Wester Hailes culvert, but crucially it preserved the future possibility of restoring navigation into Edinburgh.

The focus of campaigning shifted from the Union when the Forth & Clyde Canal Society was formed by SIWA activists in 1980. It made an instant impact by buying an old Clyde ferry and converting it into a canal trip-boat (see Figure 5). It was a public relations master-stroke, one of Glasgow's dearest objects of folk memory preserved by a canal society. The Authorities took notice. Strathclyde Regional Council and Falkirk District Council got together to prepare a Local Plan, a set of planning guidelines for the canal. It was unusual in that it crossed many boundaries, but all of the affected

Figure 5. The former Clyde ferry No 8 in a new role as the Forth & Clyde Canal Society trip boat, *Ferry Queen*. (Douglas Johnstone)

Regional and District Councils signed up to the final plan. It was unusual too in that its monitoring committees included canal society volunteers as well as councillors, council officials and representatives of all interested statutory bodies. It was a model for the future.

With the political will now favouring the canal, improvements started to flow. Two new bridges, at Temple and Kirkintilloch, were built to a fixed navigable height above the surface. It was a defining moment; both were on unused sections of the canal and it would have been easier to build them lower. Towpath upgrading began and lock gates were replaced. In 1988 British Waterways took up the challenge with the Glasgow Canal Project, a partnership-funded scheme, based on the European Regional Development Fund. It was designed to replace blockages with bridges and partially restore navigation between Hamilton Hill and Kirkintilloch. Three bridges, at Firhill Road and Ruchill Street in Glasgow, and the Glasgow Road Bridge near Kirkintilloch, were all rebuilt.

Commercial developments began to appear too. Pub/restaurants came to the rescue of old canal structures at the Glasgow Road Bridge, Underwood Lock near Bonnybridge and a whisky bond at Camelon Bridge. Two pub/restaurants at Camelon and another at Ratho also maintained old structures. New housing developments were built at various canalside locations. The old Saint Magdalene Distillery buildings at Linlithgow were converted for housing, as were the magnificent bonded warehouses at Spiers Wharf in Glasgow. They had been built in the mid-nineteenth century as a sugar

Figure 6. North Spiers Wharf from the west with the old Port Dundas Sugar Refinery on the left.

refinery and grain mills and comprised some of the finest surviving industrial buildings of their age and type in the city (see Figure 6). The wheel had turned full circle from the negative press copy of the 1950s and 60s to estate agents' eulogies about canalside locations in the 1980s.

By now the volunteers were no longer the prime movers as the authorities surged ahead with other partnership projects. The West Lothian Canal Project, based on the Glasgow Project, restored navigation between Linlithgow and the Avon Aqueduct on the Union Canal. It replaced the drowned culvert at Preston Road with a bridge and repaired the badly breached embankment at Kettlestoun. Back on the Forth and Clyde, the Clydebank Canal Project restored three manually operated bascule bridges, re-gated Lock 37 at Old Kilpatrick and upgraded about three miles of towpath.

Although significant progress was made, it was dependent on scarce finance and was inevitably slow. Large sections of the canals remained derelict, and it would be a long time before all the damage of the 1960s and 70s could be undone. More money was needed to maintain the momentum and the National Lottery presented an opportunity to tap into a substantial new source of funds.

In October 1994 British Waterways announced their intention to bid for money from the lottery's Millennium Fund to pay for a restoration scheme called the Millennium Link. At the time the Millennium Commission, the grant awarding body, was in its infancy and conditions which bids had to meet were unclear. As they clarified, British Waterways' case seemed to be enhanced. The two canals united much of the country in a way that made the idea 'Millennial'. They linked the east and west coasts and the two great cities of Scotland – suddenly that aqueduct over the Edinburgh by-pass was very important.

Bids had to be visionary, they had to look back

over past millennia and forward to the next. For the canals, looking back was easy. The Antonine Wall ran parallel to the Forth and Clyde for most of its length, coming within touching distance at many points. The canal itself was a valuable industrial monument with its great Luggie and Kelvin aqueducts and fine freestone lock chambers (see Figure 7). The Union was a masterpiece of the later period of canal construction with numerous cuttings and embankments, over-bridges and under-passes, the three magnificent aqueducts and the only canal tunnel in Scotland.

Looking forward offered a bigger challenge. British Waterways planned to dig out all the culverts and restore navigation, but they also sought to build on the scheme's potential for regeneration. The canals passed through many areas blighted by industrial dereliction and social deprivation. A revitalised canal system could bring life and colour back to them. The lost link at Falkirk also presented an opportunity to build on Scotland's reputation for quality engineering. It was not possible to restore the old locks and so an eighty-foot diameter, energy-efficient, wheel-like boat lift was designed to replace them. The proposed location was to the west of the old route on the former Scottish Tar Distillers site at Lime Wharf, Tamfourhill. It would be a unique structure: nothing like it had been built on a canal anywhere in the world. The full development included an aqueduct from the boat lift leading into a tunnel under the Antonine Wall and the Edinburgh to Glasgow railway. From there, more locks would join an extended section of canal from Port Maxwell. It would be a structure for the new millennium that would hopefully capture imaginations and become a focus for regeneration of the area.

Partnerships were important too, not only because the Commission wanted schemes to have the widest possible public support, but also because they required their grant to be equally matched by other funders. The working partnership, established through the Forth and Clyde Canal Local Plan, again seemed to enhance the bid's prospects.

The optimism was misplaced: the bid was delivered in April 1995 and placed on a B-list by the Commission two months later. Crucially it had not been rejected and the Commission expected it to be resubmitted. The bid was revamped, re-costed and sent back to the Commission in November 1995. It was accompanied by a £30,000-name petition gathered in six weeks by the voluntary sector to demonstrate the level of public support. By Easter the following year it was back on track and the Commission's consultants and British Waterways were engaged in evaluation exercises.

There were high hopes of a decision in June 1996, but instead there was a request for more information and guarantees of matching funding. October came and went and in December the hoped-for decision was deferred again. Some supporters of the scheme greeted this with accusations that the Commission was diverting money to pay for the Millennium Festival and its dome at Greenwich. They proved to be unfounded, and on 14th February, Saint Valentine's Day 1997, the Commission announced a grant of £32.2 million.

After the celebrations, British Waterways set about calling in the promises of matching funds from the project's partners. The scheme was budgeted at £78.3 million. Scottish Enterprise and its network of Local Enterprise Companies were due to contribute £16.5 million, British Waterways £5.5 million, the combined Local Authorities £5.5 million, and the European Regional Development Fund £16.5 million. The residue would be mopped up by the private sector, and the voluntary sector in kind. By late summer only the European money had to be resolved, but the hold-up was due to budget delays in Brussels. There was no hint of trouble.

The first problem emerged in late November when the Strathclyde European Partnership awarded the project less money than had been bid for. The East of Scotland Partnership followed suit a few days later.

An emergency meeting of the Lowland Canals Steering Committee was convened. It had been formed earlier in the year by expanding one of the Forth and Clyde Canal Local Plan monitoring committees to include councillors and officials from the seven local authorities along the two canals. They resolved to fight for the project and

Figure 7. The Kelvin Aqueduct at Maryhill, Glasgow, on the Forth and Clyde Canal.

delegated a sub-group to lobby in any quarters they saw fit. Government Ministers, Scottish Enterprise, MPs, European MPs and the Scottish Office were all drawn into a last push to secure the final funding.

It worked. The announcement that the Millennium Link was to go ahead was made by the Secretary of State for Scotland on 6th April 1998. What started as a campaign by concerned enthusiasts had ended with a commitment from the highest echelons of Government.[1]

A ceremony to launch the project was held on 12th March 1999 at Blairdardie to the west of Glasgow. The Secretary of State for Scotland, Donald Dewar, accompanied by the Earl of Dalkeith representing the Millennium Commission and Bernard Henderson, Chairman of British Waterways, unveiled a commemorative plaque and dug the first spadeful of eatrh. Restoration had begun.

The restored canals will not be quite the same as those that were closed. The Forth and Clyde will have fixed headroom bridges and there will be public houses, restaurants and marinas lining the banks instead of factories and warehouses. The challenge for all concerned with the scheme is to ensure that in the rush to make these valuable industrial monuments fit for the new millennium, the essential character of the old one is maintained.

NOTE

1. At least one of those early enthusiasts had been operating for some time at a lofty level of a Government office, John Hume. John always supported the campaign to bring the canals back to life. He was closely involved with the work of the Seagull Trust as a trustee, and as chairman from 1978–1993 and has served for many years on the Government's advisory body on canals, the Inland Waterways Amenity Advisory Council. John's contribution, much of it lobbying behind the scenes, has been vital to the successful outcome of a long struggle.

TED RUDDOCK

Telford, Nasmyth and Picturesque Bridges

WHILE efforts continue in the late 1990s to raise the quality of bridge designs by collaboration of engineers with architects and, in a few cases, with artists, contemporary relevance may be found in the collaboration in 1803–05 of Thomas Telford, first president of the Institution of Civil Engineers, and Alexander Nasmyth, often called the father of Scottish landscape painting, in a bridge design. The incident lies at the centre of this study of prominent bridges built between 1796 and 1826 in which architectural quality was sought in the use of castellated parapets and various Gothic forms and details.

Precedents

Such styling was not unprecedented and some precedents in the work of important architects of the previous fifty years will be mentioned first. The Adam family did not include any castellated bridges in their early practice, but a sketch by Robert Adam dated about 1750 shows the elevation of a bridge (or perhaps a gateway?) with three pointed arches.[1] When two bridges were built over the fosse for entry to the Gothic castle of Inveraray in 1755–56 they were each of two high pointed arches and the design, presumably by Roger Morris, architect of the building, was conveyed to the masons by a scale model kept in the shed used by John Adam as an office in his role of superintendent of construction.[2]

Three years later a three-arch bridge was built over the mouth of the River Aray, within sight of the Castle, and predictably in matching Gothic style. A plate in *Vitruvius Scoticus* shows a design attributed to John Adam but the bridge seems to have been built in conformity with a rather different drawing attributed to John, though not signed, and now in

the Inveraray Castle muniments. There were circular towers, or turrets, on both sides over each pier and each abutment; they rose above the parapet and were topped by corbelled-out castellations. The parapets were balustrades, as in the Inveraray drawing, not castellated as *Vitruvius Scoticus* showed.[3] Unfortunately it lasted for only about thirteen years, being destroyed by a severe flood in 1772 and replaced by the non-Gothic design of Robert Mylne.[4]

A design with castellated parapets which was almost certainly not built had been made by an unnamed architect, probably in 1770, for an aqueduct to carry the Forth and Clyde Canal over a road at Camelon near Falkirk.[5] But a fine design by the Adams, presumed to be drawn by Robert,[6] was built at Alnwick for the Duke of Northumberland, probably in 1773 and called the Lion Bridge because it bears a lion sculpted in lead on the middle of one of the parapets. It has three segmental arches with horizontal road and parapets from end to end and the castellated parapets stopped over each pier and abutment by a thick semicircular turret, embellished with a vertical mock arrow-slit covered by a hoodmould and above the string course three cross-shaped slits.

Alexander Stevens's designs in the 1780s featured castellated parapets in an estate bridge at Oxenfoord Castle, Midlothian (1783);[7] he also frequently used Gothic decoration, most lavishly in the Bridge of Dun over the South Esk near Montrose (1785–87)[8] and Stockbridge in Edinburgh (1786). Stockbridge also had 'visual castellation' (tapered slots visible only from the outside) of the parapets over four wide pilasters suggesting towers which are applied to the ends of the side walls;[9] most of the decorative details being retained through the widening and other changes made by Daniel Proudfoot in 1900–01. Stevens's use of 'rustication' of the arch rings – alternate voussoirs protruding from the plane of the facade – in his bridge at Ancrum in 1783 heralds another motif which will recur in this study.

Robert Mylne designed a single-arch bridge near the mouth of Loch Dubh at Inveraray in 1783 in a rustic style that the author has already interpreted as a response to the wild surrounding landscape of rising pastures and moorland.[10] At the ends of the arch span there are vertical 'turrets' of quadrant shape in plan and castellations in their parapets.

An Architectural System (1797–1800)

The bridges so far listed show that castellated parapets – 'battlements', as Telford was to call them – and Gothic details, while not common in eighteenth-century bridges, were used sporadically and were much favoured by one leading designer, Alexander Stevens. In two bridges built in 1797–1800 similar design elements were used to compose a complete architectural 'system' and both survive with the system, as well as some important structural features, intact. The larger of the two is Dunglass New Bridge, the name adopted in 1797–98 when it was built as the most expensive element of a two to three mile realignment of the Edinburgh-to-Berwick post road; the smaller spans the Bilsdean Burn about half a mile to the west.[11] The main road, which is now the A1, was moved northward again in the late 1920s, leaving the two bridges serving only a side road that provides access to the gate of the Dunglass Estate and farm properties.

As was usual at the time, Sir James Hall, the owner of the estate, was allowed some choice in the architecture of the bridges and he donated freely to the road trustees all the ground occupied by the new road and bridges and the use of his quarries, as well as taking a leading part in meetings about the project.[12] Bids for the larger bridge were canvassed from favoured architects – all of whom were probably architect/builders – before a contract was made with James Burn of Haddington on 8 November 1796 to build it for one thousand pounds. His brother

George Burn contracted on 27 July 1797 to build the smaller bridge for one hundred guineas.[13]

Dunglass New Bridge is a substantial structure of a single arch on a difficult site (see Figure 1). The Dunglass Burn at this point runs between sheer walls of rock and the single arch springs from ledges on both sides some forty feet above the burn bed and spans eighty-three feet rising thirty feet to the crown. The roadway is horizontal from end to end and the approaches also horizontal. In the trustees' minutes it was noted that in Burn's design the 'elevation [was] to be built in a bold rustick manner' and the bridge therefore has no smooth-dressed surfaces at all. Spandrel and parapet walls are of squared rubble work in courses of varying heights and stone of colour varying from yellow to pink, which has turned green where permanently damp. The parapets are castellated with merlons and embrasures each six feet long, and the slightly overhanging copings and the string courses have a struck rockface finish. The arch is a segmental ring of constant thickness, emphasised by alternate voussoirs protruding about six inches, again with rockface finish. The stout protruding pilasters or towers over the abutments are of bull-faced coursed work. It was a distinctly stylish bridge, but of a style unusual at its date.

It is said to have been in use by 1798 but completion was not recorded until March 1800 when Sir James reported to the other trustees that he 'had examined in particular the four places where the first bridge was seen to give way and found that the method of hollow work now followed had been so effectual that there is no appearance of failure whatever'. (Lady Helen Hall noted in a memorandum book in November 1798 that 'the new bridge is fallen'). In the structure as it now exists, there are three longitudinal voids within each spandrel separated by longitudinal internal walls,[14] a few small holes in each external spandrel wall providing ventilation to the voids. This is the system of spandrel construction developed from about 1770 onwards after several failures of large spandrels,[15] and Sir James's report seems to indicate that Burn first built the spandrels with earth filling and experienced local problems, probably cracks or bulging of the outer

Figure 1. Dunglass New Bridge (NT770721), designed and built by James Burn of Haddington 1796–1800, the first example of the full architectural system later adopted by Nasmyth and Telford.

walls, which persuaded him to remove the earth and make voided spandrels, which have been successful. There is an entrance to the voids from a passage which runs through the structure behind the abutment pilasters at the east end of the span.

The structural detail of the castellated parapet is also interesting. Burn had found it necessary to use 'large sea stones', presumably from the sea-shore nearby, for the copings, most of them single stones six feet long each covering a whole merlon. Because their durability was suspect he was required to maintain the copings 'for a reasonable time'.[16] This occasions some doubt as to whether the iron fixings

of the copings seen today date from the first construction. A wrought-iron bar of square section with both ends bent over stands up each merlon face with one bent end holding down the coping and the other anchored under the similar coping stone forming the floor of the embrasure. Protective railings across the embrasures also exist, and are of old iron, but they are more likely to be additions made sometime after the bridge's first construction.

George Burn's design drawing for the Bilsdean bridge shows two segmental arches of twenty feet span with the same pattern of protruding voussoirs.[17] The parapets also copy those of the larger bridge with string course and castellations, the merlons and embrasures each three feet long. On the spandrel between the arches George drew a quatrefoil device but in construction, or perhaps in a later rebuilding, it was simplified to a circular roundel. The width matched that of the New Bridge at seventeen feet clear between the parapets, but it has since been widened to thirty feet.

Tongland Bridge (1803–08)

Tongland Bridge, which spans the Dee near Kirkcudbright, bears strong similarities to Dunglass New Bridge but its design history is quite different. Like Dunglass, it was first conceived as an important improvement to a post road, in this case the road from Carlisle to Portpatrick and Ireland. Thomas Telford suggested it in his report to the Treasury on the state of the 'coasts and central highlands of Scotland' dated 15 March 1803 estimating the necessary cost at two thousand five hundred pounds.[18] The route and the bridge featured in subsequent reports on Telford's works and he described it in his article in the *Edinburgh Encyclopaedia* in 1812 [19] and again in his autobiography which was published in 1838 after his death,[20] each description being illustrated with a detailed plate (see Figure 2). Of the architecture he said only on the first occasion that 'the whole [had] a bold effect' and on the second that 'the external elevation ... is turreted and embattled'. The cost had been seven thousand, seven hundred and ten pounds for reasons to be explained below. As well as a main segmental arch spanning one hundred and eighteen feet and rising thirty-eight feet, there were three tall and narrow Gothic arches through the approaches at each end to provide extra passages for high flood- and tide-water and also reduce the bulk of the approach structures. Solid semicircular turrets up the sides at the abutments had arrow-slits and castellated parapets and at the road level provided generous refuges from traffic. The castellations also stretched across the main span, with a level roadway across all the arches and the approaches. The details of the castellations, the finishes of the general masonry and the rustication on the face of the arch all correspond to those of

Dunglass New Bridge, although there are no iron anchors or railings. The large spandrels were also hollowed in the same manner as at Dunglass, and were fully described in the autobiography:

> ... in the spandrills (instead of filling them with earth) were built a number of longitudinal walls, in fact interior spandrills, their end abutting against the back of the archstones and the cross walls of each abutment; these longitudinal walls are connected and steadied by the insertion of tie-stones, and at a proper depth under the roadway the spaces between them are covered with flat stones, so as to form a platform for the road; and in these spaces are arched openings for occasional examination and repair (if ever it become necessary).

And Telford added:

> I have ever since practised this mode, in order to lessen the weight incumbent upon large arches, and the pressure outward against high wing walls and spandrills ...

His statements were true but have caused confusion of two kinds. Firstly, many subsequent authors have inferred wrongly that he was claiming to have invented the technique of hollow construction described. Secondly, opinions have differed about the meaning of a note published in the *Scots Magazine* just after the bridge was finished. Written by Patrick Nasmyth, it described the bridge as built 'by the gentlemen of the county from a design by Mr. Nasmyth [i.e. Alexander Nasmyth, Patrick's father], and surveyed by Mr Telford, engineer.' The finished bridge was shown in a plate which is incorrect only in the shape of the tops of the turrets.[21] The plate was very clearly derived from a pencil sketch by Nasmyth senior which was sold by Phillips in Edinburgh in December 1994 (see Figure 3).[22] It shows a sailing boat and a dinghy which are also in the engraving in only slightly changed positions; and the ends of the parapet are not finished in the sketch but completed in the engraving. The sketch bears a pencil scrawl in Alexander's hand: 'Kirkcudbright. The Bridge at Tongland, Galloway – [illegible] – A N'. (The sale catalogue notes that on

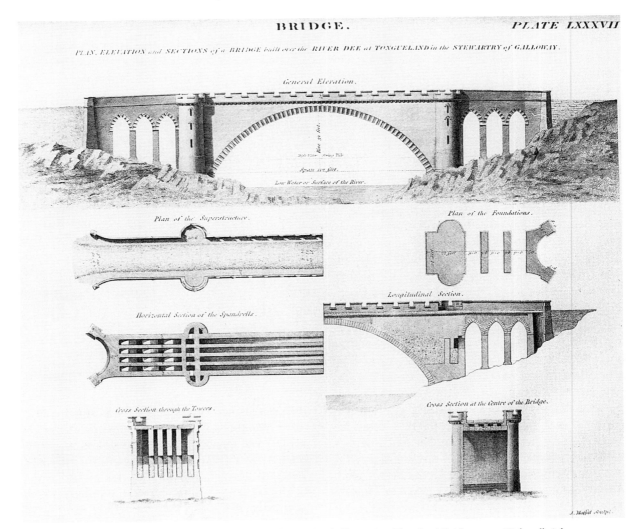

Figure 2. Technical plate in the *Edinburgh Encyclopaedia* IV (1812) illustrating Tongland Bridge, near Kirkcudbright.

the back of the sheet was 'another sketch of the bridge' but no other information about it.) In both the sketch and the engraving the parapets are castellated. Another sketch, this one in ink, is in the National Gallery of Scotland's collection of Nasmyth drawings[23] and shows the bridge from a similar stance but a narrower angle with the near end unfinished and the rest of the facade correct except for a lack of castellations. It must, obviously, have been drawn at just about the same time. It is inscribed in pencil 'Kirkcudbright' and also, in the hand of James Nasmyth, another son of Alexander who held many of his father's papers for a long

period and annotated them, 'Design for a Bridge Drawn by my Father Alexr. Nasmyth for his Friend the Earl of Selkirk. Thomas Telford was responsible with Alexr. Nasmyth for the construction of the Bridge'. At this point it should be noted that Nasmyth senior had also been a close friend of Selkirk's brother-in-law Sir James Hall of Dunglass since they met on Continental travels in 1782–84. Sir James was actually godfather to the son just mentioned, who was christened James Hall.[24]

Yet another sheet in the Gallery's collection[25] is inscribed by Alexander in pencil 'Designes for a

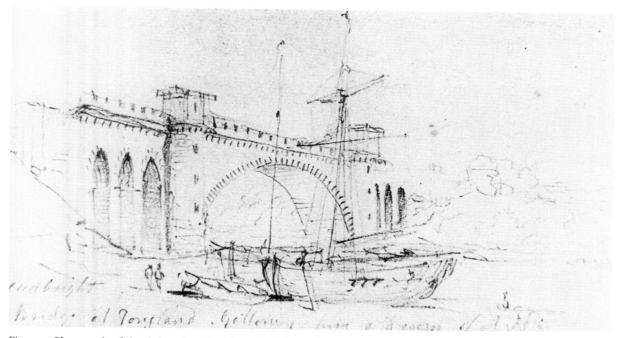

Figure 3. Photograph of sketch by Alexander Nasmyth, 'The Bridge at Tongland, Galloway' nearing completion (1808?), printed in catalogue of sale 1994. (Phillips Scotland)

Bridge over the Dee at Toungland. Kirkcudbright A N', and in a different place 'Now Built 1816 A N' (see Figure 4). It bears two sketch elevations in landscape, one of a three-arch bridge, the middle arch longer than the side arches and square pilasters between, the other a bridge of the form built with round turrets and three tall Gothic arches at each end. However, the first of these sketches appears to show an open balustrade over the large arch and plain parapets over the side arches, and the second shows plain parapets throughout. Nevertheless, it must be supposed that these sketches were drawn and the first inscription written about the time the bridge was designed, and the second inscription added by the artist years later.

Luckily, there is a clear statement of the part played by Alexander Nasmyth, written by 1813. The Reverend Samuel Smith wrote:

It was projected in the year 1803, when Mr Telford, the celebrated civil engineer, was employed to examine the situation, and to furnish a plan. But as the plan which he gave required a smoother style of masonry than could easily be executed in the country, or than seemed to accord with the bold and rugged scenery on the banks of the river, it was, with his approbation, altered, in so far as related to the external architecture, agreeably to a drawing, by Mr Nasmyth, an eminent painter at Edinburgh.[26]

His comment on the masonry finish was:

The blocks [of stone] are massy, and accurately jointed but very roughly hewed, a style of finishing, equally suited to the situation, and to the architecture of the bridge.

There can be little doubt that Nasmyth's contribution, as identified by Smith, is represented by the sketch of two alternative designs, the second being chosen and altered to have castellated parapets. Since the sketch seems to have remained with the artist, another copy was probably drawn, perhaps in plan and elevation to a larger scale, for the trustees and for Telford.

Figure 4. Sketch by Alexander Nasmyth of 'Designes for a Bridge over the Dee at Tongland'. (National Gallery of Scotland)

Smith goes on to tell that a contract for construction was made 'with country tradesmen' but in August 1804, when they had begun building the arch their centring was swept away by a flood and Telford advised that their experience was not sufficient for a structure of this scale, whereupon they were relieved of their contract and he sent a 'superintendent' from England to complete the bridge 'by day labour'. After eighteen months it was opened to traffic in November 1806 and fully finished by May 1808. Over three thousand pounds is said to have been spent before the first contractors were dismissed.

Sequels

Telford had studied architecture before he turned to engineering and held clear views about the architecture of bridges; but his large bridges in England in the 1790s had been built of ashlar[27] and that

must surely have been the 'smoother style of masonry' that was found too difficult in Galloway. The story shows that the major change in his practice which Tongland Bridge represents was not due to a personal change of taste, but to practical circumstances. The style which resulted, however, appealed to him and he began to adopt it to varying extent in other bridge designs. As early as 1810 in his *Edinburgh Encyclopaedia* article he described his seven-arch bridge at Dunkeld, built in 1805–09, as 'the finest bridge in Scotland ... The facade [had] castellated turrets over the piers and abutments' – which was not strictly true, for there is a detail at the turret-heads which may suggest castellations but is not the real thing. There are slits lower down on the turrets and alternate voussoirs of the arches protrude but not as much as in Tongland and Dunglass New bridges. A few years later he built two castellated towers at each end of his famous iron arch at Craigellachie, with no practical function other than support for a plaque announcing the place at which the ironwork had been cast. Later in his career he built the pylons of his suspension bridge over the Conwy in North Wales (1821–26) as Gothic towers with vertically elongated castellation, this form chosen, it was said, to harmonise with the adjacent towers of Conwy Castle.[28]

Nasmyth continued the style more directly. In 1811 he exhibited a painting in Edinburgh with catalogue entry 'Bridge of Almondell, built from a design of A. Nasmyth', and both the painting and a pencil sketch from which it appears to have been made survive.[29] It is known today as Nasmyth Bridge (see Figure 5). All the elements of the style of Dunglass New and Tongland bridges are present in both sketch and painting and on the bridge as built, except the iron anchors and railings in the embrasures at Dunglass. The site, with a steeply rising bank on the south and low flat ground on the north bank, posed a problem for design of a bridge worthy of the estate improvements in which the owner Henry

Erskine, former Lord Advocate of Scotland, was engaged. Nasmyth's answer was to build a bridge of one large arch, seventy-two feet span, to the south, with a significant rise of the road and parapets to the crown and a much longer downward gradient to the north over a second, smaller arch. To give the design some visual symmetry and to emphasise his large arch, he placed over its crown a length of balustrading, high, horizontal and smooth-hewn; and refuges, containing stone seats, were made at each end of the central feature, while further refuges were incorporated with the castellated parapets over pilasters on the facades at the pier between the arches, at both abutments and at the ends of the wingwalls. It was a distinctively picturesque bridge whether seen from the river banks or while crossing it. It was apparently well built, though it is questionable whether Nasmyth took responsibility for the construction, and it would be consistent with his involvement in Tongland Bridge that he should have been engaged only to produce initial drawings. A potential weakness was built into it in the fact that the interior was filled with waste quarry stones,

Figure 5. Nasmyth Bridge in Almondell Country Park, West Lothian. View from the south-east after restoration 1997.

followed by gravel and earth: and when in 1973 a partial collapse of the bridge took place the condition of the filling was probably the main cause. If Nasmyth's design is represented, as the exhibition catalogue infers, by his sketch and painting (though these pictures seem likely to have been made after it was built), photographs from the period 1900–1970 confirm that the design was executed accurately,[30] and the restoration of the bridge completed in 1997 (see Figure 5) has adhered faithfully to the original elevations and style of masonry.[31]

Connections and Picturesqueness

The marked similarity of Nasmyth Bridge to the two bridges at Dunglass demands some discussion. Nasmyth had taken part in plans for improvements to the Dunglass estate by making several sketches for a new house of well-defined architecture placed in the existing landscape [32] – the project being taken over later by the Edinburgh architect Richard Crichton to produce a classical house described by Colvin as 'a remarkably early essay in picturesque asymmetry'.[33] Such evident friendship and activities makes it very possible that Nasmyth contributed the picturesque ideas for the bridges at Dunglass; but it is also possible – though in this author's view less likely – that James Burn made the first design 'in a bold rustick manner' and that it was copied by Nasmyth in his designs for Tongland and Almondell. Moreover, whichever is true, it would be implausible not to guess that Sir James Hall's architectural thinking exerted a measure of influence on the whole sequence of bridges. He had begun during his travel on the Continent to develop a theory about the origin of Gothic architecture and pursued it by experiments with structures of wicker and branches at Dunglass, resulting in a paper which he presented to the Royal Society of Edinburgh, of which he was president for many years, in 1797, and culminating in his folio volume entitled *Origins, Principles and History of Gothic Architecture*, published in 1813.[34] Nasmyth is said to have made many of the drawings for the book, and it would be natural that any contribution by Sir James to the bridge designs should be channelled through Nasmyth as amanuensis.

It is natural to place all four designs from Dunglass to Nasmyth Bridge in the Picturesque movement. In the light of known facts of the design for Tongland and the possibility that equivalent processes took place in the designs of the other three bridges, 'picturesque' is more than a style label. It describes the method of design: Nasmyth made a picture or pictures of the proposed bridge in its context to submit to his client, and when they were agreed on a picture as the preferred design, construction could proceed, sometimes, and possibly always, with others assuming responsibility for construction.

It remains to note a further bridge which cannot be disassociated from the four. The entrance drive to Ormiston, a house only one and a half miles as the crow flies from Nasmyth Bridge, is carried by a bridge of one semicircular arch on high abutments. All the elements of the architectural system used in Nasmyth Bridge are present but at somewhat smaller scale and with fully horizontal road and parapets. Nothing is known at present about who designed or built it, but the style was surely copied from its neighbour at Almondell.[35] Are there others yet to be identified?

Further Sequels

In the eclectic world of nineteenth-century architecture, elements of the style of the bridges discussed here occurred widely and direct sources of their style probably varied. However, the bridges of two men who owed their introduction to engineering largely to Telford and can be suspected of having absorbed their evident preferences from him are worthy of mention. Alexander Nimmo, a brilliant Scottish schoolmaster who went to Ireland to take up engineering on Telford's recommendation, chose Gothic arches and details for several fine designs of bridges in rural settings (see Figure 6),[36] while many of the bridges and viaducts on Scottish railways designed in the 1860s by Joseph Mitchell are in similar style. Mitchell had had training in Telford's office in London before returning to take control of the works of the Commissioners for Highland Roads and Bridges in 1824 and later he was engineer for the railways from Inverness to Perth, to Elgin and to Wick and Thurso. Notable examples of his bridge

Figure 6. Bridge over a gorge at Poulaphouca on the (former turnpike) road from Dublin to Blessington. Design attributed to Alexander Nimmo, potentially in the mid to late 1820s.

Figure 7. North end of Dalguise Bridge which carries the main line from Perth to Inverness over the River Tay about five miles north of Dunkeld. Designed by Joseph Mitchell and built *circa* 1865. There are two iron lattice girders of 210 and 141 feet spans with castellated stone towers at each end and over the intermediate pier.

style are the viaducts at Killiecrankie, Calvine, Dunphail and Allness, the last with its castellations sadly mutilated in recent years, and the masonry abutment towers of girder bridges at Dalguise (see Figure 7) and Blair Atholl, the latter made specially fulsome in deference to the Duke of Atholl.[37]

NOTES

1. J Fleming, *Robert Adam and his Circle* (John Murray, London, 1962), p 85 and plate 28.
2. I G Lindsay & M Cosh, *Inveraray and the Dukes of Argyll* (Edinburgh University Press, Edinburgh, 1973), pp 86–7.
3. *Ibid*, pp 136–7, figures 45, 46, 77.
4. *Ibid*, pp 234–5, plates 25, 26.
5. Designs of John Smeaton FRS, Vol 5, fols 36v, 37, at the Royal Society of London.
6. D King, *The Complete Works of Robert and James Adam* (Butterworth, Oxford, 1991), figure 447.
7. A Rowan 'Oxenfoord Castle, Midlothian', *Country Life*, CLVI (1974), pp 430–3, has a photograph.
8. T Ruddock, *Arch Bridges and their Builders 1735–1835* (Cambridge University Press, Cambridge, 1979), pp 121–3.
9. T Ruddock, 'Civil Engineering', in S Jamieson (ed), *The Water of Leith* (Water of Leith Project Group, Edinburgh, 1984), p 61.
10. Ruddock, *Arch Bridges*, pp 91–2.
11. For development of the road, see A Graham, 'Archaeology on a great Post Road', *Proceedings of Society of Antiquaries of Scotland*, Vol XCVI (1962–63), pp 318–47, plate LIV.
12. Minutes of road trustees of Haddingtonshire 1783–1800, ref CO7/2/1/2 at SRO.
13. Ibid, and estimate with drawing for a bridge at Bilsdean by George Burn, ref GD206/2/157 at SRO.
14. Inspection by the author during repairs by Borders Regional Council in 1992.
15. T Ruddock, 'Hollow spandrels in arch bridges', *The Structural Engineer*, vol 52 (1974), pp 281–93.
16. Minutes, 18 March 1800.
17. See note 13.
18. 'A survey and report of the coasts and central highlands of Scotland made by command of the Lords of the Treasury in the autumn of 1802'. Ordered to be printed 5 April 1803. A copy is in University of Edinburgh Library, ref SBF 385(41)04/1. Also printed as an appendix to J Rickman, ed, *The Life of Thomas Telford, civil engineer, written by himself* (Payne & Foss, London, 1838).
19. T Telford, 'Bridge: history' and 'practice', *Edinburgh Encyclopaedia* (1830) Vol IV, pp 479–545. Vol IV was issued in 1812.
20. Rickman, see note 18, pp 31–2 and plate 8.
21. The *Scots Magazine*, vol 69 (1808), p 883 and plate.
22. Phillips, Scotland, *Catalogue of Sale* 3291, 2 December 1994, p 10.
23. National Galleries of Scotland (NGS) Print Collection, D3727/14.
24. S Smiles (ed), *James Nasmyth, engineer: an autobiography* (1912 edn).
25. NGS Print Collection, D3727/15.
26. Rev Samuel Smith, *General View of the Agriculture of Galloway* (1813), pp 324–7. I am indebted to Mr Alexander Anderson of Dumfries for bringing this reference to my attention.
27. See Ruddock, *Arch Bridges and their Builders 1735–1835* (1979), especially pp 148–54.
28. Photographs of all the bridges named in this paragraph are in S M Johnson and C W Scott-Giles (eds), *British Bridges: an illustrated technical and historical record* (1933). For Conwy Bridge see also Rickman (note 18), p 233 and plate 78.
29. J C B Cooksey, *Alexander Nasmyth HRSA 1758–1840* (Whittingehame House, Whittingehame, 1991), reproduces both and cites references.
30. Photographs are held by the National Monuments Record of Scotland, Edinburgh, and the Visitor Centre, Almonddell and Calderwood Country Park, West Lothian.
31. T Ruddock, 'The restoration of Nasmyth Bridge', forthcoming.
32. The drawings are in the NGS collection, and some reproduced by Cooksey, see note 29.
33. H M Colvin, *Biographical Dictionary of British Architects* (3rd edn, Yale, New Haven, 1995), pp 279–80.
34. *Dictionary of National Biography* (1890), Vol 24, pp 68–9.
35. I am grateful to Mr Stuart Eydmann of West Lothian Council for drawing this bridge to my attention.
36. See Ruddock, *Arch Bridges*, pp 196–200, and P O'Keeffe, and T Simington, *Irish Stone Bridges* (Irish Academic Press, Blackrock, 1991).
37. Some of Mitchell's bridges are described and illustrated in *Engineering* (1865), September 13 to October 4, pp 205–7, 257, 264, 289, 320–1; and in M Smith, *British Railway Bridges and Viaducts* (Ian Allan, Shepperton, 1994), pp 90–3.

13

FRANK LAWRIE

A Future for Scotland's Railway Past?
Disused Railway Viaducts

DEVELOPMENT of the railway network through-out the United Kingdom in the nineteenth century was primarily a function of two factors. On the one hand, there were considerable commercial benefits to be gained from using railways as a means of conveying marketable goods, particularly minerals, so many of the earliest railway endeavours were for the conveying of lucrative freight traffic. The other major driving force was the interest of local landowners both as an investment opportunity and because of the prestige which might be associated with bringing the railway and its benefits to 'their territory'.

Scotland had its share of early mineral lines. When Johnny Cope 'gang'd wi the coals in the mornin'' after the Battle of Prestonpans, he was as the song accurately recorded making his escape down the Tranent to Prestonpans mineral line. The first known viaduct specially built for railway traffic was the Laigh Milton Viaduct near Dundonald in Ayrshire. Built in 1812, the viaduct was no longer in operation by 1845, but it has recently been re-stored as a major feature in the walkway and cycleway to the Ayrshire coast (see Figures 1 and 2).

Two subsequent mineral lines constructed in the 1820s were the Dundee & Newtyle Railway and the Edinburgh to Dalkeith line – the so-called 'Innocent Railway'. Traces of all of these lines can be seen to this date, though they are effectively archaeological traces (albeit a large one in the Laigh Milton Viaduct!). The terminal station at Newtyle exists today, and is a scheduled ancient monument.

Although Scotland had a number of early mineral lines, and had an intercity route between Glasgow and Edinburgh as early as 1842, the development of the railway network throughout Scotland – and indeed links with the rest of the United Kingdom – took perhaps a little longer to effect than one might have expected. There were several reasons for this – the initial attitude of a few large landowners who were initially unenthusiastic about the impact of the railway on their property, the relative lack of worth-while mineral deposits outwith the central belt, and the sparsity of large areas of the country.

However, during the course of the nineteenth century, the railway network developed to the corners of Scotland so that, in time, very few significant communities were not served by at least one railway link. Lines were promoted by companies which amalgamated and reformed into larger and larger concerns. By the time of the 'Grouping' of railways in 1923, Scotland's railway network was the province of five separate companies, namely the Caledonian Railway, the North British Railway, Glasgow & South Western Railway, The Highland Railway and the Great North of Scotland Railway. Although the Grouping was intended to rationalise railway systems throughout the United Kingdom, it did not as one might have supposed put all the Scottish railways into one single group, presumably because it was then considered that such a group would not be viable. The North British and Great North of Scotland became part of the London and North Eastern Railway, whilst the Caledonian, Glasgow & South Western and Highland became part of the London Midland Scottish Railway.

Figure 1. Laigh Milton Viaduct, Dundonald, South Ayrshire, the first known viaduct specially built for railway traffic in Scotland. Built in 1812 to serve a mineral line, the viaduct was out of operation by 1845, and can here be seen prior to restoration (see also Figure 2). (Historic Scotland)

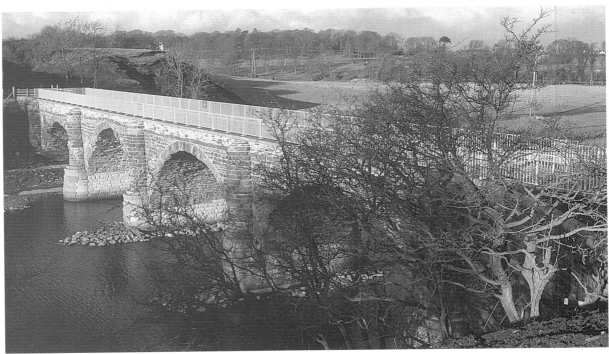

Figure 2. Laigh Milton Viaduct restored (see also Figure 1), now a major feature in a walkway and cycleway to the Ayrshire coast. (Historic Scotland)

With the Grouping came rationalisation, though route closures generally did not start to appear until the 1930s; the split of Scotland between the LNER and the LMS had ensured continued competition for business. After World War II, and the nationalisation of the railway system in 1948, there were further route closures in the 1950s. The Beeching rationalisation of the 1960s bit deeply into the total Scottish route mileage, removing many branch lines throughout Scotland – particularly in the North East of Scotland – together with three main trunk routes, namely the Waverley route between Edinburgh and Carlisle, the former Caledonian Railway route between Perth and Montrose and the route from Dumfries to Stranraer.

Railways and the Landscape

A practical consideration in drawing up the route for a railway line had to be ability of relatively inefficient locomotives to deal with gradients. Gordon Biddle has noted that 'engineers and surveyors everywhere took maximum advantage of the contours, particularly on secondary and branch lines where costs was paramount and the speed of trains little consequence, producing some remarkably serpentine routes'.[1] He also notes that this phenomenon was particularly true in the Highlands, where 'gradual though longer and more devious assents' minimise the need for the major capital expense of tunnels. The expense of bridges and viaducts was less easy to avoid, however; as Vallance notes, the nine mile branch of The Highland Railway opened in 1865 from Ballinluig to Aberfeldy required no fewer than forty-one bridges![2]

Listing of Railway Bridges and Viaducts

Given the impact of railway development across Scotland, it is not surprising that many railway structures are listed as buildings of special architectural or historic interest. The earliest statutory lists, developed by Ian G Lindsay and others from the lists which Lindsay had prepared in the 1930s for the Fourth Marquess of Bute, have been the subject of a rolling programme of national resurvey since the late 1970s. It is generally held that the original

statutory lists paid insufficient attention to Victorian and Edwardian architecture, and to industrial archaeology, though as David Walker has noted, Lindsay himself in his 1949 *Notes for Guidance of Investigators* – basically, instructions for professional staff involved in listing – comments on industrial archaeology that 'engineering works must be considered carefully, and particularly the achievements of the early railway builders …'[3]

With the national programme of resurvey now approximately halfway completed, there are forty listed railway bridges and eighty-two listed railway viaducts in Scotland. As a general rule, a viaduct may be distinguished from a bridge in that the former has three or more arches or spans. As elsewhere, however, the exception proves the rule. The Glenesk Viaduct, near Dalkeith, has a single large semicircular arch (see Figure 3), whilst the Forth and Tay Bridges arguably meet the criteria to be styled as viaducts!

Prior to 1971, the only railway listings in Scotland were the Haymarket train shed (now relocated to the Scottish Railway Preservation Society's premises at Bo'ness) which had originally been the eastern terminus of the Edinburgh & Glasgow railway, and Warriston Road Bridge, a three segmental skew arch structure – and thus a 'viaduct' – carrying the Edinburgh, Leith & Granton Railway across Warriston Road and the Water of Leith (see Figure 4). In early 1971, however, a substantial number of viaducts joined the statutory list, ostensibly as a tidying up exercise as part of the issue of statutory lists to local planning authorities following the Town and Country Planning (Scotland) Act 1968.

Listing of a building recognises its special architectural or historical merit, but does not guarantee its future. The statutory act of listing requires that anyone seeking to alter, extend or even demolish a listed building must seek listed building consent, in the first place from the local planning authority. The contraction of the railway network, and particularly that in the 1960s post-Beeching, left British Rail with a number of redundant bridges and viaducts in their portfolio. These structures were very often in relatively isolated locations and relatively expensive to maintain. It is understandable that

Figure 3. Glenesk Viaduct, Midlothian, an exception to the rule of thumb in the definition of a viaduct, in possessing only one arch. (Historic Scotland)

British Rail should have wished to target their spending on operational structures and to relieve themselves of the financial burden of redundant structures.

Leaderfoot Viaduct

Matters came to a head in 1981 when British Rail sought listed building consent from the then Borders Regional Council to demolish two redundant railway viaducts, Shankend, between Hawick and Riccarton Junction; and Drygrange, near St Boswells. This latter viaduct, more usually referred to as Leaderfoot Viaduct, had been built in 1865 for the Berwickshire Railway, a line built to connect from the Waverley route just north of St Boswells to Reston, on the East coast main line of the North British Railway.

The Leaderfoot Viaduct was the major engineering structure of what was primarily a local agricultural line. It is a slender and elegant structure

crossing the Tweed alongside the eighteenth-century Drygrange road bridge and a not inelegant concrete bridge carrying the modern A68 across the river.

The Berwickshire railway branch had been a casualty of the Beeching cuts and, in 1981, some sixteen years after the Leaderfoot Viaduct had last seen 'active service', British Rail decided to seek consent for its demolition. A local author and broadcaster, Liz Taylor, organised a vigorous campaign within the Borders which resulted in a substantial petition being laid before the Council objecting to the proposal to demolish the viaduct. In the face of this opposition, the Council was clearly going to refuse consent, so British Rail withdrew the application for consent to demolish, and that for Shankend, so that they could re-appraise options.

It should not be thought that British Rail were blind to the importance of redundant viaducts as

Figure 4. Warriston Road Bridge, a three segmental skew arch structure serving the Edinburgh, Leith & Granton Railway, one of the earliest listings in the field of viaducts. (Historic Scotland)

landscape features. Indeed, British Rail as an organisation was very acutely conscious of the unique legacy of important structures which they had inherited. In 1983, British Rail commissioned the publication of a major volume entitled *The Railway Heritage of Britain*, which was an illustrated guide to the historic buildings and structures in their care. This was a suitably prompt response to the publication two years earlier by the Property Services Agency of a similar volume illustrating the range of historic buildings in the care of the Secretary of State for the Environment.

In *The Railway Heritage of Britain*, Bernard Kaukas, then Director – Environment to the British Railways Board, commented that though repairs to Victorian railway structures were cheap compared to remedial costs of repairing motorway flyovers, in cash terms considerable sums still had to be found. He argued that redundant railway buildings which cannot be sold off or released as commercial propositions could be passed across to responsible outside bodies, such as local authorities or building trusts together with some financial contribution to help with necessary repairs. He noted too that, in the light of a successful partnership between British Rail and the Greater Manchester Council in tackling decaying parts of Manchester Victoria Station, 'British Rail offered to enter into joint partnership with any local authority or other properly constituted body to improve the environment and its lands and buildings, and that offer remains open'.[4]

In the light of this, it might be supposed that, following their failure to secure listed building consent to demolish Leaderfoot Viaduct, British Rail would attempt to persuade Borders Regional Council or other local interests to take over responsibility for caring for the viaduct – after all, many thousands of local people had signed the petition against the proposal to demolish the structure. Discussions did indeed take place, but floundered because neither British Rail nor the Council was prepared to meet the substantial costs which would be required to make the viaduct sound – it had been the cost of the repairs judged necessary to make the viaduct safe which had prompted the 1981 application for consent to demolish. However, British Rail and others remained concerned about the future of this and other disused viaducts and, following discussions between British Rail and the Scottish Civic Trust, there appeared in the Glasgow Herald on 10 March 1994 an article by Anne Johnston under the headline 'Lament for the Viaducts'. In that article, Anne Johnston reviewed some of the dealings between British Rail and local authorities over the future for disused viaducts and reported that the Scottish Civic Trust had approached British Rail to call for a forum of interested parties to discuss possible solutions.

Following publication of that article, the Scottish Civic Trust wrote to a number of interested organisations inviting attendance at a meeting in British Rail's Scottish headquarters, Buchanan House, in May 1984. Actual attendance at the meeting indicates the concern which was generally felt about the problem of disused railway viaducts and the willingness to seek positive solutions. Chaired by John Gerrard, Technical Director of the Scottish Civic Trust, the meeting brought together senior British Rail representatives, including Bernard Kaukas and David Lawrence, British Rail's Chief Estate Surveyor, several chief planning officers, representatives of the National Trust for Scotland, the Countryside Commission for Scotland, the Scottish Georgian Society (the forerunner of the Architectural Heritage Society of Scotland) and the Scottish Railway Preservation Society (SRPS). Also present were a representative of the Historic Buildings Division of the Scottish Development Department (the predecessor of Historic Scotland) and, in a private capacity as one of Britain's foremost industrial archaeologists, but shortly to become an Inspector of Ancient Monuments, John Hume of the University of Strathclyde and a member of the Ancient Monuments Board of Scotland.

Several key decisions were taken at that meeting. Although British Rail had some in-house figures for costs of urgent maintenance, it was agreed that there was a need to seek expert external advice on the overall costs of the problems which British Rail faced. British Rail agreed to pay for external consultants to survey four viaducts which were held to be representative, namely East Calder Viaduct (also known as Camps Viaduct) over the River Almond; Bilston Glen Viaduct; Teviot Viaduct and Leaderfoot Viaduct. A similar survey was already being prepared for SRPS for Birkhill Viaduct. Historic Scotland also agreed to compile a list of redundant listed viaducts and to re-assess the listing categories of these – this work was done jointly by Anne Riches, Head of Listing and John Hume.

The Group agreed to reconvene in August to receive the independent report. Although the Group had not, at that stage, been accorded any formal status, they were effectively about to assume the mantle of the Scottish Joint Viaducts Committee, with John Gerrard as Chairman and British Rail providing full secretarial services.

Although the impetus for the setting up of the Committee had come from the Scottish Civic Trust, by this stage they had found British Rail to be a very receptive partner. Publication of *The Railway Heritage of Britain* had provided an inventory of Britain's railway heritage, and in doing so had highlighted many of the practical problems which British Rail faced in dealing with obsolete or obsolescent structures. But the publication had suggested no answers, other than Bernard Kaukas' comments on the need for partnerships to which reference has already been made. It was recognised that some national follow-up would be required to address the problems identified in the volume. As a result, a conference was held in October 1984 in the Royal Society of Arts in London. The conference was convened by a panel bringing together RSA's Committee for the Environment and the Thomas Cubitt

Trust. But it was in practice planned in direct collaboration with British Rail as it provided the latter with a forum to announce the formation, with effect from April 1985 and with a budget of one million pounds, of an independent Railway Heritage Trust. The Trust would have as its Chairman the Honourable William McAlpine and Leslie Soane, formerly General Manager of the Scottish Region of British Rail was appointed as Director of the Trust.

Against that national background, it is tempting to assume that the Scottish Civic Trust was pushing at an already open door. It is important to remember, however, that many in British Rail regarded the formation of the Railway Heritage Trust as a means of ensuring proper conservation attention to heritage assets in British Rail's ownership *which remained operational.* Even under partnership arrangements, there was no interest within British Rail in spending significant sums of money on the upkeep of structures for which there was now no operational need whatsoever.

As it happens, two things occurred which must have given British Rail some heart in believing that the new Scottish viaducts group would be worth pursuing. Firstly, in August 1984, the independent reports generally pointed at lower repair and/or maintenance costs for the four sample structures than British Rail's own internal estimates had suggested. Owners are perhaps understandably often nervous and over-pessimistic about the cost of repairing listed structures. Whilst there may on occasion be justification in opting for an absolutely tip-top and fully authentic repair scheme, the security and, as importantly, the character of 'workaday' structure such as railway viaducts can be protected in most cases through something less than a full-blown repair scheme.

The other encouraging factor for British Rail must have been the positive attitude of the Scottish Civic Trust and other partners. The group did not dwell on the faults of the past, but sought to find practical solutions for individual redundant viaducts. The group also adopted four main principles on becoming the Scottish Joint Viaducts Committee which demonstrates the pragmatic approach

taken. As John Gerrard explained in a talk he gave to a conference of the Association of Conservation Officers in Edinburgh on 29 March 1990, these four main principles were:

1   The rescue formula for an individual viaduct must include a financial contribution by British Rail at least equivalent to alternative demolition cost.

2   There should be a broadly based search for the remaining elements of the funding package, targeting the individual aspects of each viaduct.

3   It was axiomatic that the responsibility for the future ownership and maintenance of each viaduct would pass from British Rail to another responsible body – this might for example be a local authority or a local trust set up for the purpose.

4   That all redundant viaducts in British Rail's ownership would be graded by architectural/historical/engineering importance and by structural condition, with those ranking highly in both aspects receiving priority.

Impact of the Scottish Joint Viaducts Committee

How successful then has the Scottish Joint Viaducts Committee been in the fifteen years since its inception? The first official recognition of the value of the Committee came relatively early. In response to a Monopolies and Mergers Commission report on British Rail's property activities, the Department of Transport carried out a review of funding arrangements for British Rail liabilities for 'burdensome properties'. Referring to the Scottish Joints Viaducts Committee, the review noted that;

There is general agreement among participants in the Committee that it is proving a helpful forum for highlighting and discussing the problems associated with the Scottish Viaducts; and that is helping to pool ideas for overcoming the problems. The Property Board [of British Rail] believe it is a good experience and in the right direction and they say that they have found the presence of an industrial archaeologist seconded to the Scottish Office particularly helpful.[5] Progress is being made slowly and patiently. The Government might therefore assist further by helping to establish a similar committee to look after BR's problems with the listing of redundant viaducts in England and Wales.

In the light of that report, the Department of Transport invited interested parties to meet and discuss the possibility of forming a similar committee for England and Wales; after a preliminary meeting which discussed experience in Scotland, the English and Welsh Viaducts Committee had its first full meeting in December 1987.

But while imitation might be the sincerest form of flattery, the Scottish Committee itself did not stand still. Membership was opened so that any other local authority interested in finding a solution for a disused viaduct in its area could come along. The Strathclyde Passenger Transport Executive – a major rail 'player' in the West of Scotland – also took a permanent seat, as did the Institution of Civil Engineers' Historical Panel. SusTrans, a charity actually engaged in converting disused railways to footpaths and cycle tracks, also usefully joined the Committee.

As the Department of Transport Review envisaged, progress has been inevitably slow and steady. In the vast majority of cases, options for putting redundant railway viaducts to some worthwhile use are somewhat limited. In almost all cases, the only option is some kind of footpath or cycleway and for that reason, a long term solution can only usually be found once a national or local group decides to set up some kind of route in which the viaduct can play a part. That said, formal rail routes do have the advantage mentioned earlier in that the

Figure 5. Lower Largo Viaduct, handed over to North East Fife District Council by British Rail in 1990 with an endowment equivalent to the hypothetical cost of demolition. (R Hobbs, from *Scottish Steam in Colour*, by H Ballantyne (Jane's Publishing Company, 1996)

ruling gradients which the railway engineers provided for steam locomotives provide very easily graded routes for pedestrian and cycle traffic. As more and more local authorities turn to the needs of these forms of transport, former railway routes become particularly attractive – and a viaduct is often a major landscape feature within the route.

Three of the four viaducts identified by the Committee as top priority have been, or are being, restored as part of a countryside route. Camps Viaduct in West Lothian is now a major feature in the Almondell Park and North Water Viaduct in Angus has been taken into local authority ownership as part of a cycleway. Bilston Glen viaduct Midlothian has been restored and taken over by the Edinburgh Green Belt Trust as part of its network of routes. All three viaducts have been resorted with

a combination of funding, including a grant from Historic Scotland and some input from the Railway Heritage Trust. Other viaducts have also found satisfactory new 'homes'. The Balmossie viaduct, near Dundee, was handed over by British Rail to the City Council in 1988. Two years later, North East Fife District Council took over ownership of Lower Largo Viaduct (see Figure 5). In both cases the transfer was accompanied by an endowment from British Rail to the level of demolition costs which they would otherwise have had to incur. In this climate of seeing redundant viaducts as more useful than simply as landscape features, a fair number of viaducts are today facing a much more certain future than was once the case. Even Laigh Milton Viaduct – not strictly a former British Rail property – has been the subject of a comprehensive repair scheme.

Figure 6. A casualty of redundancy, Loudounhill Viaduct, near Kilmarnock, demolished in 1986. (J R Hume, 1974)

Figure 7. Leaderfoot Viaduct in majestic stride across the Scottish Borders, one of the four viaducts singled out for survey by British Rail as representative of the redundant stock across Scotland. (Historic Scotland)

Not all viaducts have survived, of course. Loudounhill Viaduct, near Kilmarnock, was for example demolished in 1986 following the granting of listed building consent on appeal to the Secretary of State (see Figure 6). But whilst losses are, of course, unfortunate, liaison through the Scottish Joint Viaducts Committee does provide a forum through which every avenue can be explored.

Leaderfoot

What, then, of Leaderfoot, the viaduct which started all the fuss and the fourth of the four major viaducts identified at the outset by the Committee? After both Borders Regional Council and the National Trust for Scotland had considered taking the structure into ownership, an agreement was reached between Historic Scotland and British Rail that the viaduct could be taken into care after it had received a comprehensive scheme of repairs (see Figure 7). The repairs were carried out between 1991 and 1994

at a cost of close on one million pounds, with approximately one-third of the cost each coming from British Rail, Historic Scotland and the Railway Heritage Trust. The British Rail Property Board then worked to put together a clean title including all necessary wayleaves to allow adequate access to keep the viaduct in good order. These legal arrangements have been rather more protracted than anyone would have wished or hoped. Amazingly, not all of the arches of the viaduct turned out to be in railway ownership, but the underlying issue being looked at now is how best to manage and curate the viaduct into the future, not whether it has a future.

There is, of course, a delightful irony in the fact that a class of structures as utilitarian as nineteenth-century railway bridges and viaducts has come to be fully accepted as part of Scotland's built heritage – so much so that the Forth Bridge (our largest Category A listed building and a proposed World

Heritage site) is probably the only Scottish structure whose silhouette would be recognised internationally. It was, after all, no less a personage than William Morris who, at a meeting in Edinburgh in 1889, said: 'As for an iron architecture, there never was and never could be such. Every improvement in the art of engineering made the use of iron more ugly, until at last they had that supreme specimen of ugliness, the Forth Bridge'.[6] By no means all of our railway viaducts are high architecture, but they were generally built with an economy and fitness for purpose which look well to our late twentieth-century eyes. It is encouraging that so many have managed to survive redundancy to get a 'second wind'.

NOTES

1. Gordon Biddle, *The Railway Surveyors* (Ian Allan, BR Property Board, 1990).
2. H A Vallance, *The Highland Railway* (1938).
3. David Walker, 'Listing in Scotland: Origins, Survey and Resurvey', *Transactions of the Ancient Monuments Society*, Vol 38 (AMS, 1994).
4. Gordon Biddle and O S Nock, *The Railway Heritage of Britain* (Michael Joseph, London, 1983).
5. This was, of course, a reference to the input of John Hume!
6. William Morris, *News from Nowhere and Selected Writings and Designs* (Harmondsworth, Penguin, 1984).

14

MARK WATSON

Change for the Better: Luma Lamp Factories, Glass-clad Modernism and Reworked Textile Mills

Paradoxically, conservation of the built heritage has more to do with the future than the past. The best use for a historic building is often that for which it was designed, but we do not know that a better use might not arise at some point in the future.[1] 'Conserve as found' is a mantra appropriate to the repair of most traditional buildings, but not in all cases to the exclusion of a well researched and considered modern intervention.[2] Currently these are more likely to be found in industrial and modern architecture than in more conventional architecture, but the lessons learnt in the adaptation of industrial buildings will be increasingly applicable to all building types. This paper examines through case studies some of the consequences of grasping the nettle of radical change. Each case had to be assessed on its own merits. Incisions, extensions, re-claddings and remodellings can, in the right circumstances, be done in such a way as to preserve or enhance the essential character of a historic building.

Background

The production by the State of national inventories of British buildings and monuments lagged behind most European countries. The first lists came after the Second World War, in tandem with Town Planning legislation. More recent lists build on exhaustive fieldwork, such as John Hume's exemplary work in Scotland in the 1960s and 1970s. Thanks to the interest in the subject by David Walker, his predecessor as Chief Inspector of Historic Buildings, industrial buildings in Scotland were probably better represented in early lists than their equivalents in most other countries.

The identification stage has not yet run its course, and there will be a continuing need to update and advance as the patrimony of the future is still being built. Heritage is a finite resource, but history does not come to a stop, and neither does the construction of new buildings, a small proportion of which will be regarded as key monuments to the end of the millennium. A perhaps unforeseen consequence of the addition of international modernism to the canon of historic architectural styles has been the introduction to Historic Buildings inspectors, conservation officers and conservation architects of modernism as a way of thinking, altering and conserving. Increasingly, conservation decisions and interventions made in historic buildings and places will themselves be seen as worth conserving: witness concern raised by the Twentieth Century Society over proposed alterations to the late Sir James Stirling's work for the Tate Gallery at Albert Dock, Liverpool. The most striking alterations, which may or may not be seen as meritorious by our successors, occur when buildings change use.

A change of use is sometimes in itself sufficient to change attitudes: witness the discovery by Peter Brook for his *Mahabarata* in 1988 of the old Museum of Transport, Glasgow. It was expected to be demolished on relocation of the museum from the leaking Coplawhill Tram Depot. Brook saw it as 'an industrial cathedral which connects art and humanity', and suddenly the place had a new lease of life, without substantial physical change to the building, and experimental theatre in Scotland was revolutionised.[3]

Most changes of use do require some change to historic fabric. As such alterations increase in number, and as sustainability turns development from green to brown fields, there has been a perceptible shift in conservation thinking away from all-or-nothing preservation towards the more flexible approach offered by design briefs, management agreements, conservation plans and character appraisals, whether of a building or a landscape. This is already evident in other developed countries, from Finland to Australia, and is particularly applicable when functions change.

The Manes Gallery was built, abutting a Renaissance water tower in Prague, in the international modern style in 1923. The resulting horizontal and vertical, light and dark contrasts today seems the only natural and appropriate way of fusing new and old in that location. It has taken considerably longer for such an approach to be accepted in Britain.

In Germany, perceptions of the most devastated parts of the Ruhrgebiet have been transformed by the Emscher Park IBA (Internationalen Bauaustellung), started in 1989. Here, the Meiderich Steelworks in Duisberg Nord, which closed in 1985, is the focus of an ecological landscape park that comes astonishingly alive at night thanks to Jonathan Park's multi-coloured lighting scheme (see Figure 1). A restaurant, night club and concert halls have been fitted into the power station and blowing engine house, over and around surviving plant, and the Piazza Metallica casting floor aptly hosts heavy metal performances to a backdrop of blast furnaces built in 1954–73. At Oberhausen, a 116-metre high dry gasholder of 1928 is now an outstanding exhibition space and lookout point. Zollverein XII pit near Essen, a 1930 symmetrical modernist coal mine complex of steel frames and brick infill, is being developed for a variety of purposes, including a design museum by Foster Associates, and its coking plant is to be illuminated by Lighting Architects Group.[4]

The sculptural treatment by French architects Reichen et Robert of former textile mills in Lille (see Figure 2) and Tourcoing shows that older, and some not so very old, industrial buildings are ca-

pable of receiving creative interventions.[5] These robust rectangles of blackened brick have responded well to the changes made to them, using the successors to the modern materials that the building type spawned in the first place. Another example of such an innovative stance, by Stephenson Architecture, is a tar warehouse, now offices and music studios at Eastgate, Castlefield, Manchester (see Figure 3), with water tower remodelled, a sharp glazed corner added, and windows knocked together into vertical strips.

While such a wilful approach is not often inflicted on listed buildings in Scotland, there are circumstances where a radically new approach is warranted. These may be summarised as where it is necessary to distinguish new from old, and where openings are inadequate in buildings designed to perform a specific function that has now ceased. A prime exponent is Richard Murphy, in his remodelling of the Fruitmarket Gallery, Edinburgh, and a 1930s garage to create Dundee Contemporary Arts. He describes his approach as 'ruining buildings' in the manner of Carlo Scarpa.

The following case studies will concentrate on buildings which have intrinsic merit beyond simply offering a foil to creative architects. They will, however, be grouped according to the form of intervention adopted.

Glazed additions

Modern glass structures are sometimes the most appropriate ways to extend an old building, to link old and new, or to link two old buildings. An emphatic switch from solid to void may serve to better define the original building than would a pastiche repetition in the same style. An example of the first case is Port Glasgow Town Hall, with a striking glazed box added by Page and Park Architects towards a vacant parking lot and vistas opened by new roads and missing townscape. The Town Hall in Lisburn, County Antrim, has similarly been turned round to better dominate the street scene, a glazed link clearly distinguishing old and new elements of the Irish Linen Centre (Chaplin Hall Black Douglas, 1995). A barn at Tadcaster has been joined by glass to a new swimming

Figure 1. The Meiderich Steelworks in Duisberg Nord, Germany, closed in 1985, and now one of the principal features within IBA Emscher Park, begun in 1989. (Mark Watson, 1996)

Figure 2. Former Le Blan flax mill in Lille, France, now 'La Filature', converted *circa* 1979 (Mark Watson, 1991)

Figure 3. Eastgate tar warehouse, Castlefield, Manchester, England, after conversion. (Mark Watson, 1996)

Figure 4. Bank Mills, Leeds, England, after office conversion incorporating glazed links. Left: spinning mill; right: raw flax warehouse. (Mark Watson, 1996)

pool with wave-like roof (architects Goddard Manton Partnership). The Bradford Wool Exchange (Lockwood and Mawson) now has a planar glazed link which works better than the dull elevation that preceded it. A modern balconied link by Pollard Thomas and Edwards between two parts of the Anchor Brewery next to Tower Bridge, London pays homage to the originally louvered area that cooled the wort. On a smaller scale is the lift tower added to St Francis Friary, Glasgow, also by Page and Park, the stair at Wellpark School, Glasgow by Elder and Cannon, and the bridge between engine house and Mill Number Three at New Lanark, following the route once taken by rope drives.

Perhaps more controversially, modern glazed structures have been used to replace parts of existing building where superior performance and aesthetics can be achieved. Law and Dunbar-Nasmith have transformed the impression made by the Festival Theatre, Edinburgh, on the street, and views that may be obtained from it of Surgeons Hall opposite. It was the auditorium of the existing theatre which was of interest, not its humdrum 1920s front-of-house, nor its inadequate stage and backstage facilities. Whilst the auditorium was retained and refurbished, other areas were dispensible.

Glazed links

Bank Mills, Leeds (see Figure 4) comprised three detached brick buildings of the 1830s within a conservation area designated by the Leeds Urban Development Corporation. One of the spinning mills has now been linked to a warehouse by means of a fully glazed service tower, stair and lift. The choice of modern systems has allowed the two buildings to be read as retaining their own distinctive functions, separated to protect against fire, whereas a brick-built solid link in a similar style would have blurred that distinction ...

The Aberdeen Maritime Museum, so as to adequately represent the oil industry, required further space and higher ceilings than were offered by Provost Ross's House. The solution, by Aberdeen City Council Architects, was to expand to absorb an empty Victorian church (Trinity Congregational, 1877), and fill the space between with a glazed curtain wall (see Figure 5). This had the full support of the National Trust for Scotland and of Historic Scotland. A pastiche infill to mimic two such disparate buildings was not even considered. The result, best seen at night, won an RIAS award.

Drumlanrig's Tower, Hawick, has been made to stand out from the accretions of an 18th–19th-century coaching Inn by a glazed link on several levels by Gray Marshall Associates for the Scottish Historic Buildings Trust.

Other modern glazed atria have turned around architectural perceptions, such as the roofing of Princes Square, Glasgow, and of the courtyards between Aberdeen Town House and Sheriff Court, or between the two ranges of Cromarty Brewery, for Robert Gordon's University.

Glazed incisions

Another scenario that sometimes arises is the need to introduce light into a building inadequately supplied with natural light for its new purpose. In some circumstances the appropriate solution is to repeat the fenestration type and rhythm already suggested by the building in question: examples are the additional rows of horizontal attic level windows above the cornices of Seafield Works in Dundee, West Bridge Mill in Kirkcaldy, and Mid Mill, Stanley Mills, Perthshire. Further north, the Gaelic Free Church at Inverness, on being abandoned by the congregation in favour of a large bungalow, was acquired for use by a bookseller. Owing to road levels lowered in the mid-nineteenth century, the existing arched windows were too high to serve as shop fronts. Rather than elongate the original windows and face the issue of designing complex new astragals, here it was put to the applicant that simple new windows well beneath the cills would

suffice, and so it has proved. Other cases suggest an entirely different approach, introducing windows of alternative scale and proportion.

At Plockton Free Church the roof was sagging. The building was very important to the history of the area, due to the wholesale transfer of allegiance in the 1843 Disruption from the adjacent Parliamentary church. But by 1990, the congregation had fallen to six, none of whom would permit use of the church for any purpose that might involve alcohol or music, or give over for parking or amenity any of the sizeable garden of the manse next door. Skye and Lochalsh District Council obligingly submitted an application to demolish the church and build new houses on the site. This was resisted, just short of a public local inquiry, but it became apparent that only a residential use could be accepted, at the expense of the pews, integral communion table and tiered pulpit.

The main design issue was: how to introduce windows to a street elevation that, true to its fundamentalist origins, looks more like a barn than a church? The solution, promoted by the area Historic Buildings Inspector, and following the barn theme, was a series of glazed vertical slots to either side of the boarded main door. This allowed the original big windows to the gables and the loch to come into their own. Repairs by architects Philip Cocker and Partners were part funded by the Secretary of State under the Historic Buildings Repair Scheme.

Bonnington Bond, Leith, has been converted to offices occupied by a number of organisations, including Scottish Natural Heritage. It was evident that natural light was insufficient in each of the four buildings on the site. That in the centre, a sugar warehouse, was demolished, while that to the south forms phase one. In order to retain on three sides the appearance of regular rows of small windows that characterise its original use as a floor maltings, it was decided to cut two great gashes into one elevation, and line them with glass. The existing structure and regular iron columns have been retained, and those columns that came out of the incisions have been used within a new projecting stair well.

In Dundee, the Dundee Industrial Association was set up to offer communal managed workspace to small businesses. The withdrawal of Tay Textiles from a number of small jute mills gave the opportunity to concentrate a small industrial estate in the centre of the Scouringburn, re-designated the Blackness Industrial Improvement Area. The core of the area is now a conservation area, and Dundee

Figure 5. Aberdeen Maritime Museum, Scotland, showing the glazed link connecting the sixteenth-century Provost Ross House with the neighbouring Trinity Church. (Positive Image, Mike Davidson, Aberdeen, 1997)

Heritage have their textile interpretation centre at nearby Verdant Works. The Association lets out four former mills (Meadow, South Dudhope, Burnside and Douglas) and demolished two more (Anchor and West Dudhope).

Douglas Mill (see Figures 6, 7 and 8) was built for Robert Gilroy in 1835, and has a number of characteristics of that period: two storey and attic, with built-in engine, boiler house and chimney. While the beam section in the stair and in the fireproof ceiling over the boiler-house corresponds to that of other mills of the period, the rest of the mill has beams with a broad lower flange, and columns with Egyptian papyrus capitals (a stylistic feature favoured by the Dundee engineers Robertson and Orchar, established in 1857, and who employed the column type until at least 1885, when they completed Bowbridge Works). The single-span, two piece arched cast-iron roof is unique of its type in Scotland.[6]

The chimney was long ago reduced by removal of its upper brick part, leaving the stone base projecting at eaves level. To prevent water ingress, a little roof has been fashioned for it. The alternative of lowering it in height and continuing the roof slope over it was rebuffed, and now it reads very clearly as an engaged mill chimney similar to that at Verdant Works. Another early chimney, that of Claverhouse Bleachworks, 1838, has also been roofed at a reduced height, as part of a housing development.

At first the easily accessible ground floor was all that was let. The first floor was loaned to Dundee Heritage for the storage of machinery from the College of Technology, which is now either part of the working display at Verdant Works or scrapped. The fact that only a single stair served the upper floors inhibited more intensive use. The solution was to insert a second stair to serve as the principal access to the upper floors, which could then be divided to provide a variety of different lettable

Figure 6. Douglas Mill, Dundee, Scotland, before intervention. (Crown Copyright: RCAHMS)

Figure 7. Douglas Mill, Dundee, Scotland, during insertion of stair into the former engine house. (Mark Watson, 1994)

Figure 8. Douglas Mill, Dundee, Scotland, after insertion of the new fanlight, and the installation of upturned columns as lamp standards. (Mark Watson, 1995)

spaces. The easiest route for a new stair proved to be via the engine house because this already occupied a vertical slot through the building adjacent to the old spiral stair. The work allowed access to the engine foundations: a slot for a 16-foot diameter flywheel, a bearing wall for the column and two tall ashlar bearing blocks for the cylinder, laced through by grooves for anchor bolts. The engine, rated at 30 hp, was of a similar size and, in mirror image, layout, to that still at Garlogie in Aberdeenshire. Power take-up appears to have been via a vertical shaft on the other face of the engine house wall. At attic level it was geared to directly drive the rope drum of a goods hoist, which survives.

So, in terms of cultural value, the Douglas Mill engine is of lesser importance than that at Garlogie, the only surviving *in situ* rotative engine in Scotland.[7] On the other hand, more can be learned about the linkages between engine and mill as the whole mill survives. The structural fabric reveals ways it was used to transmit power, accommodate workers and carry goods. Its value in establishing typologies lies in its being part of an identifiable group. Other mills in the city that had similar engines have had some of that evidence lost on the installation of larger engines of different types (e.g. at Dura, Pitalpin, Upper Dens and Tay Works). Verdant Works' slightly broader (double windowed) engine house retains archaeological potential, as does the Boulton and Watt engine house of 1799 at East Mill, and there is scope for comparison with the bigger engine houses at Logie Works, recorded by RCAHMS prior to alteration in a housing conversion.

The engine at Douglas Mill was externally expressed by a single high window, possibly once arched, later crudely divided into two by the addition of a mezzanine. Given the elevated position of the engine, the ground floor was blind. The solution here was to cut a single slot down to the ground. The resulting tall and clearly modern fanlight makes the stair very light (Figure 8). Two upturned columns salvaged from another mill stand sentry to mark the entrance. The stair was so oriented as to arrive at the ground by removing one of the two stone pillars that carried the cylinder. The rest of the foundations are preserved and capable of illustrating the form of engine that was installed here. Now access is given to a number of small but high-tech businesses, some working in the field of bio-technology. So at the cost of some original fabric, and a changed appearance, the building is more intensively used, has a more secure future and is better able to be interpreted. The architect for the adaptation was George Reid of the William Wilson Partnership.

Beam engine houses also proved to be the natural route for stairs and lifts in the conversions of Upper Dens Mill, Dundee (1833/50, converted 1984 by Baxter Clark and Paul for Hillcrest Housing Association) and West Bridge Mill, Kirkcaldy (1857, converted to a foyer in 1996 by David Bell of RPS Cairns for Link Housing Association). In each case the foundations were already missing due to replacement of engines, and the open void allowed impressive new stairs to reach as far as the fireproof engine house ceiling before adopting more modest scales in the top two floors. Some persuasion was required in the case of West Bridge Mill to demonstrate to consultant engineers that the iron frame was sound. A new tripartite Georgian door was installed, perhaps anachronistically, in Upper Dens Mill, whereas a more modern approach could be taken at West Bridge Mill through an existing mysteriously large arch.

The conversion to housing of nine mill buildings in Dundee, and one in Kirkcaldy, is a remarkable success story, so much so that it is said that the market for tenement flats has been depressed by the availability of new flats with better views in converted mills. Funding for these came from Scottish Homes, housing associations and the private sector.

In only three cases was a Historic Building Repair Grant from the Secretary of State also needed. Seven of the Dundee buildings were primarily spinning mills, the other two being for dyeing and finishing. A balance, to reflect the variety of building types in the industry is obtained by three power loom weaving factories in Forfar, Brechin and Arbroath, a hand loom factory, now a hotel, in Montrose, and a damask warehouse in Dunfermline. In most cases the development package necessarily included a degree of demolition and new-build to cross-fertilise the conversion.

The glass curtain wall

As more twentieth-century buildings are being recognised as historically valuable, the question will increasingly arise as to whether an external skin can be expendable. Where conservation thinking is slanted towards external appearances, as it has been where most protected buildings are of solid masonry construction, it can be disconcerting to find that some relatively modern claddings have finite lives.

In the context of ways that many vernacular buildings have been repaired over the years, the concept of an exchangeable external skin may not be so alien after all. It is now recognised that ancient buildings like Scottish tower houses have a history of repeated applications of harl both as protective coating and as architectural embellishment in a variety of rich colours. The ideal of pure and maintenance-free exposed stone is the exception, not the rule, and depended on the application of nineteenth-century technology in sawing stone and pressing bricks. Even the Ancient Greek and Egyptian monuments that inspired severe neo-classicism were originally gaudily painted. In this Scotland has much in common with the architecture of central Europe. The analogy applies equally to weatherboarded and tile-hung houses, timber-framed buildings, cob and turf houses, thatched and slated roofs. The covering is more or less ephemeral: a sacrificial layer which may be replaced sooner or later, and a building so treated may be no less authentic than one stripped clean, or 'scraped', so long as its internal frame exists.

With this in mind the conservation of a steel

skeleton or reinforced concrete framed building becomes less of a philosophical quagmire. The role of the Essex firm of Crittalls in developing a glazing system capable of cladding a building was critical in the development of modern architecture, being used even at the Bauhaus in Dessau, so it is important that some original examples of their work should be protected as such. However, there are some instances when replacement becomes unavoidable. Provided the replacement is of sufficient, or arguably superior, quality, a pioneering modern movement building can still have meaning when reclad.

Sir E Owen Williams led the adoption in Britain of curtain walling hung from mushroom slab reinforced concrete framed floors. His three buildings for the *Daily Express* take this to extremes, to the extent that the entire front facades are glass and vitrolite in slim-section steel Crittall frames. These are coming to the end of their lives: they leak and suffer from excessive solar gain. Modern glazing systems offer unquestionably superior performance, and to prevent the possibility of upgrading would be to force eventual abandonment. *The Manchester Daily Express* building (see Figure 9), Ancoats Road, completed in 1939, and now occupied by the *Sunday Sport*, was therefore reclad in 1995 by architects MHA in a different but roughly matching system. At the same time the opportunity was taken to enlarge the building in a similar style, fill in the cantilevered loading bay and install a set-back mezzanine. The Glasgow equivalent, now occupied by the *Glasgow Herald* (see Figure 10), has listed building consent for similar upgrading, not yet carried out, obtained by architects BDP.

Figure 9. The former *Daily Express* building (now *Daily Sport*), Manchester, England, after alterations in 1995. (Mark Watson, 1996)

Figure 10. The *Glasgow Herald* building (formerly *Daily Express*), Glasgow, Scotland, as built. (Mark Watson, 1996)

One of the best example of upgraded curtain walls to date are those at Boots D10 Wet Processes building, Nottingham, within a model industrial estate far from public roads. This masterpiece of functionalism was designed by Sir Owen Williams in 1930–33. Some criticism has been levelled at the substitution in 1992–94 of highly reflective, hermetically sealed glass, in place of the original transparent and hinged windows evident in photographs of 1931.[8] However the renewed elevation is far closer to the spirit of the original than the factory had become in the 1980s and remains in parts not yet upgraded. The neat dark green framing had by then been repainted in lighter eye-catching colours, and much of the glass had been coated in films or painted, or obscured by external blinds in attempts to repel the sun.

The reinforced concrete (mushroom columns and flat slabs) has been repaired where necessary, and the internal atria are still astonishing. The new glass and galvanised steel framing (Crittall again), and re-coated concrete, means that the external finish of the main elevation is new, but is a considerable enhancement over the original fabric. Jan Sosna of AMEC carried out the design work, and the considerable negotiation with English Heritage and two local authorities to demonstrate that the existing glazing should not be kept to the main elevation.[9] The bulk of the factory to the rear retains the original glazing system for comparison. 'D10 is no living Museum. This magnificent building is still central to the company's manufacturing interests', say Boots.[10] Changing the building allowed its essential character to be enhanced without requiring a change of use.

Green's Playhouse in Dundee (see Figures 11 to 14) was outstanding on a number of counts: its sheer bulk, as became apparent with the construction of the inner ring road; its capacity, which at 4,126 was the second largest number of seats in a single cinema auditorium in Europe (the largest, also Green's, was the Apollo, Glasgow, which was demolished in 1988); as representative of a city which had more cinemas per head than any other, albeit the majority were much more makeshift; a lavish interior of gilded Corinthian columns by John Alexander; and

lastly, an advertising tower taller than any other in the UK, the ultimate in night architecture, overtaken only by Tait's Empire Exhibition Tower of the same year. Here, and for the stylish cafe and vestibule, the modernist design skills of Joseph Emberton (also of buildings in Blackpool and Simpsons, Piccadilly) were employed.[11]

The tower was until recently the least highly regarded attribute. In 1972 when the glass started to show signs of decay, it was simply reclad in a dull profiled sheet metal (Figure 12). The lights were extinguished and the tower looked quite hideous. The reason for the listing of the cinema, and at Category A, of national importance, lay in the stupendous auditorium. However when this burned down in 1995, attention focused on the need to encourage Mecca to rebuild their bingo hall in the city centre, to explore the archaeological potential of a site within medieval Dundee,[12] and to reinstate the advertising tower (see Figure 13).

This last proved controversial, given proximity to a great medieval church tower and, next door, a tolerably good, or at least worthy, Victorian gothic spire by Charles Wilson. Even when first built, the Dundee Institute of Architects and Dundee Arts Society had soundly condemned 'the Nethergate Offence'. However the tower had the support of The Royal Fine Art Commission, and of the area Historic Buildings Inspector, and an application to demolish was withdrawn.

It proved necessary to remove the tower temporarily to give access to the site. This permitted a close inspection of the original bolted and riveted steel structure, and refabrication of the flanking cylinders, before re-erection under the supervision of architects Cooper Cromar. The rear rendered brick tower was shortened, emphasising the verticality of the tower, and incidentally exposing it to startling effect at night from across the Tay. The area devoted to lettering was reduced. A state of the art lighting system was brought in, using all of Mecca's many colours, and in a yo-yo fashion rather than the original waterfall effect.

Because all of the glass was renewed, it might be considered that the tower is simply a new building. However the skeleton is original, and without it

Figure 11. Green's Playhouse, Dundee, Scotland, as it was *circa* 1936. (Crown Copyright: RCAHMS)

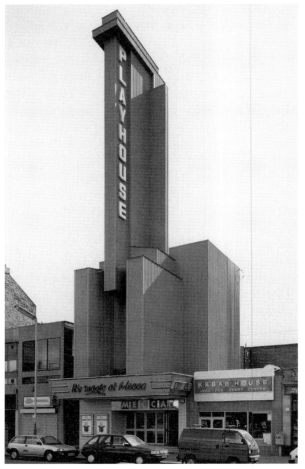

Figure 12. Green's Playhouse, Dundee, Scotland, after re-cladding with sheet metal in 1972. (Crown Copyright: RCAHMS)

planning permission might never have been granted for such a striking advertisement. This case illustrates ways in which perceptions of what constitutes the significance of a monument may change. That which had recently been a glorious auditorium within an undistinguished rump has been transformed into a modern auditorium with a glitzy art deco exterior missing since the hey-day of cinema.

Of course, many attempts at re-cladding set out to alter architectural appearance, rather than conserve the qualities of the original design, and the results are often abysmal. Examples include aluminium replacements in another pioneering curtain wall in Nottingham, Viyella House, by F A Broadhead, or the overcladding of J J Burnet's Wallace

Scott Tailoring Institute, Cathcart, now happily removed by Cooper Cromar for Scottish Power. However the achievement at Boots, Ancoats, and Green's in Dundee, show that conservation of modern buildings can and should be more than skin deep.

Remodelling within a steel frame

Lastly, the Luma Lightbulb factory in Glasgow is an example of a building radically transformed, with listed building consent, in a way that has enhanced its meaning, or cultural value, despite the extent of the changes to it. The original Luma Lightbulb factory in Stockholm was a co-operative enterprise. The factory is an E-shaped pile of modernist

Figure 13. Green's Playhouse, Dundee, Scotland, after sheet-metal cladding had been removed following the fire. (Mark Watson, 1995)

Figure 14. Green's Playhouse, Dundee, Scotland, after reinstatement of tower by Mecca (Mark Watson: 1998)

reinforced concrete buildings by the architect Artur von Chmalensee, begun in 1929 and completed in the 1940s. The most striking feature is a rectangular lamp testing tower, fully-glazed excepting the reinforced concrete frame. The factory is now occupied by a multitude of small businesses.[13]

The Scottish and Swedish Wholesale Co-operative Societies developed a number of mutually beneficial linkages during the 1930s. The Swedish Luma Lightbulb Factory of 1939 was the most prominent result in Scotland, and is today the main survivor of the once extensive Shieldhall industrial estate established by SCWS in Glasgow. The Society's architect, Cornelius Armour, created a curved 26-metre high lamp testing tower which, like

the light bulbs made there, was redolent of the spirit of the age. The factory was prominently situated on the arterial road that led in 1938 to the Empire Exhibition Ground.

However, following a period in the 1970s as 'Caravanland', it fell into severe dereliction (see Figure 15). The building was listed in 1988, but various schemes for hotel and office uses in the early 1990s came to nothing. The potential of the tower was briefly highlighted by an art student's temporary lighting installation, but it is thanks to the drive and determination of the community-based Linthouse Housing Association, recognising a strong local affection for the building, that funding obstacles were overcome. The original factory was

Figure 15. The Luma Lamp Factory, Glasgow, Scotland, after several years of dereliction, *circa* 1990. (Crown Copyright: RCAHMS)

Figure 16. The Luma Lamp Factory, Glasgow, during conversion work. (Mark Watson, 1996)

adapted to provide 43 homes for sale (they went rapidly), a two-storey office in the lamp testing tower, and 12 new social housing units for rent in three new blocks at the rear.

The main assembly area to the right of the tower had been on two floors, the upper one of which, where the filaments were wound, had no windows at eye level, all natural light coming from above to reduce glare for the workers. As it stood, the building was quite unsuited to a housing use without removal and remodelling of all the rendered brick infill. So architects Cornelius McClymont created within the existing robust steel framework to the right of the tower four four-storey tenements, in classic Glaswegian fashion, but with all the emphasis on long horizontal window bands, and judicially placed additional portholes. The three bays to the left of the tower and a new atrium had their windows slightly reduced, but otherwise corresponded more closely to the existing arrangement. Crittall supplied all the new steel windows, double glazed and with a slightly heavier section that was disguised by a reversion from cream to the original black colour scheme. The new flexible 'cement free anti-crack' acrylic render is expected to retain a brilliant whiteness much longer than did the original cement harl (coming full circle, investigation of the damage now known to be done by cement to traditional lime-built buildings was used as an argument against cement even when originally used on this building).

Described as one of Glasgow's 'best known art deco buildings'[14] (although it is doubtful that it was seen as such a style when built) the factory now is considerably more art deco than it was in 1938. It is as if an ocean liner were docked there, having picked up *en route* some tips on proportion and massing from Eric Mendelsohn. It is '... a vigorous intervention, not one for purists', according to Building Design.[15] The project was planned in 1993–94, completed in 1996 (see Figure 16), and won the RICS Regeneration Award in 1997. The role of the building as a beacon of light is highlighted by an imaginative lighting scheme, and the lamp testing tower shines out as it did before the war. Its past function is therefore not forgotten and the project may be considered a conservation success thanks to, not despite, radical alteration.

NOTES

The views expressed in this paper are those of Mark Watson, and not necessarily those of Historic Scotland.

1. The rumination on which this paper is based stems from a panel discussion staged in 1997 by the Architectural Heritage Society of Scotland between the author, Mia Scott, John Gerrard and James Simpson. He thanks also Bernie Goslin, Richard Emerson and Deborah Mays for their suggestions.

2. See James Strike, *Architecture in Conservation: Managing Development at Historic Sites* (Routledge, London, 1994), or Giles Worsley, 'Breaking the Aspic Mould', in *Perspectives*, May 1995.

3. Theatre Programme, *La Tragédie de Carmen* (1990) and *Scotland on Sunday* 5 July 1990, p 19.

4. TICCIH Intermediate Conference 1995, reported by Peter Wakelin in, *Industrial Archaeology News* 93, 1995; IBA Emscher Park *Katalog zum Stand der Projekte Frühjahr* (1993); Robert Holden, in *Architects' Journal*, 9 November 1995, pp 23–6; *Building Design*, 17 January 1997, pp 12–13.

5. Lise Grenier and Hans Wieser-Benedetti, *Les Chateaux de l'Industrie* (1979), pp 294–301, and see Binney, Machin and Powell, *Bright Future: The Re-use of Industrial Buildings* (Save Britain's Heritage, London, 1990), pp 28–9.

6. Mark Watson, *Jute and Flax Mills in Dundee* (Hutton Press, Tayport, 1990), pp 36, 46, 49, 135, 168, 173, 204.

7. G D Hay and G P Stell, *Monuments of Industry* (RCAHMS/HMSO, Edinburgh, 1986), pp 131–5. Garlogie Engine is now in the care of Aberdeenshire Heritage.

8. S MacDonald, in S MacDonald (ed), *Modern Matters* (Donhead, Shaftesbury, 1996), pp 95–6, and *Architects' Journal*, 25 July 1996, p 14.

9. Information gathered at Docomomo UK Nottingham Symposium, 1996, and in *Architects' Journal*, 3 November 1994, pp 31–41. The *Manchester Daily Express* is described in *Architects' Journal*, 18 January 1996, pp 24–5.

10. The Boots Company, *Celebrating the renovation of D10*, 1994.

11. C A Harkins, *We Want U In: the Story of a Glasgow*

Institution (Amber Valley Print Centre, Erdington, 1995), pp 101–37, and Richard Gray *Cinemas in Britain* (1996), pp 113–14.

12. Archaeology rewardingly explored by SUAT, *Tayside and Fife Archaeological Journal*, Vol 4 (1998), pp 179–201.

13. Stockholms Stadsmuseum, *Vardifulla Industrimiljoer I Stockholm* (1983).

14. Stuart Blakley, *Scottish Art Monthly*, April 1997 p 11, and also Charles McKean in *Ex-S* (BBC Scotland).

15. Robert Bevan, in *Building Design*, 14 November 1997, pp 14–17.

John Robert Hume OBE: A Select Bibliography

THE following list contains only major writings by John R Hume. It does not include reviews and short articles in the daily press, and other non-specialist publications.

Books: Sole author

The Industrial Archaeology of Glasgow (Blackie, Glasgow and London, 1974).

The Industrial Archaeology of Scotland: Vol 1, The Lowlands and the Borders (Batsford, London, 1976). *Vol 2, The Highlands and Islands* (Batsford, London, 1977).

Isle of Bute (HMSO, Edinburgh, 1988).

Dallas Dhu Distillery (HMSO, London 1988).

Vernacular Building in Ayrshire: an Introduction (Ayr Archaeological and Natural History Society, and Scottish Vernacular Buildings Working Group, Ayr, 1988).

Harbour Lights (SVBWG, Dundee, Edinburgh, 1998).

Books: Joint author

With John Butt, *The Industrial Archaeology of Scotland* (David & Charles, Newton Abbot, 1967, also with I L Donnachie).

With John Butt and I L Donnachie *Industrial History in Pictures: Scotland* (David & Charles, Newton Abbot, 1968).

With Michael Moss, *Clyde Shipbuilding from Old Photographs* (Batsford, London, 1975).

Glasgow as it Was, 3 vols (Hendon Publishing, Nelson, Lancs, 1975–76).

Workshop of the British Empire: Engineering and Shipbuilding in the West of Scotland (Heinemann, London, 1977).

Glasgow at War (Hendon Publishing, Nelson, Lancs, 1977).

Beardmore: the History of a Scottish Industrial Giant (Heinemann Educational, London, 1979).

Old Photographs from Scottish Country Houses (Hendon Publishing, Nelson, Lancs, 1980).

The Making of Scotch Whisky (Ashburton, Devon, 1981)

A Bed of Nails: a History of P MacCallum & Sons Ltd (Lang & Fulton, Greenock, 1983).

Shipbuilders to the World: 125 Years of Harland & Wolff, Belfast, 1861–1986 (Blackstaff, Belfast, 1986).

With Michael Moss and Stephen Elson, *A Plumber's Pastime: Photographs of Victorian Life in the West of Scotland by Matthew Morrison* (Turner & Earnshaw, Burnley, Lancs, 1975).

With Michael Moss and I L Donnachie, *Historic Industrial Scenes, Scotland* (Moorland Publishing, Buxton, 1977).

With Anne Ross, *A New and Splendid Edifice: the Architecture of the University of Glasgow* (University of Glasgow Press, Glasgow, 1975).

With B F Duckham, *Steam Entertainment* (David & Charles, Newton Abbot, 1974).

With Colin Johnston, *Glasgow's Stations* (David & Charles, Newton Abbot, 1979).

With G Douglas and M K Oglethorpe, *Scottish Windmills: a Survey* (SIAS, University of Strathclyde, Glasgow, 1984).

With T Jackson, *George Washington Wilson and Victorian Glasgow* (Keighley Kennedy Bros in association with Aberdeen University Library, Collins Gallery and University of Strathclyde, Aberdeen 1983).

With C Tabraham, *New Abbey Mill* (HMSO, Edinburgh, 1983).

With John Burnett and others, *Scotland's Industrial Past: an introduction to Scotland's industrial history, with a catalogue of preserved material* (NMS and Scottish Museums Council, Edinburgh, 1990).

With J D Storer, *Industry and Transport in Scottish Museums* (The Stationery Office, Edinburgh, 1997).

Edited books

Early Days in a Dundee Mill: Extracts from the Diary of William Brown, an Early Dundee Spinner (Dundee University Library, Abertay Historical Society, Dundee, 1980).

Bothwell Castle (HMSO, Edinburgh, 1985; revision of 1958 first edition by W Douglas Simpson).

Caerlaverock Castle (HMSO, Edinburgh, 1986: revision of first edition by B H St John O'Neill).

Articles in or other contributions to books

Field survey work, documentary research and illustrations in John Butt, *The Industrial Archaeology of Scotland* (David & Charles, Newton Abbot, 1967).

'The Industrial Archaeology of Scotland', in John Butt (ed)

Robert Owen, Prince of Cotton Spinners (David & Charles, Newton Abbot, 1971).

'Industrial Archaeology', in *Discovery and Excavation, Scotland* (1972), pp 52–3.

'Shipbuilding Machine Tools', in John Butt and John T Ward (eds), *Scottish Themes* (Scottish Academic Press, Edinburgh, 1976).

'Telford's Highland Bridges', in Alastair Penfold (ed), *Thomas Telford: Engineer* (London, 1980).

'Transport and Towns in Victorian Scotland', in George Gordon and T R B Dicks (eds), *Essays in Scottish Urban History* (Aberdeen, 1983), pp 197–232.

Section on Scottish Region, in Gordon Biddle and O S Nock (eds), *The Railway Heritage of Britain* (Michael Joseph, London, 1983).

'New Abbey Corn Mill, Industry and Action' and 'Garlogie: Industrial Experiment for the Future', in Magnus Magnusson (ed), *Echoes in Stone* (SDD, AMD, Edinburgh, 1983).

'Engineering', in John Langton and R J Morris (eds), *Atlas of Industrialising Britain 1780–1914* (Methuen, London, 1986: jointly with M K Oglethorpe).

'Industrial Buildings', in *The Buildings of Scotland: Glasgow* (Penguin, London, 1990).

'Industrial Design in Scotland', in Wendy Kaplan (ed), *Scotland Creates: 5000 years of art and design* (McLellan Galleries, London and Glasgow, 1990).

'The Paths of Progress', in Magnus Magnusson and Graham White (eds) *The Nature of Scotland* (Edinburgh, 1991).

'Iron in Building in Scotland: its Use and Conservation', in Anne Riches and Geoffrey Stell (eds), *Materials and Traditions in Scottish Building* (Nic Allen, SVBWG, Edinburgh, 1992).

'The Scottish Houses of William Leiper', in Ian Gow and Alistair Rowan (eds), *Scottish Country Houses 1600–1914* (EUP, Edinburgh, 1995).

'Building for Transport in Urban Scotland', in Deborah Mays (ed), *The Architecture of Scottish Cities* (Tuckwell, East Linton, 1997).

Articles

'Industrial Archaeology', *Scottish Historical Review*, 44, 1965.

'The St Rollox Chemical Works 1799–1964', *Industrial Archaeology*, 3, 1966, pp 185–92, 197.

'Muirkirk 1786–1802: the Creation of a Scottish Industrial Community', *Scottish Historical Review*, 45, 1966, 160–83 (with John Butt).

'Mills of River Ayr', *Ayrshire Collections*, 8, 2nd Series, 1967–69, pp 44–59.

'The Water Supply of New Lanark', *Industrial Archaeology*, 8, 1968, pp 384–7.

'Historical Survey of Scottish Ironfounders', *Newsletter, Business Archives Council of Scotland*, 1973, pp 10–13 (with Michael Moss).

'Scottish Suspension Bridges', in *The Archaeology of Industrial Scotland, Scottish Archaeological Forum 8*, 1977, pp 91–105.

'Cast Iron and Bridge Building in Scotland', *Industrial Archaeology Review*, 2, 1978, pp 290–9.

'Scottish Windmills: a Preservation Policy', *Scottish Vernacular Buildings Working Group Newletter*, 5, SVBWG, 1979, pp 36–43.

'Early Days in a Dundee Mill 1819–1823: Extracts from the Diary of William Brown, an early Dundee Spinner', in Abertay Historical Society, Publication 20, Dundee, 1980.

'Art and Industry in Scotland', in *Signs of the Times: Art and Industry in Scotland 1750–1985* (catalogue of an exhibition held in 1985).

'Industrial Photography in Scotland', in *Made from Girders: Photography in Industrial Scotland* (catalogue of an exhibition held in 1987).

'Firing Quill from the Duke of Cumberland's Bastion, Fort George', in *Proceedings of the Society of Antiquaries of Scotland*, 1991, Vol 121, pp 423–25.

'Wallhead Chimneys, Nepus and Timpany Gables – a neglected aspect of Scottish Urban Vernacular Building', in *Vernacular Building 16*, Edinburgh, 1992, pp 7–20.

'Charlestown Limeworks', in John Dorrington Ward and Ingval Maxwell (eds), *Proceedings of the Historic Scotland International Lime Conference* (Edinburgh, 1996).

'The History of Supply and Demand for Traditional Building Materials in Scotland', in Ingval Maxwell and Neil Ross (eds), *Proceedings of the Historic Scotland Traditional Building Materials Conference* (The House, Edinburgh, 1997), pp 11–14.

Periodicals Edited

Scottish Railways, an historical journal published by the Scottish Railway Preservation Society, 1967–70.

Transport History (jointly with Baron F Duckham) 1968–73, (with Malcolm Reed), 1973–75.

Scottish Industrial History (jointly with Dr C W Munn), 1976–80.